A DANGEROUS
PLACE

SIMON FARQUHAR

The Story of the Railway Murders

A DANGEROUS PLACE

The
History
Press

Cover illustrations
Front: (Author's collection); *back*: Duffy and Mulcahy as teenagers.
(PA.1390035. By kind permission of Hertfordshire Police)

First published 2016

The History Press
The Mill, Brimscombe Port
Stroud, Gloucestershire, GL5 2QG
www.thehistorypress.co.uk

British Library Cataloguing in Publication Data.
A catalogue record for this book is available from the British Library.

ISBN 978 0 7509 6589 7

Typesetting and origination by The History Press
Printed and bound by CPI Group (UK) Ltd

For Dad, from number two son

CONTENTS

PREFACE

Any writer is excited by an invitation to write. I was also surprised and intrigued when I received a message in May 2015 from Mark Beynon of The History Press, following an obituary I had written for *The Independent*. The piece had paid tribute to the broadcaster Shaw Taylor, for many years the face of law and order as the presenter of the television programme *Police 5*, the *Crimewatch* of its day.

When pinning the article up on Facebook, I had made mention of the occasion on which my father appeared on the programme, appealing for information in the case of the murder of Alison Day. I said that I still believe my father's refusal to obey his superiors and close that enquiry down, and his subsequent connecting of Alison's death with that of schoolgirl Maartje Tamboezer, did, in the long run, probably save a few lives. The pulling together of three separate police inquiries into one of the biggest manhunts in criminal history, coupled with some outstanding detection all round, surely speeded the identifying of the killers, even if one of them would evade justice for a long time.

'Sounds fascinating. Would you like to do a book?' came the message from Mark. Very few people have the chance to pay tribute to a parent in such a practical or demonstrative form, and so for that opportunity, and for his constant devotion to the project, I have Mark to thank, which I do most sincerely.

I was never going to follow in my father's footsteps professionally. But writing this book has allowed me the experience of doing so in the literal rather than the metaphorical sense. Walking the murder sites he visited, talking to his colleagues and piecing together a case that dominated the final year of his career has been by turns fascinating, disturbing, compelling and humbling.

Writing a book about someone you admire always runs the risk of resulting in a hagiography. Having not done the rounds of Her Majesty's Prisons, I have been unable to find anyone with a rough word to say about my father. But what I have found is an understanding of the job he did and an understanding of the resilience, mental discipline and determination that he needed to do it well. Like any other profession, be it nursing, bricklaying or acting, there are good and bad police officers. This book is about some of the good ones.

Many of the officers who were involved in the pursuit of John Duffy and David Mulcahy have never spoken publicly about the case before, or no longer choose to do so. Therefore I must express my particular gratitude to those officers who agreed to do so purely out of support for this project and affection for my father.

All the police officers who have contributed to this book, both serving and retired, have been invaluable in their assistance. Although I hope that the inclusion of their words within the text in itself reflects my appreciation, I must personally thank Paul Dockley for his enthusiasm, receptiveness, sincerity and superb recall throughout; all the officers of Operation Lea, specifically Brian Roberts and John Manners; two long-standing colleagues of my father's, Barry Fyffe from Operation Lea and Dave Cant from Flying Squad days, who have been unceasing in their assistance; and John Hurst, the driving force behind the arrest of John Duffy in 1986, who has been charming and supportive. Caroline Murphy took time to give me a fantastic account of her work on Operation Marford, and Mick Freeman from the outset has been unceasingly helpful, the sort of person who is a godsend to a project like this. I must also thank Gordon Reynolds, Colin Hockerday, Keith Hider and Michael Taylor. Outside of the police, special thanks also go to Marc Barrett, Professor David Canter, Richard Priestley, Riel Karmy-Jones QC, Monica Weller and, for placing his trust in me, Mr Kenneth Day.

Several organisations have been extremely cooperative, so thank you to Ian Carmichael and all at the Press Association, the staff of the British Library, Kathleen Dickson at the BFI, the BBC, James West at ITN, Fremantle, Getty Images, REX Shutterstock, the National Archives, the *Hampstead and Highgate Express*, Hertfordshire Constabulary, the Metropolitan Police and the Crown Prosecution Service.

On a personal level, Fiona Fenn Smith and Michael Fadda have been quite magnificent in their enthusiasm for this project from day one. The debt I owe my fine friend, the inexhaustibly instructive and edifying W. Stephen Gilbert, is a colossal one. As fellow writers, both Stephen and the ebullient Ian Greaves have been empathetic; as friends, they have been tonics.

Thank you also to Chris Maume; my agent Nick Quinn; friends and colleagues Octavia Lamb, Jolene McGowan, Suzanne Becker, Martin Duncan and Christina Thummanah, who make it a pleasure to come to work every morning; old friends Gavin Monks and Johnny Horth; Andrew Conway, Mark Nickol and Nick Kirby, the oldest of friends; Lu Frazer, Louise Henry, Jules Porter, Kristel McCartney, Julie Thompson, Joey Langer, Norman Eshley, Dan Austin, Howard Hill-Lines, Jill Singer, Laura Milne, Holly Brown, Kasha Gawelda, Jody Merelle, Debra Sargeant, Tony Smith,

John Goldschmidt, Bobbie Seagroatt, Joe McFadden, Pauline Lynch, Wendy Grahame, Victoria Gooch, Doremy Vernon, Linnie Reedman, Maggie Stride and Luke Healy; Twiggy, Leigh and Ace Lawson for a decade of friendship and advocacy; and my brother Martin and my mother Barbara, both of whom I hope are pleased with my efforts. And last but never least, Juliet Fletcher, for whom there will always be honey for tea.

1

DEDICATION

There is a house on a hill, overlooking the Moray Firth in the north of Scotland. This softly changing part of the world was the place where my father was born and raised. Once he and my mother had retired here, the room I'm in now is the room in which he would sit on summer evenings, reading books of history and occasionally looking out at the blurry blue of the bay and the barley fields that sway like gospel choirs. This is a place far away from the city he policed, both spiritually and geographically.

For London is a land where change is merciless, a land where the only thing that can't be bought is silence. That much never changes. My father's London was a London there is little trace of now. The scruffy London of 'George Davis is Innocent'* slogans. A city still overcast by the heavy,

---

* George Davis (b.1941) was convicted on questionable identification evidence and sentenced to twenty years' imprisonment in connection with an armed payroll robbery at the London Electricity Board, Ilford, in 1974. His innocence was protested in an extraordinary campaign that began with a graffiti epidemic throughout the East End (in retaliation, a wall on the Bethnal Green Road read: 'If George Davis is innocent, Humpty Dumpty was pushed'). It climaxed, after lorries had been driven through the glass doors of the offices of the *Daily Mirror* and the *Daily Express* and into the gates of Buckingham Palace, with the cricket ground at Headingley being dug up, sabotaging the last day of the Test match between England and Australia. The Home Secretary, Roy Jenkins, subsequently ordered Davis to be released, deeming his conviction 'unsafe' though not declaring him 'innocent'. Less than two years later, Davis was caught armed at the wheel of a getaway vehicle during a robbery at the Bank of Cyprus, Seven Sisters Road. He pleaded guilty and was sentenced to fifteen years in jail. He was released in 1984, but jailed again three years later, after pleading guilty to attempting to steal mailbags.

slow shadow of the war. A city propped up by corrugated iron fences and camaraderie. A city of police and thieves. A city which was, and still is, a dangerous place.

My father was a man of quiet pleasures. I picture him at the end of the garden, pottering away in the greenhouse. I suspect now that his garden wasn't just the place where he found solitude after a working week in a growling, dangerous city, but that it was also his way of staying connected with the land he had come from and would one day return to.

He and I stood on Sunnyside Beach* somewhere in the years between his retirement and his death, as he spoke of the ending to his favourite film, Bill Forsyth's *Local Hero*, which was shot only a few bays away, at Pennan. 'After he leaves Scotland, he gets back to his flat in Denver late at night and takes a beer out of the fridge, then he hears sirens outside. And he stands on the balcony looking out across the city, and as it fades back to that shot of Pennan, he's obviously thinking of how, just for a short time, he's been in a place so far removed from all the crime and all the madness that goes on in the city. I thought that was wonderful.'

When a man dies, a library burns to the ground, so the proverb tells us. I am now going to try to rescue what I can from the flames. For scattered about this house are the fragments that when pieced together tell the story of my father's career in that dangerous city. In a battered white vanity case in the attic are all the press cuttings my maternal grandmother kept, which have somehow ended up sandwiched between reminders of dental appointments and half-term holidays inside a threadbare 1984 Flying Squad diary. At the bottom of a wardrobe are the slight relics of my father's National Service. And in a large, deep wooden chest, or a

---

* One of Scotland's secret beaches, located between Cullen and Portsoy on the north-east coast, a mile or so from where my father was born.

'kist' as it is called in these parts, buried under three genera-
tions of photographs and cards, is a hand-sized red leather
autograph book, presented to him upon his retirement from
the Metropolitan Police in April 1987. Each page is covered
with dedications in police ballpoints from his colleagues.
The stories behind many of the inscriptions are now lost
to time, but one arrests me with its sincerity and accuracy:
'Many thanks, Charlie, for your measured, professional and
dedicated effort for justice.'

I will never know a more valiant man than my father.

This is the story of his last case. My father is not the only
hero of this story, for there are many. This is a story of suffering and of evil, but it is also a story about dedication, and
it is dedicated to my father and to everyone else who played
a part in bringing John Duffy and David Mulcahy to justice.
For this world is a dangerous place, not only because of the
people who do evil, but also because of the people who
don't do anything about them, to modify a different proverb. And this is also dedicated to all those who suffered, all
those who lost their lives and all those who lost loved ones
because of those two men.

I hesitate to call my father an old-fashioned man: traditional is the better word. He was an exemplar of his
generation, one of a breed born with so little who achieved
so much, blessed with an unimpeachable sense of duty and
discretion. He was always immaculately dressed, his top
button always done up and his tie always straight, even if
he had arrived home in the early hours of the morning
and then departed again before the milkman had been, an
occurrence which certainly wasn't unusual in our household. He respected learning and was devoted to his family;
despite the cruel hours his job demanded, I can honestly
say that he never once missed a school play, a prize-giving
day, a carol service or a birthday party. He was 40 when

I was born, and I was 40 when he died. Only now, as I piece together his working life, can I fully appreciate the might with which he achieved all he did and the depth of his commitment to being a husband and a father, as well as to being a fine detective. He was a success. Not a 'winner', as that would suggest luck played a part. What he achieved he achieved through skill, application and endeavour.

He was born Charles John Farquhar on 30 April 1932, the only boy of six children, and nicknamed 'Toux', a local word meaning 'little', as he was the youngest. His eldest sister, Betty, was twenty years his senior. His mother, Jane, went into hospital for a hernia operation when he was 12, and died under anaesthetic. Life for her had been punishing, which was why he ensured that my own mother never wanted for any household appliance that would make domesticity a little easier. After Jane's death, his sister Jean gave up her nurse's training to look after him and his father, James, was a farm labourer who was later a gardener at Cullen House, the commanding seat of the Earl of Seafield. That grand dwelling has long since been converted into flats, his work gone to waste as its gardens are now unkempt, with even the ornate faux-classical temple in the grounds conquered by towering weeds. Not all of us get to leave behind some evidence of our working lives.

My father was a quiet man with a commanding morality. At his funeral, his school friend John Bain told me that 'as boys, if any of us were getting up to evils, your dad would very firmly say, "You don't do that."' When I was 7, I tentatively stole a pencil from the stationery cupboard at school, then boasted of my little dare to him. I can still remember his reaction as he ordered me to return it, a reaction not of anger but of consternation. My elder brother Martin has a little story which perfectly illustrates this side of his character:

When I was about 16, I came home one day and triumphantly announced to him that I'd found £50 in the street, a tidy sum in 1979. All I could think of was which records I was going to buy with my new-found wealth. You can imagine my horror when he looked up over the newspaper and told me to hand it in to the police station, insisting that some elderly or less-fortunate person might be relying on that money for a week or more and may have nothing else. He tried to console me by saying that if it wasn't claimed within a week it would be mine and I would feel better for having done the right thing.

A long week passed as I planned my future investments. But then, a week later, I was told by the PC at the front desk that the money had been claimed. The final insult was that the police told the person who'd lost it where I worked and he came into the shop, said 'cheers' and left! I moaned for weeks about the injustice of it, and Dad was clearly amused, but he showed his softer side by giving me £20, saying 'consider that a finder's reward'. Still ungrateful, I told him I was £30 down, to which, in a very insightful way, he said: 'Son, £30 is a small price to pay for your integrity.'

Apart from his strong moral code, the only hint in his early life towards his future career was his reading of the double-page reports of Old Bailey trials in Sunday newspapers, though this was a national pastime of the age, immortalised in George Orwell's essay 'The Decline of the English Murder' (1946). Upon leaving school, he became an apprentice baker at John McKenzie's in Cullen. (He still made bread occasionally when I was growing up, and it was excellent.) He would set his alarm on his day off just for the satisfaction of being able to silence it and go back to sleep.

He made no secret of his admiration for the Attlee government, the founding of the Welfare State and Harold Wilson, but beyond that he rarely volunteered his political views and kept his voting habits a secret, like many of his generation. I did learn after his death, however, that as a young man he had actually been a member of the Labour Party, and had travelled as far as Brighton attending conferences.

Now I lift a tin out from the foot of the wardrobe to learn the story of his National Service. Called up when he was 18, medically examined on 26 July 1950 in Aberdeen, and pronounced as Grade 1 in terms of physical fitness with 'a fresh complexion', he was to present himself at the Royal Signals, Catterick Camp, near Richmond in Yorkshire on Thursday, 21 September. His full-time service lasted two years and two weeks; he was promoted to lance corporal in 1951, then to sergeant the following year, being based at Reading, on Salisbury Plain and at Osnabrück in Germany. He was due to take part in the Korean conflict, but contracted frostbite, which may well have saved his life since many of his fellow soldiers never returned.

Upon his discharge from full-time service, his conduct was described as 'very good', with the following testimonial:

> He has been employed as a wireless operator during his stay with this regiment. He has worked well and has shown that he can absorb theoretical detail. He can be relied upon to carry out duties without military supervision. Those serving under him respected him and did exactly as they were told or asked, proving that he had complete control.

Back in Scotland, he joined the workforce on the Great Glen Hydroelectric Scheme, constructing the mighty Dundreggan Dam. Situated in a wild, treacherous wilderness near Invermoriston, a few miles beyond Loch Ness, the dam crowned the first underground hydroelectric power station in Britain and brought affordable electricity to the people of the Highlands.

The Scots had proved themselves an indomitable breed in military service, and many of them were being welcomed into the police force in the years that followed the Second World War. So once work was completed at Dundreggan, Charlie moved to Glasgow to join the Ministry of Civil Aviation Constabulary.

The east–west divide in Scotland has blurred now, but in those times it was pronounced. Glaswegians were a noisier breed than their surly neighbours. My father rarely spoke to me of his time in Glasgow, but it was a city he held little fondness for until he returned for a weekend break the year before he died and found himself delighted by it; his earlier displeasure was probably a symptom of homesickness.

Whatever the case, his time there was short. A dissatisfaction with Glasgow but an affinity with police work inspired him to apply to join the Metropolitan Police, and he was called to a Medical and Selection Board at 201–205 Borough High Street, on Tuesday, 30 December 1958, so a torn card in a drawer tells me. Successful, after Hendon Police Training School (where one visiting lecturer was the celebrated 'Fabian of the Yard'*) he was stationed at Islington Green. He came down from Cullen early the following year and moved into police accommodation at the Olive Section House in Canonbury, bringing with him the framed black-and-white aerial photograph of his home town which now hangs on the wall behind me.

A future colleague, Dave Cant, tells me that:

So many Scots rose through the ranks to become senior officers quite swiftly; they'd proved themselves during the war or afterwards as a no-nonsense bunch and had shown they had

---

*   Robert Fabian (1901–78) was a brilliant detective who became a household name as well as the subject of a television series, *Fabian of the Yard*, in 1954.

the impetus to uproot. You and I are Londoners, but we both know London can be a very lonely place. People don't talk to each other. You had to prove you were capable of surviving, and Charlie did.[1]

The crime rate rose sharply now; 1959 saw indictable offences reach 160,000, the highest recorded figure to date. Five years later, the figure topped a quarter of a million.[2]

These were the dying days of the bobby on the beat, before Britain moved from 'deterrent to reactive policing'.[3] The early sixties were definitely not the Swinging Sixties. In fact, a few ghosts of Victorian London were still roaming around. The music halls may have been derelict and the docks running dry, but for the hobos at least, time stood still. My father used to speak of how in those days 'a genuine old-fashioned tramp would lay all his money and possessions out beside him when he put his head down for the night, so that if someone wanted to rob him, they could do it without harming him', and that 'in those days, if you gave a beggar a couple of bob, you could be fairly certain he'd spend it on a bacon roll'.

Vagrancy was rife, perhaps boosted by the number of men displaced or traumatised by wartime experiences, and therefore down-and-outs made for a significant part of a policeman's lot at that time. I remember driving through Islington with my father one Sunday evening several decades later, and him pointing to a doorway and telling a story; frustratingly, the only line of it I can now remember is 'there was a dead vagrant in the hallway and I wouldn't go upstairs'. Perhaps this had been his first encounter with a corpse (although he never got used to post-mortems, and said autopsies on meth drinkers were often the most stomach-churning).

In the days before thermal underwear, it wasn't unknown for policemen to wear pyjamas under their uniforms on cold nights. When the cold got too much to bear, a solution could be to escort a fragrant vagrant to what was known as 'The Spike' (possibly named after the metal spike on which admissions tickets issued at the local police station were placed). There, paraffins* were fed, put in a bath and given a change of clothes. It was a grim place, but taking them in kept a cold copper off the street for a couple of hours.

My father was often encouraged to write a book of his police experiences, but it never happened, probably due to modesty as much as endless DIY commitments. Nevertheless, occasionally over a flask of tea at the side of the road on holiday, he'd reminisce about incidents from those days on the beat, such as the time when a woman made a complaint that the man occupying the flat opposite was exposing himself to her every evening. When my father commented that you couldn't get a clear view from where he was, she replied, 'You can if you stand over there.'

A significant case while he was stationed at Islington began as a complaint made by the local lending library that books were being defaced. The perpetrators weren't selective; the seventy-two books ranged from children's stories to Betjeman's poetry. One of the library staff was suspicious of two rather shifty local men, who turned out to be playwright Joe Orton and his lover (eventually his killer) Kenneth Halliwell, exasperated at the library's anodyne array of reading material. They were both sentenced to six months' imprisonment and fined £262. The vandalised book covers, which viewed today are rather a scream, are now on display at Islington Museum.

My mother, Barbara, was an East End girl working in a wool shop on Essex Road when she met my father on a double date:

---

*   Paraffin lamp = tramp.

One of the first things I remember him dealing with was up at Camden Passage; long before it was gentrified, it was where a lot of prostitutes had rooms, and I remember a tale where a rich client paid one of them five pounds for her to strip off and throw cream buns at him.

'If we keep seeing each other like this we'll end up getting married', said one evening as the couple were passing The Marksman pub on Hackney Road, was the closest she got to a proposal. They married in 1962, and resided at 240c Clapham Road. My brother Martin was born almost a year to the day later, but money was tight and hours were anti-social. 'I wondered what I'd let myself in for,' she remembers. 'I was newly married with a baby, and I used to hang out of the window all night watching the traffic and wondering if he was ever coming home.'

By now he had joined the CID, with which he toured the stations of East London over the next decade. 'Some of the dregs of society you see in those thirty-odd years in the job are hard to conceive,' reflects Dave Cant, 'but Charlie being down the East End in those times would have been quite something.' Comedy was essential if you were to maintain your sanity amid the tragedy. He continues:

Charlie and I first met on 'E' division in 1966, down at Holborn. A hairdresser called Patricia Langham had been found dead in her flat in Kilburn, naked on her bed with her arms folded across her. She'd been banged on the head and sexually assaulted. It transpired that she'd had some trouble with the ballcock on her toilet and called out a plumber, then called him back when she'd not been satisfied with the job he'd done, and in a fit of temper he'd killed her.

We had no leads at all, but we noticed that the handle on the toilet chain looked very new and had a print on it.

So we set about interviewing every plumber in North London. And when we got down to the last few, this particular one was never in. Finally we saw him and he put his hands up to it and confessed, but he was baffled at what had taken us so long. It transpired that after the murder, he'd taken an overdose and when they'd rushed him into the New End Hospital in Hampstead, a nurse who was new had gone through his pockets to try and find some identification and opened a sealed envelope which contained his confession. Fearing she'd get into trouble for opening it, she'd thrown it away. And actually in the Occurrence Book at the station that evening, there were two entries, one after the other on the page, one being the murder, and the other this attempted suicide!

The other funny thing on that one was that while Charlie and I were searching the flat a second time we found two theatre tickets down the back of the sofa. The governor, Ray Dagg, sent officers to sit on either side of the seats on the night of the performance, and who should turn up and sit down there? Only a PC from the station and his mistress: the tickets had fallen out of his pocket when he'd been searching with us a few days earlier!

Charlie and I got our experience on jobs like that. Years later if Barbara was watching something on telly he wasn't interested in he'd go upstairs and telephone me and we'd laugh back at these things. He was a very shrewd man with no airs and graces. I miss him taking the piss out of me.

I came on the scene, as my father used to put it, in 1972, by which time the family had moved out to Essex, the traditional dormitory for East London folk. Around this time, as a detective sergeant, he did his first stint on the Flying Squad, then based at Scotland Yard. (It was tremendously arresting in the school playground to be able to say your dad was in the real-life Sweeney* during the time that the television series was being broadcast.)

Charlie arrived at Scotland Yard during the first exposure of widespread corruption** that changed public perception of the police forever in the mid-seventies; he said that at that time if you had a bit of information, you were scared to let anybody know because you had absolutely no idea who you could trust. The commissioner who did the most to stop the rot, Sir Robert Mark, reflected years later that for some officers 'virtue became fashionable ... the great majority of the CID must not only have been honest but anxious for reform'.[4]

A collection of engraved silver tankards glinting on the top of the Welsh dresser are the souvenirs of the stations Charlie served at through the seventies. Working his way around City Road, Forest Gate, West Ham and Plaistow as a detective inspector produced its fair share of memorable moments. At Plaistow in November 1976, he investigated an arson attack on Ye Old Black Bull pub on Stratford High Street, which had been bought by footballer Bobby Moore and renamed Mooro's. It was one of a string of ill-advised business ventures for Moore, and the fifth act of sabotage directed at him. In March 1972, the Country Club in

---

* Cockney rhyming slang (Sweeney Todd = Flying Squad) for the unit of the Metropolitan Police dealing with armed robberies.

** The first major attempt to purge Scotland Yard of corruption, targeting the Obscene Publications Squad, was an unexpected consequence of the Oz Trial in 1971, the longest obscenity trial in British legal history. The fifteen-month convictions of the editors of the counter-culture magazine were quashed at appeal when a trip to Soho to buy £20 worth of the hardest pornography the Defence could find made Oz appear extremely tame by comparison. In 1999 it was revealed that the Home Secretary, Reginald Maudling, had been so perturbed by accusations that Oz had been targeted over more explicit publications because of bribes that he launched a vast anti-corruption drive. It resulted in 400 officers, including the deputy assistant commissioner, being imprisoned or leaving the force. Subsequently, after Commander Kenneth Drury was sentenced to eight years' imprisonment on corruption charges in 1977, Operation Countryman was launched to investigate the Flying Squad, but its findings have never been fully revealed.

Chigwell that he ran with Sean Connery had been damaged in an arson attack; the following month, his office was burgled; in January 1973, thieves broke into his clothing warehouse and attempted to set fire to it; and two months later his clothing factory was vandalised. With Mooro's, an arsonist struck a week before the doors were due to open, causing £6,000 worth of damage.[5]

Speaking about the case on television in 2002, Charlie said:

> It looked as though white spirit or turpentine had been thrown about the place and set alight. We did all the forensic examinations, but in that area as usual, nobody's talking. We put it down to perhaps a little bit of gangsterism in the background, but we never got to the bottom of it. Bobby Moore was never a suspect; he was a footballer, and I think he was a bit naïve. He didn't always choose the best sort of people to get involved in business with.[6]

A policeman's experiences of humanity are frequently a cocktail of the macabre and the eccentric, and Charlie experienced one notably dreadful example of this at West Ham, when a man visiting his elderly upstairs neighbours to complain about a leak found the skeleton of the husband lying in the bed. He had died in his sleep ten years previously, and his widow, Mrs Violet Blackholly, who 'hoarded everything she obtained', had claimed ever since that he had left her. At the inquest, it was called 'an incredible story which a coroner rarely comes across in his career'.[7]

My brother recalls that at West Ham, 'a new young PC was threatened with a gun. Dad spotted him in the canteen afterwards and realised there was something wrong as he was holding his newspaper upside down. He was having a complete breakdown; his career was over. Dad was very upset by it.' Dave Cant adds, 'Charlie was so aware of those sorts of situations. He was a tough man but he had a very caring presence about him.'

A letter sent in sympathy to my mother after my father's death refers to a case which I remember my grandmother telling me was the only time she saw my father not managing to quite shake something off when he came home from work. The letter is from Dick Kirby, a former police officer and now a crime writer:

> When Charlie arrived at West Ham, morale was at an all-time low, but it did not take long before his dynamic type of leadership made itself known. Detective Inspectors at West Ham were not known for making arrests. Charlie put that to rights when he was informed of the death of a child in mysterious circumstances. He simply walked across the road to the hospital, handcuffed both of the graceless parents and marched them straight back into the charge room.[8]

It was the diligence of legendary local GP and police surgeon Hannah Hedwig Striesow,* a powerhouse of humanity who had fearlessly refused to allow the child to be returned to his parents, that had seen the boy secured with his grandparents, a couple who were, in my father's words, 'rough, but good'. When their custody of him was brought to an end, the result was tragedy. I can still recall my grandmother saying to me that 'Dad would come home at that time, lift you up and cuddle you, and say, "Hello, I've missed you," jokingly, but

---

* Despite Nazi opposition, the Jewish Hannah Striesow qualified as a doctor in Bavaria in 1933. Unable to practise, she came to England, but her German qualifications were not recognised, so she trained as a nurse before finally becoming a GP in 1949. Her practice was next door to her house so she could be available at all times to both her patients and her family. At 76, she took on a partner so that she could have alternate Saturdays off. She was the oldest full-time doctor in the country when she retired at 81. She continued to work as a locum until she was 90. Reporting her death at the age of 100, the *Guardian* said 'in her life and work, she repaid her adopted country a thousand-fold for the refuge it had provided'. (*Guardian* obituary, 6 April 2009)

you could tell that this had weighed on his mind'. The case would not be the last time that my father was critical of the actions of social workers in cases involving children.

A second stint on the Flying Squad in the late seventies placed him under the command of Michael Taylor, who tells me that:

> his reputation was very high indeed. A very determined detective with a bulldog quality. I wouldn't have wanted him chasing me if I was a villain, that's for sure. Notably at this time he arrested armed robber James Moody* after a siege in South London. Actually, Moody subsequently escaped from Brixton and years later was shot dead in a Hackney pub while playing a solitary game of pool.[9]

The Flying Squad then underwent a reorganisation, being split into four units, based at Rigg Approach, Tower Bridge, Barnes and Finchley, the last of which my father was posted to in 1981. It becomes clear to me now that the next three years were the happiest of his life. Thoughts of the early eighties create a myriad of happy impressions in my mind, and I fancy that this is in no small part due to him reaching the peak of professional satisfaction at this time, and that somehow enthusing us all. He made the first of many television appearances soon after he arrived at Finchley, clad in his duffle coat, at the scene of a violent robbery outside Barclays Bank in Marylebone High Street.** When I went into school

---

* James 'Jimmy' Moody (1941–93) was a gangster and contract killer who worked for the Kray Twins, the Richardsons and, after his escape, the Provisional IRA. He was dubbed by his peers 'the hardest man in London'.

** The robbery, on 11 January 1983, perpetrated by a prolific gang, was interrupted by four plain-clothes policemen who happened to be passing, One of them, Stephen O'Rourke, was shot in the arm; he and two civilians who gave chase were awarded the Queen's Commendation for Bravery in 1986. The gang carried out a further robbery in Bristol which climaxed with the hijack of a lorry and the driver being forced at gunpoint to take them down the M4 with the police in pursuit. The full story is told by Flying Squad Commander Frank Cater in his book *Sharp End* (Bodley Head, 1988).

the following morning, it seemed as if everyone in my class had been watching.

I once got talking to two former armed robbers in a Fulham pub, who spoke wistfully of a golden age of smash-and-grabs now long past (because most cash is moved around electronically nowadays, and also, there is more money to be made through drugs). I was struck by how they used the words 'job' for a raid and 'working' for the planning stages, without any hint of irony, perhaps to give their activities a veneer of respectability. Armed robbers ('blaggers') and gangsters may be two of the least defendable breeds of villain, threatening people's lives with no psychological motivation beyond greed. Yet strangely, their public images render them as folk heroes to many. Buster Edwards,* who my father described as 'a vicious little bugger', was the subject of a rom-com, *Buster* (1988); similarly, the Krays' legend seems indestructible, due to a combination of nostalgia and cunning spin. My father once told me of how, during their reign of terror, the twins menaced the owner of a television shop into giving them a free set, which they then donated to a local old people's home – with maximum publicity.

Cops and robbers is a game for two teams, and as much as the bad guys talk just like they do on the television, so do the good guys. Many a time I remember hearing my father on the hall telephone using phrases such as 'nick him'. My friend Jonathan and I would occasionally be chauffeured to school at this time by him and his driver, the affable and assured Harry Duncan, with the police radio chattering

---

* Ronald 'Buster' Edwards (1931–94), member of the gang that committed the Great Train Robbery. When interviewed by Piers Paul Read in 1978 for the book *The Train Robbers*, he claimed he was responsible for coshing the driver of the train, Jack Mills. He later retracted this and other claims. In his final years, he ran a flower stall outside Waterloo station. At the time of his suicide, he was being investigated as part of a fraud enquiry, and it is speculated that his death was prompted by a dread of returning to prison.

away all the while. I remember how fairly alarming exchanges would float into the car which the two old pros up front never seemed remotely fazed by; it was all in a day's work for them. Another of Charlie's colleagues, Gordon Reynolds, endorses my view of his happiness at Finchley, explaining that 'we had a tremendous team. I think we arrested more people in the process of committing armed robberies than anyone had ever done. There were seventeen successful operations in one year, we could do no wrong. And Charlie was leading that, all credit to him.'[10] But it's fascinating to discover that things didn't bode well at all at the start, as Dave Cant explains:

The previous DCI at Finchley was Tony Lundy, who ran all the supergrasses; at one stage he'd had about fifty or sixty armed robbers in custody awaiting trial. Prisoners were naming names in return for lighter sentences. But he was too successful; there were concerns about these fellas who'd done the crimes getting lighter sentences for snouting their mates. He had an informant who was getting thousands of pounds in 10 per cent rewards for information, and it was making people uneasy. So he was moved from Finchley rather suddenly, and in came Charlie. I arrived there just after he did, expecting Lundy to still be in charge, walked into the office, and this voice went: 'Canty, you bastard, put the kettle on!' To be honest, I worshipped him. I worshipped the ground he trod on, and I'm not just saying that.

But he confided in me that he was deeply unhappy with the situation he'd found himself in. Lundy was coming back to Finchley every evening, tidying up on a few jobs, and after saying hello, was going out and chatting to the other men on the team and taking them up to The Torrington, which was the pub we used. Charlie got a sense that things were being put around that he wasn't party to.

He was a very different personality; Lundy was brash and upfront, with a bottle of scotch in his desk, whereas Charlie grew geraniums on the windowsill; outwardly he might have thrown them a bit at first. But he very discreetly put a stop to what was going on, and within months the results he started getting on pavement jobs* were superb, I mean really top quality arrests. He was respected in no small part because he was straightforward and honest.

Gordon Reynolds continues:

When I arrived at Finchley, morale was very low. After a few weeks Lundy was moved on, and Charlie had the thankless task of coming in to pick up the pieces. It wasn't an easy job at all. What was so rare was that he would always back you up if he thought your intentions were good, and that is so rare.

Colin Hockerday agrees, summing him up as a 'detective's detective':

One night around midnight I got a call from a guy I knew who owned a hotel in Acton. He was suspicious about a rather cagey guest at the bar who was flying out of Heathrow the following day. I got dressed and breezed in there as if I was just passing. The bloke wanted to order a minicab in the morning so I arranged for an officer to pose as a driver, but somehow the bloke tumbled and had it away on his toes. We headed to Heathrow to see if we could spot him, but had no luck. On the way back a report came over the radio of a robbery at Kutchinsky's, the jewellers on Bond Street; they'd made off in a Rolls-Royce that belonged to Mike Yarwood.** It turned out there was a connection, but at the time

* Ambushing armed robbers during the offence.

** British comic impersonator, the first to be awarded his own television show. A huge star in the seventies, his 1977 Christmas special was seen by over 28 million people, making it the most watched programme in Christmas television history.

I had to go back to Charlie and explain what I'd been up to. It was a time when he was under huge pressure over budgets, but rather than offload that pressure on me, he heard me out and said I was quite right to have acted as I did. It was so refreshing to have a boss who allowed you to have a bit of initiative.[11]

'Armed robbery' and 'violent crime' are hackneyed phrases, but petrifying situations to be faced with. To combat them, a team needs to be fearless, loyal and staunch. Leadership of such a unit is a formidable task, but 'he was quite brilliant at getting the whole team to gel'. Gordon Reynolds explains:

In those situations, facing blokes with sawn-off shotguns, the adrenaline is pumping through your veins. We tailed a gang who were going to rob the Nationwide at Hatch End once; I remember we steamed in and your dad stuck a gun in a robber's ear at the counter. You go in very hard and don't give them the chance to do anything, but it's afterwards when you're sat in the canteen having a cup of tea that as you stand up, your legs turn to jelly and the danger you were in hits home.

But there were plenty of laughs at Finchley, as Dave Cant testifies:

One morning Charlie was issuing the guns, while my job was to do the tea. I knew my station in life. One of the men was handed his gun and thought the safety catch was on. I'd just started to pour the tea out of this huge urn when a bullet came screaming out of the incident room, through the door, into the tea urn and out the other side, liquid gushing out like in one of those old Westerns when someone shoots a water tank. Suddenly they all come running in saying, 'Canty, Canty, you all right?' I said, 'I'm fine, but the tea's fucked!' They covered up the bullet hole in the door with an Elastoplast that stayed there for years. Actually, it's probably still there now.

Underneath the camaraderie, life was being risked on a regular basis, but the only hints I ever got of this were my mother occasionally saying, 'Oh he woke up with a start in the night, dreamt of being shot again,' and my memory of him enduring a stomach ulcer for a time.

This was a London of rogues and rascals, a London of blaggers, of crime reporters with Sohoitis* and con men preying on the outwardly honest: Charlie knew well both the streets and the characters that pestered them. After he had retired, I was with him one afternoon in the West End when he was spotted by a man doing the three-card trick,** who promptly did a runner. 'Some of the characters he knew,' says Dave Cant. 'He could talk to people, a great skill. If he needed a bit of info, he knew where to ask around.' Having gleaned the term from *The Sweeney*, as a child I asked him once, 'Dad, do you have informants?' 'Don't ask such things,' was his gentle reply.

After three years, he was promoted to detective super-intendent, and his time at Finchley was at an end. After a modest celebration with his team, he came home and sat quietly in the living room. It was one of the only times I knew him not quite manage to keep his emotions in check. Only now, after getting an insight into those glory days, do I understand why.

He was now appointed one of the superintendents on '3 Area' (East London) Major Investigation Pool, and stationed at Romford. Those final three years were to prove powerful and triumphant, although the mystery of

---

* A disease which causes a sufferer to become addicted to Soho, staying in its drinking dens day and night and never getting any work done. Jeffrey Bernard (1932–97), columnist for *The Sporting Life* and *The Spectator*, was the most famous victim of the condition.

** Confidence trick in which a victim bets on the assumption that they can find the money card, which has actually already been substituted for another.

80-year-old local eccentric Dorothy Cleveland,[12] who was found strangled in her flat, remained the only unsolved murder he investigated. (He did confess to me he was fairly certain that a door-to-door salesman was responsible, the motive being theft, though he could never prove it.)

Immediately preceding the case that this book centres on was one that was equally harrowing, equally significant criminologically, and one that must also be remembered.[13]

A 14-year-old girl, Keighley Barton, disappeared one morning in August 1985 while walking her dog on Wanstead Flats. The dog, a German shepherd, whose appearance alone would have warded off an unknown attacker, returned home to Keighley's mother, Theresa, visibly traumatised.

The police soon unearthed a horrific history of sexual abuse that had been committed by stepfather Ronald Barton for most of Keighley's life. Theresa had initially been unaware of his appalling record of past offences, which included convictions for grievous bodily harm and seven sexual offences against teenage girls, one of which had resulted in a jail sentence. When Keighley was 8, Barton had been charged with two acts of gross indecency towards her, for which he had received a twelve-month suspended sentence. He had been arrested again in 1982, but the case was dropped on the day of the trial because Keighley refused to testify against him. Two years later, he was arrested and charged again, only for Keighley to again withdraw her allegations at the eleventh hour.

The child was placed in council care, but regularly ran away and returned home. The abuse of mother and daughter by Barton, sometimes at gunpoint, continued until 1985, when Theresa called the police again and took out a court order to protect them both from him. Shortly after this, she met a new partner. Barton was incensed, and began spying on her and making abusive telephone calls.

That this had been allowed to persist paints a deplorable picture of social services and the legal system at that time. At last, however, Barton was under arrest, though he denied all knowledge of Keighley's disappearance. My father believed he had abducted her to abuse her again, and had then murdered her to prevent her testifying against him, as well as to enact revenge on her mother. I recall him telling me that when he visited Barton's parents to search the house, Barton's father quipped, 'I'm not going to lift a finger to help you, but if anything's happened to that kid, he'll have done it.'

The search for Keighley lasted for fifteen months. Her mother received two letters from her claiming she was alive and denying any abuse had taken place, but my father was convinced she was dead and had been forced to write them in her final moments; and so, despite no body being found, he charged Barton with murder. There were unlikely sightings of Keighley as far afield as Ireland in the months that followed; one of her teachers also reported seeing her shopping locally, which was a serious challenge to the already almost unprecedented aim of securing a murder conviction without a body being found.

On a Sunday afternoon a few weeks before the trial, my father was just about to carve when the telephone rang. The message was that Barton, on remand at Brixton, had 'something to say'. Charlie drove across London, and when he confronted him, found that all he'd wanted to say was 'fuck off'. Barton then turned to the prison officer and said, 'Take me back to my cell.' My father jovially replied, 'I hope you look forward to the Christmas cards I'll be sending you counting down the years, Ron. Inside they'll read "one over thirty", "two over thirty" … keep an eye out for them.' I understand now why my father would always jokingly refer to him over the years as 'my pal, Ron'. How else do you cope with spending several months of your life dealing with such a creature other than to cast them as an object of ridicule?

In October 1986, the jury took five hours to find Ronald Barton guilty of murder. He was sentenced to life, the judge describing him as 'an evil, cynical and depraved man from whom society, your wife and family deserve to be protected for many years'. My father had achieved one of the only convictions for murder without a corpus delicti in British criminal history.

The day after his sentence began, Barton revealed to the governor of Wormwood Scrubs that Keighley was buried in Abney Park Cemetery, although he would give no clues as to where. The search of the heavily overgrown 32-acre site lasted several days. Finally, bones and clothing were taken to the mortuary, where Dr Peter Vanezis confirmed that they were all that remained of Keighley, and that she had been stabbed eleven times. One of the bones was from her forearm, and from an indentation on it, it was clear that she had put up a fight so one of the knife blows had struck her there. Also among the remains was a cheap ring she had bought on a market stall.

Keighley Barton's life had been short and pitiful. I was not quite her age, but close enough, and gradually becoming aware through watching the news reports after school each evening of just how safe my brother and I had been kept throughout our happy and well-furnished childhoods, and of how very different Keighley's experience of the world had been to ours.

When my father retired, he brought home two boxes of paperwork from his office, and stored them in the toy cupboard until he could find the time to sort through them. One afternoon, seized by a tidy fit, while stacking up board games I opened one up in an act of youthful inquisitiveness.

The first folder contained the transcript of an interview he had conducted with Ronald Barton. I only lasted reading it a few minutes before stuffing it back in the box. The details were far beyond anything ever mentioned in what had seemed to be exhaustive media coverage of the case.

'Don't believe everything you read in the newspapers' is healthy advice. But additionally, don't believe what you read in the newspapers is everything. The full horrors that people suffer and that police officers have to deal with never reach the printed page. One would hope this is to allow victims what little dignity remains available to them. But when I remember my father was fond of reminding me that some journalists 'never let a fact get in the way of a good story', perhaps 'never let a fact get in the way of a good breakfast' might be another motivation. For the public eagerly gobble up their daily diet of murder and cruelty through their newspapers every morning, but they don't really want too many details. Murder, for those who don't have to clear it up, is entertainment. Murder is the ultimate box-office attraction. Paradoxically, a film about death itself is usually box-office suicide.

The Keighley Barton case, looked upon now in the light of Operation Yewtree, is an appalling reminder of the lack of understanding of abuse victims in the recent past and the lack of vigilance regarding their abusers, by both the courts and by social services. Things are far from perfect now, but society at least appears finally to be making progress.

My father's role in the case remains one of the things for which I am most proud of him. Trawling through newsreel footage of him at Abney Park Cemetery before I wrote this, I truly saw what a man of decency, compassion and necessary resilience he was.

The late John Hopkins* was arguably the finest writer there has ever been of drama exploring the psychological realms the policeman occupies. Shortly before his death in 1992, he explained that:

> [T]hey confront the full range of darkness. Their life is a constant confrontation with horror. We ask from them a commitment to our safety and livelihood, and we say, 'You will do that for us, it all comes with the territory of being a policeman', but we don't pay them the respect of understanding what a cost it is to them, how much in terms of ordinary life they sacrifice to be our guardians.[14]

I now turn to my father's last case. Retracing his steps, I am on a journey towards a deeper understanding of him and the world he endured: that dangerous place from which he protected the child I once was.

---

* John Hopkins (1931–98) wrote over ninety episodes of *Z Cars* in the 1960s. His work is stark and torturous; particularly penetrating works focusing on crime and policing include the film *The Offence* (1972) and for television *Play for Today: A Story to Frighten the Children* (BBC, 1976).

2

COLLUSION

What causes two men to become monsters? The most we can offer here in response to that question is the sequence of events that moved John Duffy and David Mulcahy from anonymity to notoriety. But although these events may appear to provide us with the reasons why they became multiple rapists and ultimately serial killers, caution should be advised. It would be foolhardy to proclaim that these experiences *caused* their criminality. It is clear that these experiences *fashioned the nature of it*; beyond that, we cannot know for sure, and must resist the temptation to apply the logic of ethical behaviour to such men. Sex and money are the traditional motives for murder, and there is no doubt that early experiences of emasculation and humiliation, together with feelings of inadequacy and resentment for the world around them, had devastating effects on the personalities of Duffy and Mulcahy. Yet the events alone do not suffice; for every man that will turn to murder as a result of humiliation and alienation, a million others will not.

Much is made today of the suggestion that human beings are inherently selfish creatures, and that perhaps even our most selfless acts are only born out of a desire to gratify ourselves and avoid the torment of a guilty conscience. But surely this depressing-looking theory contains within it an uplifting truth: that by and large, our natures are good and cooperative;

why else would we suffer guilt when we act selfishly, unless we had been doing something which was against our nature? Modern man is persuaded to murder far more easily by king and country or by religion than he is by himself, because king and country offer him motivation, relieve him of guilt and spare him demonisation. The story of Duffy and Mulcahy is in part a story of sexual and social inadequacy, but it also contains telling militaristic imagery: a leader and a second-in-command dehumanising their enemies, striving for masculinity through violence, dressing up in uniforms, acquiring weaponry, meticulously planning, aspiring to become 'warriors' and swearing an oath of allegiance.

John Francis Duffy was born in the Irish border town of Dundalk, County Louth, on 29 November 1958, the eldest of three children born to Philomena and her bricklayer husband Frank, a couple described as 'good, hard-working, decent people who believed in decent values'.[1] Thirty years later, the press would claim the boy was named after Pope John XXIII, which may be pure invention, though his saintly names do suggest an effort by his parents to bequeath him with their religious sensibilities, sensibilities which for a time went unchallenged. His early childhood, including a stint as an altar boy at the St Nicholas School chapel, seems to have been contented and undramatic. He attended De Le Salle's Infant School, where the mother of a fellow pupil later described him as 'one of the sweetest children you could ever meet',[2] but in 1965* unemployment forced the family to move from Ireland to Kilburn in North London, a traditional destination for Irish immigrants.

* According to *The Hampstead & Highgate Express* for 4 March 1988. Some other sources claim Duffy's family moved to London when he was 7, others that they were already domiciled there when he was born, and that his birthplace was Dundalk because his mother was on a return visit there to see relatives at the time. Recordings of police interviews with him in 1997 suggest no discernible Irish accent. *The Daily Mail* of 27 February 1988 has the year of his move to England as 1964.

The family lived in the Du Maurier House flats on Lawn Road and Duffy attended Kingsgate Infants', Rosary Catholic School and St Dominic's. A neighbour said that Duffy's parents were:

> the nicest of people, and John was brought up to be very polite. If ever I was walking in the block at the same time as he was, he would open the door for me. He was no different from any other schoolboy and would play in the woods with the other children. He was probably quieter than most, but was only a loner if you call that the don't-get-yourself-into-trouble sort of boy.[3]

The well-brought-up lad who played with his friends on a patch of wasteland overlooking his home, within earshot of the North London Line – the railway that was to become the scene of many of his crimes – was, however, soon drowning in the brutality of city life in the troubled decade that was the 1970s, when, at 11, he began his fateful time at Haverstock School.

Future pupils would include Ed and David Miliband, but Haverstock in the early seventies was for many a place not of encouragement and education but of violence and exclusion. There were over a thousand pupils, but only 1 per cent of them made it to the upper sixth form.[4] It was hardly unique in its gang fights, regular police presence and class and racial divides, but any hopes Duffy's parents may have held of a constructive future for their son were brutally sabotaged upon his arrival there in the autumn of 1970.

Runty and ravaged by acne that would leave his face permanently pockmarked, this 'leprechaun of a boy'[5] who would never grow taller than 5ft 4in was an easy target for bullies. Fellow pupil Richard Priestley remembers:

He was in a tough year, with a lot of big lads. The school went
through some very bad times in the late sixties, and through
the seventies things did improve, but he did get bulled and
pushed around quite mercilessly. He didn't fit in.[6]

Duffy took to wearing a parka jacket with the hood up
regardless of the temperature in an attempt to hide himself,
specifically the ginger hair which drew much of the ridicule, from the world around him. Classmate Alan Bulman
said, 'I used to have to stick up for him. He'd come to me for
help; he would not hit back. He was a wimp, but a decent
enough sort of wimp, or so we thought. He was always
easily led, one of life's victims.'[7] Another classmate said, 'He
was useless with girls, useless at lessons and totally unin-
terested in things like sport and music. No one liked him.
He was short and spotty-faced, the sort no one could get
on with. And he was always rubbing people up the wrong
way.'[8] However, he wasn't the only target for bullies in the
school. On his first day at Haverstock, Duffy met another
child of Irish immigrants: David John Mulcahy.

The son of a garage mechanic turned pub landlord, David
Mulcahy was born on 23 May 1959. At school he was stocky,
more confident and better looking than Duffy, though his
large forehead was the feature his bullies ridiculed him
over. The pair quickly found they were safer together, and
as Mulcahy began to grow taller and stronger, he assumed
the role of Duffy's minder. It's not hard to see how being
protected by Mulcahy would have made Duffy grateful
almost to the level of sycophancy. Mulcahy responded to
his predicament at Haverstock with aggression towards the
world as a whole, and now, basking in his protective shadow,
Duffy followed suit. It is theorised that serial murder is often
motivated by a desire for 'regulation of self-esteem, either
the recovery of lost self-esteem or an attempt to establish

self-esteem which [the perpetrator] never had',[9] and in this respect, the pair were a textbook example.

It would seem that Duffy's retarded personality was weaponised by Mulcahy, who would come to call his protégé 'the midget'. Duffy would later explain, 'We did everything together; we were in the same classes, we played truant together … if he got up to some mischief I was always there and vice versa.'[10] They were now on the road to becoming what one victim would describe as 'two bodies with one brain'.[11]

Abuse often has a domino effect (verbal and physical bullying are both forms of abuse), so Mulcahy dominating Duffy, and ultimately both men dominating their victims, can be seen as a dreadful result of the cruelty shown towards them by other pupils at Haverstock, though not an inevitable result. Duffy in particular would go on to suffer what he construed as serious challenges to his masculinity, and yet, as has been said, other men who experience far greater traumas go on to live lives of decency, sociability and achievement.

At the age of 13, Mulcahy was suspended from school for repeatedly clubbing a hedgehog with a plank of wood, pretending they were a cricket ball and a bat, then killing the animal by stamping on its head. He was found splattered with blood, Duffy laughing by his side.[12]

Wicked men commonly experiment in early life with inflicting suffering on animals. In adulthood, John George Haigh,* the so-called 'acid bath murderer', experimented with dissolving mice in acid before later attempting to destroy one of his victims, Mrs Olive Durand Deacon, the same way. While for Haigh this was primarily 'practice'

---

* John George Haigh (1909–49) was convicted of six murders that were motivated by money. He believed he had perpetrated the perfect crime by dissolving bodies in acid, but forensic evidence still remained and proved sufficient to hang him.

(something which makes him 'one of the few murderers who actually practised before he committed the crime'[13]), it was surely also to gratify his desire for the God-like power he felt over others by stopping a life. Mulcahy too would later refer to a 'God-like' feeling when committing murder.

Although Duffy had initially shown no interest in sports, soon the pair were taking judo lessons, not as an outlet for their aggression but as a way of sharpening it.* Mulcahy wanted them to become 'warriors', so they also joined the Army Cadet Force. They were now beginning to target females in the school playground, playing a variant of kiss-chase in which they would pursue girls and touch them inappropriately. Behaviour of this nature would ring very loud alarm bells today, or at least one would hope so; it has been demonstrated repeatedly of late that the 1970s were prehistoric times in regard to such matters.

The pair were also finding inspiration in the kung-fu craze that was sweeping through Britain at the time, a fad that starred Bruce Lee** as its poster boy and for which Carl Douglas provided its soundtrack.*** Richard Priestley recalls, 'It was the height of Bruce Lee and kung-fu, and there was also a large Chinese population. There were fights where the boys from Camden Town tried to take on the boys from Chinatown.'

For Duffy and Mulcahy, Haverstock was a depressing existence; by the time they left, without any qualifications, their personalities were grossly disfigured, their only ambitions

---

* *The Kensington News & Post* of 29 October 1976 reported that there had been a dramatic rise in young people enrolling in judo and karate courses at this time, which it attributed to 'London's mugging situation'.

** Born Lee Jun-fan (1940–73), Hong Kong-born martial artist and film star.

*** Carl Douglas's novelty hit, *Kung Fu Fighting*, a homage to martial arts films, sold 11 million copies worldwide in 1974.

self-preservation and gratification. Mulcahy found work as a plumber and a painter and decorator before qualifying as a plasterer. In April 1975, meanwhile, Duffy was working at a local youth club, where he was described as 'withdrawn and quiet'. It might seem curious for someone like Duffy to be helping children to learn snooker, but he was probably hoping to experience something of what it was like to be a leader. (Much later, he would take a bolder step in trying to imitate Mulcahy, by trying to recruit his own partner in crime.) He then trained for a City and Guilds certificate in carpentry and joinery with a building firm in Camden, but he was denied an apprenticeship due to frequent absences.

The pair were both emotionally immature, dressing up as soldiers, relentlessly practising martial arts moves and by night donning freakish carnival masks before jumping out and spooking gay couples on Hampstead Heath. Steered by Mulcahy, they began experimenting with petty crime.[*] A vicious misogyny also began to make itself known. Mulcahy developed a vendetta against the female owner of a house in Talbot Crescent, Hendon, who he had been working for, and decided she needed 'teaching a lesson'. He and Duffy broke in and lay in wait twice, but both times she failed to come home. They then broke into a house in Kensington Park Road with the same intention of rape (Mulcahy had decided the lady owner was 'stuck up'), but were thwarted and fled when the female resident returned home with a male friend in tow.

On 13 December 1976, Mulcahy and Duffy received a conviction for ABH. Mulcahy's parents were running The Prince of Teck pub in Earl's Court at this time, and at 3.10 p.m. on Sunday, 22 August, he and Duffy had been

---

[*] Editions of the *Hampstead & Highgate Express* for the mid to late 1970s seem to suggest a surge in petty crime in the area, particularly vandalism and theft.

arrested for firing an airgun at pedestrians from the upstairs bathroom window. Five people in total were shot at, four of whom required hospital treatment.* The pair also began stealing cars and joyriding at this time.

On the Spring Bank Holiday weekend of 1977, they had a night out at the Empire Ballroom on Leicester Square, where Mulcahy met Sandra Carr, who was 16 and still attending school. The following June, the couple were married at Euston Registry Office. Speaking to the *Daily Mail* in 2001, she remembered that two days after that first meeting, she and a friend travelled down to the coast for the day with Duffy and Mulcahy, who she found to be 'a prankster who made me laugh'.[14] The couple then worked behind the bar at the Bond Street pub Mulcahy's parents were now running; she referred to Duffy, who she claimed did not attend their wedding, as 'sly'.

Duffy had by now found work as a carpenter for British Rail, being based at the Vehicle and Furniture Department at Euston station. The job allowed him free travel on the rail network, a network he would quickly develop an unhealthy knowledge of. He and Mulcahy also regularly attended an ice rink in Queensway, where they would further test the waters by deliberately colliding with other skaters. It was here that Duffy met nursery nurse Margaret Byrne. The couple married in secret, due to parental disapproval, at Camden Register Office in 1980, not actually moving in together until several months later.

---

* Two other incidents in the area involving an airgun were reported in *The Kensington News & Post* that summer. The edition for 13 August 1976 tells of an 18-year-old store porter who was caught 'with two youngsters' at Trellick Tower firing at tin cans while children played nearby. The youths were unlikely to have been Duffy and Mulcahy, since the culprits were obviously too young to be named in the article; therefore this event must have been purely coincidental. However, Duffy and Mulcahy may well have been behind the second incident: the edition on 27 August tells of the closure of an open-air pool after a rooftop sniper with an airgun had fired at sunbathing girls at the end of July.

Despite Mulcahy's wife giving him an ultimatum when she learnt of his conviction for car theft, in 1981 he and Duffy were both arrested, this time for stealing wine and spirits from a storeroom, and given suspended sentences. Many male acquaintances of Mulcahy's have spoken of his hyperactivity and of his constant need to impress; indeed, he earned the nickname 'Crazy Dave' for his readiness to perform dares and play with danger. Duffy himself later confessed to finding him exciting to be with. But around women, repellent attitudes could erupt; in late years, when he was moonlighting as a minicab driver with Crystal Cars of Dulwich, Mulcahy regularly referred to women as 'fucking slags' or 'sluts', 'that fucking slut who makes my tea', and at one point put his hands around the neck of controller Lola Barry, asking, 'Are you scared?' before exiting, laughing. Another employee, Carla, who Mulcahy referred to as 'an 18-stone feminist', physically ejected him from the office at one point for his behaviour.

At this time, Duffy was at a point of confusion, and ready for orders. His appetite for aggression and transgression had been unleashed but lacked direction. He and Mulcahy were 22 years old, but Mulcahy was by now a father, while Duffy's own attempts to produce a child with Margaret had proved unsuccessful. The couple instead invested in an Alsatian puppy, Toby, which Margaret doted on and Duffy ill-treated. It fell from the roof of their flat and died, a grim metaphor for their marital crisis.* Margaret borrowed £250 from Duffy's parents to consult a Harley Street specialist about their problems conceiving, the results of which showed that her husband had a low sperm count.

---

*   DS Mick Freeman told me there was a strong suspicion that Duffy had thrown the animal from the roof.

Duffy attempted suicide sometime in 1982. Whether this was a reaction to these events, or whether it was connected with the first attacks, is not known. His wife would later say that their four-year marriage was a journey from him being 'a nice person' to him becoming 'a raving madman'.

Margaret went away on a training course one weekend, giving Duffy a window of opportunity. He and Mulcahy hatched a plan to abduct a woman and torture her. They fantasised that after snatching her, they would blindfold her, drive her around London, walk her across rooftops and then hold her hostage in Duffy's flat.

A woman at home in her flat in Abbey Road one evening felt someone was watching her, turned off the light and was confronted with Duffy standing on the first-floor balcony staring at her through the window. She rushed downstairs, opened the door on to the garden and screamed. She heard the voice of a second man as they fled. She described the man at the window as short, with red hair and 'pig-like eyes'.[15]

The pair were angered and determined to prove themselves to each other.

On 10 June 1982, two men drove along North End Way, a road bordering Hampstead Heath, and at midnight, noticed a girl walking home alone. The 20-year-old au pair was dragged into the undergrowth, where she was raped by both of them.

After their first attack, Duffy and Mulcahy fled to Duffy's home in 'a high state of excitement'. They agreed that the attack had been easy and thrilling. As they began to plan another, a pact was made that if ever one was caught, the other would always stay silent.

Duffy would later say:

We'd talk about what type of girl we'd like to rape … for me it was exciting at the time, doing [the attacks], and the going out and the actual waiting. We used to call it 'hunting', and the actual waiting was the game. Afterwards I'd feel remorse, but as soon as the next time come [sic], that was all forgotten. The cycle started again. But David, he seemed to be going further and further. I mean his eyes were ablaze when he was doing it, he was a totally different person. He was in total control. He liked the dominance.*

Three months later, a woman was attacked in Golders Green. When an initial attempt to rape her was unsuccessful, the two men bundled her into a car and drove her to wasteland where the Jubilee line runs over the North London Line, beside Westbere Copse in West Hampstead.

Six days later, they struck again, this time in Arkwright Road, again close to the railway line and again at around midnight. A 17-year-old girl was attacked, and a belt tied around her neck. She was then dragged to an isolated spot and raped.

The last two attacks being just days apart considerably raised the level of attention the crimes were receiving. Blank-faced artists' impressions of both men stared out from the top of page two of the *Hampstead & Highgate Express* on 22 October. One man was described as 'early to mid-20s, 5 foot 8 inches tall with dark, curly or wavy hair, fairly dark skin and wearing a St Christopher. The second has blond, longer hair, is heavier built and shorter.' The car the second victim was abducted in was described as 'a yellow or cream saloon', and the belt used as 'maroon leather with an interlocking diamond design'.

---

* Robert Hazelwood, an FBI agent, said that one American serial rapist confessed to him that rape was 'the least enjoyable part of the crime', that it was from the planning that the real thrill was derived. Hazelwood said that this substantiates the idea that 'sexual assaults service non-sexual needs. It's power needs, anger needs, it's control'. (*Horizon: Traces of Murder*, BBC2, 9 May 1988)

Looking at the sketches now, with the benefit of hindsight, there would be little chance of anyone who knew Duffy and Mulcahy making an association, for, accurate though much of the information is, the faces are distractingly strange. Victims of attacks tend to exaggerate the features they do remember, resulting in misleading sketches that are dominated by one or two grotesque components.

Two days after that edition of the *Hampstead & Highgate Express* came off the news stands, there was another attack, this time in Kilburn, close to Duffy's home in Barlow Road. He and Mulcahy were driving down Kilburn High Road (they had airguns with them, and had probably been shooting at windows from Hampstead Heath, something they continued to do throughout this period) when they spotted a woman coming out of the Kentucky Fried Chicken shop, on her way home from a party and clutching a teddy bear. Mulcahy said, 'Let's hunt that,' and parked the car in a side road. Wearing balaclavas and tracksuits, they pulled her into Burton Road. She tried to shout but a plaster was immediately put across her mouth and a blade pressed against her as the taller man said, 'Don't worry, it's a knife.' They taunted her that all they wanted was the teddy bear. The blade was then held to her throat and she was manhandled over a wall into a partly built house, where both men raped her.

On 26 March 1983, Duffy and Mulcahy attacked the 29-year-old manageress of a French restaurant as she was walking home from work. She would later describe the pair as being 'two bodies with one brain', due to their almost telepathic communication with one another, a nod of the head from one being enough for the other to know what he was thinking. She was grabbed from behind but desperately fought back during Mulcahy's assault of her and bit his hand. This drove him into a frenzy, during which, after beating her to the ground, he kicked her repeatedly. The pair then ran off.

In July, an arts student was on her way to visit her boyfriend in South London at 11 p.m. when a man asked her the time. Twenty yards on, another man grabbed her from behind and held a knife to her back. She was then dragged off the road and on to a piece of land next to railway sidings. She was pinned against the wall by one of the men, who said, 'My name is Dave and I've never touched a woman before.' She tried to engage him in conversation, and he relaxed his grip slightly. She then tried to escape, but as with the victim who fought back in West Hampstead, this disobedience prompted him to explode with violence. He dragged her along the ground with even more aggression, before 'swiftly, angrily raping her'.[16]

The victim was seen by a police doctor, who collected forensic evidence and prescribed the morning-after pill. There seems to have been no aftercare offered to her whatsoever, something which would be unthinkable today.*

It seems there were no more attacks by the pair for six months. It has been suggested that this was related to a brief return to stability in Duffy's domestic life as he and his wife continued to try for a baby; however, there are a number of unsolved attacks on file which may well have been perpetrated by them, and others may simply not have been reported.

At the end of the year, Duffy's wife left him, prompting a terrifying proliferation of offences, doubtless due to anger

---

* It should be remembered that only months before the first rape committed by Duffy and Mulcahy, the BBC had broadcast *A Complaint of Rape* (18 January 1982), an episode of Roger Graef's fly-on-the-wall documentary series *Police*, which had spent a year following Thames Valley's E Division. The episode in question, which showed two officers bullying and dismissing a woman with a history of psychiatric treatment who claimed to have been raped by three men, was devastating evidence of something rotten in the attitudes of some police officers, and it also highlighted the shocking lack of care being offered to victims. The programme caused a public outcry and led to vast changes in the way such complaints are dealt with, but progress was clearly slow. A follow-up programme, *Panorama: Rape on Trial* (BBC1, 25 June 2006), assessed how much police behaviours and procedures had improved.

as much as opportunity, and quickly escalating in violence and frequency. Concentrating on the areas they knew best, namely Hampstead, Kilburn, Finchley and Cricklewood, Duffy and Mulcahy would recce lonely railway stations, 'the quieter ones … we had our favourite places', planning their attacks and their escapes with a militaristic precision.

The pair had stolen a cassette tape of Michael Jackson's recently released *Thriller* album from a car, and played the title track repeatedly to psyche themselves up as they drove around hunting for victims. They carried with them their trademark balaclavas, a knife and sometimes a blindfold. Mulcahy would affix strips of masking tape to the inside of his coat that would then be used to silence his victims. They both carried Swan Vesta matchboxes, which contained tissue paper as well as matches. The tissue was used after each attack to wipe semen from the victims, and was then burnt. They were now also tying their victims' hands together in a praying position, using coarse string. While one raped the victim, the other acted as lookout. 'Sometimes there would be arguments as to who would go first', according to Duffy. The nauseating disregard for human life is exemplified by the fact that such arguments were usually settled with the toss of a coin.

On 20 January 1984, Mulcahy collected Duffy from his flat and, after doing some decorating work for Mulcahy's parents, they drove to Barnes Common, where a 33-year-old social worker who was walking to the station was accosted by two men wearing masks. She was punched to the ground, threatened with a knife and gagged with a rag. The pair made horrific threats to mutilate her before dragging her into the woods; once there, the taller man failed to achieve an erection, and instructed the shorter man to gouge out her eyes. She was then raped by both men; the threat itself seemed to cure the taller man's impotence.

On 3 June, they trapped a 23-year-old woman in the waiting room at West Hampstead railway station. By now they were attempting to adopt different accents (on this occasion, Northern) to evade detection, a skill Mulcahy proved to be more adept at than Duffy. They marched the woman to the railway bridge and ordered her to strip before assaulting her, then told her to continue walking along the tracks. By the time she reached the next bridge and got back up on to the road, they were driving by and spotted her staggering down the street, Mulcahy jokingly suggesting to Duffy that they offer her a lift. Duffy later said, 'It was exciting in the car, although I felt a bit guilty about that one as the girl actually reminded me of my wife.'

On 8 July, a 22-year-old woman was walking along Highgate West Hill on her way home from a party. After they sprung on her, she collapsed in fear and was dragged across the road towards the cemetery. There, a knife was run across her lips. As she struggled to avoid being silenced with tape, one of the two men said to the other, 'Stab her, stab her,' then told her, 'You had better keep quiet, you bitch.' However, residents nearby heard her screams, and the two men vanished. They actually drove past the scene of the attack on their way home and saw that the police had arrived. This fuelled their excitement, as did their discussion about how attractive the girl had been, and of how 'she could have been a model'.

Duffy later said, 'we were playing a game with the police and generally making it fun. We never thought we'd get caught,' and that as far as the victims were concerned, 'we thought we were better than they were', the belief that allows those who commit such acts to justify their actions.

Thwarted on their last attack, they returned to Hampstead Heath on Sunday, 15 July, this time with Duffy carrying an imitation Colt Python gun as well as a knife. After driving around for a long time repeatedly playing the stolen *Thriller* tape, at 2.30 a.m. they spotted two 18-year-old Danish au pairs who had missed the last northbound train, walking up Spaniards Road, which runs across Hampstead Heath. According to Duffy, 'Being two of them, we had our doubts, 'cause it's easier to control one person. But we had a little talk first, split them up and they were both raped by me and Dave. He raped one girl, I raped the other.'

The two girls were followed and then confronted by two men wearing balaclavas, who forced them into a wooded area, seconds away from the main road but at a lower level, out of sight of any passing motorists. The tall man said, 'Now you have to be real nice to me. Okay?' After the attack, Duffy apologised, then robbed the girls of the £2 they had on them, and reprimanded Mulcahy for using his first name during the attack. The two girls were found by a minicab driver and taken to Hampstead Police Station, while Duffy and Mulcahy drove home, discussing how much more exciting it was to have two victims. Duffy was probably also electrified by the fact that, even though he had lost his grip on the imitation firearm when he had first pushed it to the victim's stomach, for the first time he had controlled a victim all by himself.

Duffy was repeatedly truanting from his job, preferring to spend his days at home watching violent movies. This was the height of the 'video nasty' era, when, due to a loophole in film classification laws, films which would otherwise have been heavily censored or banned easily found their way on to the rental market. Martial arts films were his favourite, many of them appallingly made and cartoonish; one particular film in his collection, *Jaws of the Dragon*, notably contained a prolonged strangulation sequence.

Finally, Duffy was sacked from British Rail, though he continued to travel about the network for free, identifying suitably dangerous places along the North London Line. His next and final employer was Westminster City Council; at his suggestion, Mulcahy then found work there too. On 19 October, the pair were stopped in Mulcahy's Talbot Horizon and found to be in possession of stolen building materials and plasterboard, for which they received a fine at Hampstead Magistrates' Court three days later. A balaclava was found in the car too, but Mulcahy claimed it was worn when he was working as a plasterer on dusty ceilings, and the arresting officer failed to appreciate its significance.

This close call did nothing to dissuade them. Nor did an appeal on the television programme *Police 5**** for information concerning the rape of the Danish au pairs, which unfortunately repeated the misperception that the two balaclava-wearing attackers were black.

On 26 January 1985, a 20-year-old German au pair was blindfolded with her own scarf, marched at knifepoint under a road bridge near Brent Cross shopping centre, then raped under a bridge that crossed the River Brent. She was then told to count to 100 before moving, and warned, 'We know where to find you if you tell anybody.' Four days later, they pounced again on Hampstead Heath, but this time events took an unexpected turn.

The victim, a 16-year-old girl, came out of the railway station at about 7 p.m., and immediately heard footsteps behind her. The taller of the two tracksuited men knocked into her with some force. He then put a hand over her mouth and pulled her head back. The shorter man put his right hand around her waist and pressed something, presumably

---

*   *Police 5* ran for thirty years, with editions in a number of ITV regions. As a result of the 25,000 appeals it staged, around 7,500 arrests were made.

a knife, against her left side. They both repeatedly told her, 'Don't speak or you're dead.'

The victim was dragged on to the Heath and asked how old she was and if she was a virgin. She then remembered the watching Duffy saying, 'Let's forget it, let's go. I told you, none of that.' Mulcahy took no notice, and apparently Duffy tried to push him off her. But then Duffy warned that there were people close by, and the pair ran.[17] Duffy would later claim that he had become worried by how aggressive Mulcahy was being, suspecting that perhaps he had intentions even beyond rape. 'I was so worried I went back and told him there was someone and to run. I actually had to pull him by the collar.'

Duffy's sudden assertiveness towards Mulcahy is as perplexing as his sudden panic over the level of violence being deployed. It is generally accepted now that for Mulcahy, the violence was becoming the dominating element of the attacks, and many of the victims assert that Duffy was generally the less violent of the two. Certainly the violence was moving beyond overpowering the victim and issuing terrifying threats to mutilate them, and it is probably at this point that Mulcahy became aware that he needed Duffy to be as much of a perpetrator of the violence as he was if he was to move things to even more appalling depths.

Two days later, they attacked a 23-year-old au pair in Church Row, Hampstead; she screamed for help so loudly that her voice gave out. She sustained severe facial bruising before her attackers ran off. In March, a 23-year-old woman was attacked as she walked to a petrol station to buy cigarettes in Swiss Cottage. A knife was put to her throat and she was punched in the stomach. As she struggled with Mulcahy, in desperation she told him that she had AIDS. Duffy intervened again, leading Mulcahy off. The following evening, they dragged a 25-year-old legal secretary on to the Heath by North End Way and raped her; this time Duffy punched her in the face when he became aware that she was looking at him through a gap in the blindfold.

Duffy's wife was living with him again at this point, making her final hopeless attempt to save their marriage. She found he was staying out more and more in the evenings, and that his nightly jogs could sometimes last as long as four hours. She found that:

> He could be very gentle and then without any reason he could be like a raving madman. On one occasion we were talking quite kindly and then he suddenly said he had raped a girl, that she had enjoyed it and that she had asked him to come back with him. He said it was my fault that he'd done it. I just didn't believe him.[18]

He then produced a personal stereo which he claimed to have stolen from his victim, and offered it to her as a present.

As the marriage collapsed completely, Duffy subjected his wife to a campaign of sexual, physical and verbal abuse, beating her, gagging her and, during sex, tying her hands behind her back:

> It got to the point where I couldn't stand looking at him or touching him. He couldn't understand it and demanded sex every day. Once he forced a handkerchief down my throat. He sat me down nice and calmly and told me to open my mouth and close my eyes. He said he had something nice for me. I thought it was a piece of cake, but he pushed a handkerchief in and then held me. He squeezed his hands around my throat and I pushed him off. He later apologised and said he didn't know what had come over him. I thought he was going to kill me.

He had become adept at tying her up with remarkable speed, sometimes managing it with just one hand, while the other held her throat. He mentioned suicide again around this time, the previous year having tried to stuff pills down Margaret's throat, which she had spat out. In June, she left him for the last time; a month later, he raped her at knife-point in a park in Hendon. She reported him to the police and he was arrested, charged with the offence and bailed. Margaret also took out an injunction forbidding him to come near her.

If it wasn't for the events that had transpired with his wife since the last attack, one would presume that Duffy was becoming disturbed by the mounting violence from Mulcahy. However, the attack on his wife suggests he was instead becoming inspired by it, and determined to prove himself in his own right.

By now, he was regularly offending alone. His first solo attack had been the previous year on Barnes Common; now he was growing more confident, attacking girls in Richmond Park, at Hadley Wood and West Hampstead rail-way stations, abducting another in Camden Town and then another at Hendon, who after the attack was ordered to comb her pubic hair to remove any he may have left on her. This was knowledge he had gleaned from the forensic examination he had undergone after his arrest for the attack on his wife.

A charitable mood was sweeping across the country on Saturday, 13 July 1985, the day of the Live Aid concerts in Britain and America. As the evening drew to a close, Mulcahy and Duffy took to the streets, attacking three times in one night. Their first victim was a dancer, walk-ing home along Warren Mews, off the Euston Road near Great Portland Street underground station. An hour later, they seized a nursery school assistant in Kentish Town Road. Finally, just a short distance away in Marsden Street, a 24-year-old secretary became the third victim of the night.

A massive police operation was underway to desperately try and find the two men who were terrorising North London, and who the press had nicknamed 'The Spiders'. It was codenamed Operation Hart, and initially based at West Hampstead, under the command of Detective Superintendent Ian Harley,* and then the late Ken Worker. The operation had been disbanded in 1983 but reformed the following year when more links had emerged; the 'Mica' computer, with advanced cross-referencing capabilities, was released to a divisional police station for the first time and the team moved to Hendon, where the computer eventually held 100,000 pieces of information on suspects. The team linked twenty-seven cases,** but even though a considerable amount of information had been amassed, progress proved slow. In October, Harley appealed in the press to the smaller of the two men, who was 'weaker than the other and sometimes apologised to his victims … a dominated man', to give himself up.[19] Speaking about the enquiry in 1988, Worker explained that:

We knew that one was a tall man and one was a short man. We didn't know a great deal about the tall man, but the shorter one was an A-secretor blood group and from witnesses, we were told that he had fair hair. He'd also given the witnesses information about being in prison and in prison hostels, but we thought a lot of that was deliberate lies to put us off the scent. We also knew this man often worked alone, and he

---

* Operation Hart's name was an acronym of 'Harley's Area Rape Team'.

** We will never know precisely how many attacks were perpetrated by Duffy and Mulcahy.

had very distinctive methods in the way that he operated.
He would always carry a knife, he would engage the girls in
conversation before he attacked them, he would steal property from them on occasion, and he would often attack near
deserted railway stations.[20]

They also knew that the taller man wore an earring, often
had problems maintaining an erection (which may have
prompted, and also been rectified by, some of his violent out-
bursts) and according to one victim, had a mole on his chin.

Operation Hart had compiled a database of sexual
offenders with an A-secretor blood group, which were
labelled 'The Z Men'. After the attack on his wife, Duffy's
name was routinely added to it, and it was noted that he
lived in Kilburn, where many of the attacks had taken place.
It was now a matter of working down the list and interviewing every suspect. Duffy was number 1,594.

Despite the injunction, while still on bail for the offence
against his wife, Duffy telephoned her asking to meet.
Tellingly, the place he chose was outside a North London
railway station; once there, he became abusive and aggressive, and when she left, he followed her back to the home
of her new boyfriend. He forced his way in, produced a
spring-loaded cosh from his pocket and attacked them both.
The couple required hospital treatment for head wounds,
and Duffy was charged with malicious wounding. At West
Acton Crown Court on 19 September, the judge-in-cham-
bers bailed him again, despite police opposition.

At 3.30 p.m. on 20 November, Duffy waited by a footpath
at the back of the Copthall Sports Centre in Mill Hill. There
he confronted a 20-year-old woman at knifepoint, dragged
her into the bushes and raped her. Because there was a very
good description of the attacker, the case was featured on
the BBC's *Crimewatch* programme the following month,

although not as part of any larger enquiry, as it had not yet been connected to Operation Hart. Duffy had been noticed by a number of witnesses (apparently walking with a dog that answered to the name Bruce). Along with an artist's impression, he was described as 'only 5ft 3in tall, with light ginger hair and pock-marked skin'.[21] Later in the evening, the response from viewers was described as 'very heartening': many local people had contacted the BBC after seeing the artist's impression, and one girl reported that she too had been raped by a man fitting this description.

On 2 December, Duffy appeared before the Hendon Magistrates on domestic abuse charges. The court automatically renewed the bail terms that had been approved by the Crown Court. An officer dealing with Duffy noticed his similarity to the Copthall attacker, but the victim failed to identify him. (Duffy did recognise her, however, and it was later speculated that this close call may have brought home to him the realisation that the more victims who survived, the more who could potentially identify him.)

Posters with sketches of Duffy and Mulcahy were building up across North London in what was now Britain's biggest-ever rape manhunt. Duffy said:

> We always knew the police were going to be involved at some stage and that they were going to start linking the crimes, but I think it came to a head when they put up the wanted posters for the North London rapists. We started to look for other places to go to.

On Christmas Eve, a woman travelling the North London line eastbound from West Hampstead became so frightened of a man in the carriage staring at her that when the train stopped at Homerton, she leapt on to the platform and rushed to the two men waiting there, pretending one of them was her husband.[22] She was fortunate. One stop further east, four days later, Duffy and Mulcahy would take a woman's life. One day in the future, a jury would be told that the pair 'now needed to be fed a higher level of cruelty and violence. This time Duffy did not pull back.'[23]

It is possible that up to sixty women suffered at the hands of Duffy and Mulcahy. With a vile inevitability, these two men were now to become murderers. Already their catalogue of depravity had made them Britain's most prolific serial rapists. That was no longer enough.

These crimes had been committed mostly in cheerless places disturbingly close to main streets and railway lines. Visiting these sites, one realises that both men must have been looking for potential attack sites everywhere they went. They operated in the cracks in the city, the narrow alleyways, the railway sidings and the unfenced roads that border the dark heaths and parks. In the press, police were now warning, 'No girl is safe after dark.'

My grandmother lived on a council estate in Harold Hill, Essex. It was mostly populated by decent retired East End folk, but by the middle of the 1980s, its crime rate was increasing distressingly swiftly. One particularly winter evening around this time, perhaps even during the winter in question, my father came to collect me and as we walked towards the car, I noticed a young girl walking alone in that dangerous place. I commented that surely she shouldn't be walking there by herself. My father replied, 'Son, she should have every right to walk wherever and whenever she wants to by herself.'

3

ALISON

A pitiless winter announced its arrival at the end of 1985. By Sunday, 29 December, only a few parts of the country were reporting temperatures above freezing. Snow had fallen in East Anglia and was now approaching London. It was one degree below freezing when Alison Day, on the last night of her life, set out from the home she shared with her parents and brother, a few hundred yards from Upminster Bridge underground station.

A manicured 'Legoland', Upminster, where my family also happened to live, lies at the far east of the District Line and just over the Essex border. A garden suburb with a fast mainline rail link into London that has led it to become a desirable finish line for commuters, it wasn't a very exciting place to be young in, but nor was it troublesome. Sir John Betjeman, who unashamedly adored the peculiarities of suburbia, spoke often of the need for us all to use our eyes, something my father, having the enquiring mind of a good detective, did unceasingly. On my Sunday evening walks with him as a boy, he would find something to stop and remark upon even in the most regimented of those avenues. I understand now that while a son or daughter might find the suburbs sober and banal, a parent views them as protective and uncorrupted.

Alison Jane Day was born on 23 May 1966 at Hackney Hospital. A few months later, she was adopted by Kenneth, a postal worker, and Barbara, who suffered from poor health and was undergoing dialysis by 1985. Alison, now 19, had been dating Paul Tidiman, a printer from nearby Rush Green, for three years; they were engaged and had planned to set a date for the wedding when they were more confident of their finances. Like my brother Martin, she had been educated at Gaynes School. He says, 'Sadly, I remember Alison Day. I never really knew her well but she was a pretty girl, with blonde hair. It's strange … I can see her now standing with her friends in the playground under the cycle sheds.' When she was 16, she helped to run the local Brownie pack at St Lawrence's church and, after leaving school, she worked as a clerk for a firm of solicitors in Hornchurch, a short bus ride away. The staff there found her to be bubbly, popular and reliable.

On the corner of Alison's road was a newsagents, which my father and I drove to most Sundays to buy a newspaper, as it was the nearest one to us that was open. Sundays were still quiet days in 1985. This one was particularly quiet because the Christmas break was proving a long one, Christmas Day having fallen on a Wednesday. Most factories and warehouses were still in darkness.

Paul Tidiman's firm, Fairway Graphics, were based at Hackney Wick, about 11 miles away from Upminster as the crow flies but a world away in atmosphere. The area beside the canal was home to a number of workshops and printworks. Because of problems with the machinery that evening, Paul was asked to stay behind and work overtime. He telephoned Alison in the afternoon and suggested that she come over there to keep him company. She'd never been to his workplace before, so he gave her directions and said that if she left home between 5.30 p.m. and 6 p.m., he would start looking out for her from 7 p.m. She had a meal with her parents, then set off, having borrowed £2 in 20p pieces from her mother.

Hackney Wick not being on the underground, her journey meant taking a bus to Romford, from there a train to Stratford and then another train one stop further. Alison walked the 300 yards from her home to the bus stop outside the tube station, and there saw a couple of friends, who stopped to chat to her while she waited. The journey to Romford took ten minutes. Rose Lee, a ticket collector at Stratford, remembered a girl fitting Alison's description asking her for platform information at about 7 p.m. and remarking what a cold night it was. That would prove to be the last known sighting of her. What happened next would remain unclear for many years.

John Duffy had spent the day watching video cassettes at his parents' home. He was preparing to accompany them to a social club for the evening when the telephone rang. David Mulcahy had been ill and out of circulation for a few weeks, but certified fit by his doctor six days earlier now simply said to Duffy, 'Let's go hunting.'

Duffy made an excuse to his mother and, wearing dark clothing and carrying a knife, was collected in Mulcahy's van. The pair dropped Mulcahy's children at their maternal grandmother's home in King's Cross (his wife was visiting relatives in India), then drove around, following the North London railway line out of their home turf and eventually arriving at Hackney Wick, a site Mulcahy had earmarked. The area around the station was ill-lit and deserted: a dangerous place.

Today, this is a land of hipster bars and art exhibitions, basking in the silver shadow of the Olympic Stadium; back then, it was a wasteland, a monument to London's industrial decline, a place haunted by abandonment. Detective Sergeant John Manners remembers it as 'a dark and miserable place, and not somewhere for even a uniformed policeman to walk around on his own'.[1]

It is easy to forget that although the war had been over for forty years, its ravages were still a significant part of London's make-up at this time. This was a city as much of waste ground, dereliction and demolition as it was of bright lights and bustle, and on a gloomy night it wafted out the impression that it was crumbling both physically and spiritually.

Visiting today, I find that overlooking the site of Alison's ordeal there is now a bar crammed with happy, animated youngsters, all of them blissfully ignorant of what once happened here. And yet it is still a dangerous place; a moment away from the bars is still an unloved wilderness of scrapyards, ripped-out buildings and imagined footsteps. Eerily, I notice a man on the footbridge photographing that forgotten crime scene; when I then walk the route Alison was meant to take that night, I encounter him again, photographing what was once Fairway Graphics. Perhaps I am not the only person in the neighbourhood this evening aware of what once happened here, after all.

Alison was probably the only passenger on the one stop along the line from Stratford that night. When she stepped from the train and crossed the footbridge, she was actually less than five minutes from her destination. Duffy and Mulcahy were watching from the opposite platform. As she started to descend the steps, Mulcahy ran up past her, then turned and grabbed her from behind. She struggled desperately until Duffy produced his knife. Mulcahy then told her that if she was quiet they wouldn't hurt her. He and Duffy discussed taking her into the station waiting room, but instead decided to walk her along the platform and down to the canal. Duffy kept hold of her while Mulcahy walked behind them, acting as lookout. They walked her across the live tracks, down the bank and under the railway bridge, and while a quarter of the population of Britain were settling down in the warmth and safety of their homes to watch that night's film premiere on television, they subjected Alison first to relentless sexual violence, then, in Detective Sergeant Mick Freeman's words, 'tortured her to death'.[2] Less than two hours earlier, she had been having dinner with her parents.

During his assault on her, Duffy asked Alison her name, and saw from her necklace bearing the letter 'A' that she was telling the truth. He then told her to freeze while a man walked past on the opposite towpath, but this stranger who could have saved her life appeared not to notice them.[*]

After he and Mulcahy had each raped her, they gave Alison her clothes back and told her they were going to put her back on the other side of the canal. Duffy led the way, climbing back up the slope and on to the railway line. The plan, certainly in his mind, was to leave her on the towpath with orders to wait fifteen minutes while he and Mulcahy escaped. But Mulcahy wanted to continue persecuting her. Rather than allowing Alison to walk beside the tracks, he forced her to walk along the frosty, narrow ledge on the outside of the bridge. The bridge was too high for her to hold on to the top, and instead, she had to press herself against the freezing ironwork. Halfway across, she lost her footing and fell into the canal, screaming out that she couldn't swim. She waded to the edge, where Duffy pulled her out; as soon as she was on the towpath, she broke free and ran for her life, having no idea of her surroundings or where she was heading. Duffy's instinct was to make his

---

[*]   The man was never traced.

escape in the opposite direction. But as on previous occasions, a victim's defiance enraged Mulcahy, and this time more than ever before. From the other side of the canal, he shouted, 'Get the bitch, John. Get her.'

Duffy caught up with her, then remonstrated about Mulcahy letting his name slip again. 'David was annoyed she'd managed to run. He was making threats. I still believed he was going to leave her somewhere. I even said: "Why did you say my name?"' Mulcahy led Alison down to a pile of rubble and pushed her over. He attempted to remove her jeans, but they were soaked and clinging to her skin. Once he had succeeded, he raped her again, while Duffy acted as a lookout. He then marched her across a playing field with Duffy following. 'When he got to the other side, he was rough with her.' Mulcahy cut some material from her blouse, which was now on inside out. Alison pleaded, saying, 'Please, it is only the moustache I have seen. I will not tell anyone. Do not hurt me.'

But Mulcahy 'kept going on about being identified and that we would be done for attempted murder'. Mulcahy stuffed some of the torn material into her mouth, used some to tie her hands together in a 'praying' gesture, then tied another strip around her neck, knotted it, and fed through the knot a 4in-long piece of twig. He looked at Duffy and told him, 'We are in it together. We have got to do this together.' Duffy recalled, 'He was twisting it at the same time. He kept on about taking it, twisting it, which I did. I gave it about a half twist and I let it fall to the floor and walked away.'[3] Mulcahy then started to drag Alison's body back towards the canal, and told Duffy to help him. They rolled her into the water, then separated and each made their way back to the van.

Alison's watch stopped when she went into the water. The time on it was 8.10 p.m. Her ordeal had lasted an hour.

On their drive back, Mulcahy justified their actions to a worried Duffy by insisting that the killing was necessary, as they would be facing a charge of attempted murder anyway. Mulcahy was confident he could claim to have been looking after his children all evening, but Duffy's mind was racing to devise an alibi. Returning home, he quickly changed, then joined his parents at the Social Club.

By now, Alison's boyfriend had left Fairway Graphics to look for her, accompanied by his mother, and had contacted her parents. At 9.15 p.m., Alison's father telephoned British Rail enquiring if there had been any accidents on the line. The police then visited Alison's home and completed a Missing Persons Form.

Appeals and reports of Alison's disappearance began to appear on television and radio the following day. A police search of the area by helicopter on New Year's Day yielded nothing, nor did door-to-door enquiries, either in Hackney or in her own neighbourhood. Seventy officers, some with tracker dogs, searched industrial estates, open ground and derelict buildings, while divers from the Underwater Search Unit searched the canal, initially without success. An incident room was set up at Romford Police Station, where my father was at the time dealing with the Keighley Barton enquiry.

The *Daily Mirror* and *Daily Mail* were the first of the national newspapers to appeal for information, reporting Alison as '5 foot 7 inches tall, of medium to slim build, fair complexion and shoulder length blonde hair. She was wearing a three-quarter length suede jacket, jeans and pink and white flat shoes. She was also wearing a gold necklace with her name on it, and another with a horn-of-plenty emblem.'[4]

At the end of the week, the local press reported that:

Fears were growing late last night over the fate of missing teenager Alison Day. The pretty 19-year-old blonde disappeared without trace after leaving her home in Upminster at 6.15pm on Sunday. A massive police operation around East London involving hundreds of officers, tracker dogs, helicopters and an underwater search unit has so far failed to solve the mystery, searching Hackney Wick, Stratford and Upminster Bridge. Detective Inspector John Pierce said: 'We are very concerned for her safety. If Alison reads this and has a problem, she can ring me in confidence and have a talk'. Parents Kenneth and Barbara were too distraught to talk, and are being comforted by relatives as they keep a round-the-clock vigil by their phone.[5]

Paul Tidiman told the *Daily Mail*, 'She means more to me than anything else. I love her very much and I desperately want her to come back.'[6]

Detective Sergeant Brian Roberts explains that 'although it started out as a missing persons enquiry, it was John Pierce who was insistent that this wasn't just a missing person. He was convinced she would never stay away from home through choice.'[7]

At this point, although police feared the worst, Alison's loved ones were still trying to cling to the unlikely possibility that she had chosen to run away. The police enquiry was exacerbated by the fact that no one could ascertain which route she had taken to Hackney Wick, or whether she had actually got there. In spite of Paul's instructions, she could have been driven by the cold to take an underground train to Mile End and change there for Stratford instead, and even if she had gone to Romford, there were three different buses that could have taken her there, multiplying lines of enquiry that led nowhere.

The Sunday after Alison's disappearance, a roadblock was set up outside Upminster Bridge station, the place where the last positive sighting of her had taken place. Similar action was taken at Hackney Wick. Police stopped 750 cars and questioned the occupants to see if anyone had seen her. At the same time, officers armed with posters questioned travellers on buses and at twenty-five rail and tube stations along her likely alternative routes. The following week, the local press noted that they were probing a brutal knifepoint rape in Hackney Wick that had occurred on Tuesday the 7th, in which a 20-year-old girl was attacked a few hundred yards from the station. Already by now, house-to-house enquiries had gathered more than 200 interviews. On Sunday, 12 January, a reconstruction and appeal was broadcast on the London edition of *Police 5*.

Alison was still missing when the following week's *Romford Recorder* was published. The paper reported:

Kenneth, Alison's father, left his round the clock vigil by the telephone to face television, radio and newspaper reporters at a press conference at Romford police station. 'If anybody is holding her, why? Why are they holding her? Please let her go. She has done no harm to anyone. If Alison hears or reads this, then I would say come home straight away. If you are frightened to come home, then don't be. If she walks through the door now the police would not take any action against her'.

Mr Day remained composed but his wife Barbara was too upset to attend the press conference. 'The family is taking it very hard. My wife is very, very upset. She is just keeping herself busy. Alison's boyfriend is shaken just like the rest of us. There is no reason why she would have left home. She was perfectly happy. She would not have gone anywhere with anyone she did not know. If she went out and without her boyfriend, then it was with friends, and she always came home by taxi. We can't give up hope. That is all we have, hope.' He described her as a home loving girl who always discussed things with her mother when she had a problem.[8]

The only useful information came from the ticket collector at Stratford, who was certain she had spoken to Alison. Detectives were inclined to believe her, since she had made her statement the following day, with events still fresh in her mind.

'The underwater search team had to break the canal up into sections, and you can only go into water like that for short periods,' explains Detective Sergeant Barry Fyffe, one of two exhibits officers* on the case. 'There were dangers from contaminants in the water and all manner of things that had been thrown in there.'[9]

On the morning of Wednesday, 15 January, frogmen found Alison near the east bank of the canal, 200 yards south of the Eastway Bridge and 300 yards from Fairway Graphics. By chance, the Royal Navy, on a training exercise further along the river, subsequently discovered her coat, weighed down by two granite blocks in the pockets. Beside some metal fencing that had been dumped in the canal (which Alison must have been very close to landing on when she fell from the bridge) was her hair slide. She was still wearing her jewellery.[10] Her shoes were never found.

Alison's boyfriend had to face not only the news of her death but the fact that, with nothing to go on, police had to consider whether he could be a suspect. Most murders are committed by someone the victim knows, and there was no way of knowing at this stage that Alison's death belonged to any larger enquiry. Brian Roberts, the other Exhibits Officer, says that:

These days Paul would have had a Family Liaison Officer placed with him and been handled with kid gloves, but when you consider that something like 90 per cent of murders are

---

* A police officer appointed to catalogue and manage the movement of all exhibits gathered during the course of an investigation.

committed by someone known to the victim, that line of enquiry has to be investigated.

Having had to deal with bereaved parents many times in the course of his career, Barry Fyffe observes that:

> When parents lose a child, especially in circumstances like those, the reaction of a man to the loss of his daughter can be completely different to his wife's reaction. They can't always help each other as their reactions can be very different. She's your lass, and men know what beasts some men are. That eats away and men can become angry.

At the police forensic lab in Lambeth, Alison's coat, inside which were found the directions she had taken down and which her father confirmed were in her handwriting, took two days to dry out before it could be inspected. The standard way of inspecting such an item for any fibres that may have been shed by an attacker was by 'taping': placing strips of Cellotape across the material and then lifting them off to see what has clung to the adhesive.

Dr Geoffrey Roe found that:

> The coat was muddy and covered with the remains of small animals from the river, which made taping much more difficult than normal. However, we could see that we were picking up fibres on the tapings, some of which might have come from the attacker. So we knew that if the murderer was caught there was some possibility that we could match fibres on the tapings to fibres on his clothing, but the chances were very slim.[11]

Five different sets of alien fibres were eventually lifted from the coat.

Detective Superintendent Eric Brown, appointed Senior Investigating Officer of what was christened Operation Lea, told the evening news that 'in the last three weeks we've had a very good response from the public',[12] but the post-mortem appeared to yield very little, most of the forensic evidence having been destroyed due to the amount of time the body had been in the water; what remained could not exclude any individual. As Barry Fyffe explains, 'In those days, before DNA, blood was grouped very simply; you could tell if someone was a secretor* or not; that was about it.'

There was nothing apparent to suggest that Alison had been killed by two men, but pathologist Dr Peter Vanezis did find one unique element at the post-mortem. Speaking in 1988, he recalled that:

When I was asked to do the autopsy I found that this lady, who'd had a ligature round her neck, had also had this ligature tightened with a tourniquet. A branch was used from somewhere nearby. In addition to this there was also a knot which had been tied into the ligature around the front of her neck in order to tighten the neck even further and have an effect therefore on the voicebox. The fact that we had this combination of injuries led us to believe that possibly the person involved may have been someone who knew something about the martial arts or indeed possibly someone who'd been in the armed forces, but of course at that stage this was mere speculation.[13]

---

* A person who secretes their blood-type antigens into bodily fluids and secretions such as saliva and semen. Before DNA technology, blood type from bodily fluids other than blood could only be obtained from secretors, who make up about 80 per cent of the population.

Barry Fyffe continues:

> There were three lines of enquiry. We found that the tour-
> niquet concept had at one time been taught in first aid as a
> method of staunching bleeding, but it had been discontinued
> as you needed to release it on regular basis or you would cause
> more damage. And also, if you looked at the City and Guilds
> course for carpenters, a variant of it was used to hold a piece of
> wood in place while glue was setting.

In fact, although Duffy was a carpenter, it was the third line
of enquiry which would prove the right one: Dr Vanezis'
suggestion that the killer may have had a knowledge of
martial arts. The technique of using a stick through a knot
as a lever to tighten a ligature is in fact known specifically as
a 'Spanish windlass'.

Brian Roberts continues:

> The enquiry [had] begun at the station closest to Alison's
> home, but we then moved to Hackney and were based in a
> portacabin at the back of the station. There was practically
> nothing to go on, we couldn't even ascertain which side of
> the canal Alison had been assaulted on or where she had been
> thrown in.

Alison's watch was found to be in good order and almost
fully wound; a service manager from Seiko supplied an identical model which was tested in water, and this cemented the
view that she had been thrown into the canal at 8.10 p.m.

Public appeals did result in one piece of seemingly significant information. A minicab company had logged a call
at 7.13 p.m. from a young woman asking for a cab from
Hackney Wick station into Hackney. She was told there
would be a delay; the caller then hung up. The telephonist

remembered the caller sounded distressed. 'We did a lot of work following that up,' says Barry Fyffe. 'And we considered whether there had been a rogue taxi driver who could have picked her up.' We know now that it couldn't have been Alison, yet at the time it sounded plausible, and this kind of coincidence could have dangerously diverted the enquiry if it wasn't for disciplined detection. Fyffe adds, 'You stick with the evidence, you don't speculate. It's all very well coming up with theories but you have to keep to what you can prove. That was your dad's mantra when he came on to the enquiry, and mine too.'

If Alison had somehow made a call (assuming she had enough money left from the £2 she had set out with) because she was lost, or sensed she was being followed, her boyfriend or the police would have been the obvious people to contact, though as an existing line of enquiry, it had to be exhausted. (The caller was perhaps another lone female who had been uneasy at the presence of Duffy and Mulcahy.)

Eric Brown turned to the BBC's *Crimewatch* programme, and a reconstruction and appeal were broadcast almost two months to the day after Alison's death, outlining the main theories as to what could have happened that night. The first was that Alison had been followed from the train, called the cab firm and then been abducted. Or she could have left the station, got lost, made the call, failed to get a cab and then taken a wrong turn into Wallis Road, which led to a printers yard regularly haunted by men looking for discarded proofs of pornographic magazines printed in the neighbourhood. Brown also speculated that she could have been picked up by car, or caught a bus somewhere.[14]

Later that evening, *Crimewatch Update* reported with characteristic optimism that there had been at least twenty calls to the studio and more to the police directly, though these merely reported sightings of Alison on the bus and the train en route to Hackney Wick. Brown did appeal for other women who may have been attacked in similar circumstances however, and thirty-eight contacted the programme, some of them reporting the crimes for the first time. Detective Sergeant John Manners continues the story:

Eric Brown was a reasonably new superintendent, and after a few months' running the enquiry he went to Bramshill* on a course. There came a stage when I was in charge. Eric had gone and there were just a few of us and a couple of WPCs effectively running a major crime, which was absolutely disgusting. I think there was an attitude from higher up that this was unsolvable and they wanted it wound down. The working conditions were appalling considering it was a murder enquiry. It was going nowhere, and money was short because of the Wapping Dispute.** Then your dad was brought in.

Barry Fyffe explains that:

I first knew Charlie when I was still in uniform at Plaistow, years before this. We both had enormous respect for honesty. When he took over the Alison Day enquiry, he came over to the porta-cabin, sat down with us and said, 'What do you think? Do you think we should carry on?' He listened to what we'd got to say, how we'd been drastically depleted in terms of manpower and so on. But we said that we felt it was worth pressing on. He then flung all his support behind that. He went back to the governors and said that we were of a mind that there were still things to be considered, and that he was going to support that.

---

*   The Police Staff College, located in Hampshire, which was until 2015 the principal police staff training establishment for England and Wales.

** A year-long strike by workers of News International which climaxed with the sacking of virtually an entire workforce by owner Rupert Murdoch.

'He rejuvenated the whole squad,' affirms Brian Roberts.

> Eventually he got us moved back to Romford, where the working conditions were far better. That's important. We set up an Incident Room in what had been the Commander's Office, which was ideal, because you can't have somewhere where other people are wandering in and out. Eric Brown was a very nice man but I think he was maybe a bit too nice. He didn't have the push and know enough like your dad did. Charlie didn't suffer fools gladly.

John Manners calls my father:

> a brilliant detective who had a lot of time for his troops and who would stand up for any of them. It's a cliché, but he was an inspiration to everybody who worked on the enquiry. We would have done anything for him.

Charlie went back to the original suspects and inevitably had to interview Paul, Alison's boyfriend. Brian Roberts was present for this:

> He interviewed Paul at Romford and it was one of the first interviews I was party to where we had a sound feed to another room so that Charlie could be given opinions by other people during the course of the interview. It became apparent Paul had nothing to do with Alison's death, but all the way along, Charlie treated him with kid gloves. This was long before close family or friends who are suspects were typically treated this way.

Alison's disappearance and later the hunt for her killer drew heavy media attention locally, and I can vividly remember my father driving me to school the morning after that interview, and me asking if Alison's boyfriend was who they were looking for, to which he replied, 'He never did that. The boy's devastated.' 'But how do you know?' I asked. If he'd been less modest he might have said, 'After twenty-odd years dealing with murders, you know', but instead he simply said, 'You just know.'

He organised a new wave of publicity. A local medium pestered him with nonsense as a result, but even a further newspaper appeal and a whole edition of *Police 5*[*] devoted to the case, in which he and presenter Shaw Taylor walked the murder scene, yielded no useful information. There were really only the five fibres found by Dr Roe and the use of the tourniquet. Crucially, however, he was about to make the breakthrough which would turn the investigation of a seemingly unsolvable local murder into the biggest criminal manhunt since the Yorkshire Ripper Enquiry, which had finally ended five years earlier. But unlike that catastrophic chain of events, the excellent and collaborative detective work of a number of separate police forces on this occasion probably saved lives.

But prior to that breakthrough, there was increasing pressure from what he would go on to label in the press as 'penny-pinching'[15] superiors, keen to close the enquiry down. Eventually, in Barry Fyffe's words, 'he faced the governor and said, "If you want to close it down, you do that. But you can be the one who tells Mr and Mrs Day." Without him standing his ground, it would have been shut down, no question.'

At the Incident Room, the Operation Lea team continued to examine any unsolved sexual assaults, John Manners recalling that he personally probably read over 100 different statements relating to rapes in the Met area. Barry Fyffe remembers that:

---

[*]   Broadcast on ITV in the London region on 15 June 1986. Sadly the programme no longer exists in the archives.

Initially two young WPCs would read through each report to see if there were any similarities with our enquiry. After a while we realised that these young women officers were leaving the station and heading home in the dark having spent the day reading about attacks on young females. This side of things tends to get forgotten. The people on these teams are ordinary human beings. Charlie never lost sight of that.

Duffy was lying low. Mulcahy, however, was hiding in plain sight, unable to resist an opportunity to be the centre of attention. In March, he took part in a roller-skating marathon from Southend to London in aid of Guide Dogs for the Blind. The event was covered on the children's programme *Blue Peter**. Watching the programme, he is clearly visible skating alongside presenter Simon Groom, at one point cheerfully helping him up from a fall. The camera also catches him momentarily giving a rather intimidating stare. A month later, he and Duffy found their next victim, who was still a child. She may well have watched the programme.

A crime committed against one person has countless victims. A murder destroys countless lives. And even though a crime may be solved, there is no true solution to the suffering that crime has unleashed. The most that can be hoped for is to find and contain the perpetrators. The impact of a man's momentary evil endures. In Shakespeare's words, 'the evil that men do lives after them; the good is oft interred with their bones.'[16] I asked my father many years later, with regard to the parents of a murder victim, 'How do you get over something like that?' His reply was simple. 'Son, you never get over something like that.'

He had years of experience dealing with bereaved families, and I'm told that he believed that after the initial stages,

★ Broadcast on 10 March 1986.

the senior officer, having so many demands on their time, should step back and allow another officer, in this instance Barry Fyffe, to be their main contact. But on his first meeting with Alison Day's parents, offering assurance but also necessary prudence, he told them, 'We will do everything in our power to catch whoever did this. But there's one thing I can't do, and that's give you your daughter back.'

4

MAARTJE

Peering from the window of my train, the rich countryside of Surrey now regrettably reminds me of Sherlock Holmes explaining to Watson how, when he surveys rural houses, 'the only thought which comes to me is a feeling of their isolation and of the impunity with which crime may be committed there'.[1] For John Duffy and David Mulcahy took this very train journey once, looking not for beauty, but for dangerous places, and found one in the opulent village of Horsley. This is 30 miles from Hackney Wick, where Alison Day had died in December, but in every other sense it was truly a world away from that wretched wasteland, until the afternoon of Thursday, 17 April 1986.

Horsley is a verdant district, a place of high-achieving schools, riding clubs and golf courses, linked to the capital by motorway and railway but swathed in green belt. The village noticeboard is a colourful, busy display of events organised by the local Decorative and Fine Arts Society, the Classic Car Club and the History Group of the local school. The sense of community is strong in this well-behaved parish, the crime rate mostly limited to burglaries. Two weeks before Duffy and Mulcahy went there, the local paper obligingly publicised a nationwide campaign by the police warning that 'attacks on women have received a lot of publicity lately'[2] and offering basic safety advice, a well-meaning gesture which residents of this bucolic place probably felt had little relevance for them.

A pretty child, quiet but happy, Maartje Tamboezer had just celebrated her fifteenth birthday. A 'little dot of a thing',[3] she was born in Holland on 22 March 1971, the daughter of a civil engineer who was employed by Shell UK Exploration and Production, and had a younger brother and sister. Her father's work had led the family to make their home in a number of countries during her short life; on this occasion, they had been in the UK for just under a year, living in Little Cranmore Lane, West Horsley.

Maartje was bright and studious, and spoke English fluently. She attended the American Community School in Cobham, and on the day she died had been excited about a school trip back to her home country that weekend. School finished at 3 p.m.; earlier that day she had told her friends she was planning to buy some English sweets for the trip. She was collected from school by her mother, and when she got home she had a drink and ate some biscuits. Mrs Tamboezer then took her other daughter to the riding stables nearby.

Shortly after this, Maartje left the house on her bicycle, with her purse in a plastic bag hanging from the handlebars, and headed for the neighbouring village of East Horsley, which had the sweet shop with the best selection. As I retrace Maartje's route that day, a girl who could be the same age that she was cycles by and smiles easily at me, even though I am a stranger in town. An unusual occurrence in London, but a commonplace one in a safe, friendly neighbourhood.

Maartje cycled past West Horsley Garage, where a passer-by remembered her by her blue jacket and bright turquoise trousers. Her mother had always told her to keep to the main roads when cycling, but there is a well-used shortcut to East Horsley along a cinder path that runs alongside the

Waterloo to Portsmouth railway line. The Tamboezers often cycled along it as a family, but the children were instructed never to take it if they were alone.

David Mulcahy, still employed by Westminster Council, had spent the morning replacing a doorstep. Thursday was payday; at lunchtime, he went to the depot to collect his wages, where he met Duffy, who was on sick leave but had come in to collect his pay packet too. Mulcahy told him he had found a new location for 'hunting', where he had recently given a woman a fright. He promised Duffy that he could 'go first' if they found a victim. They arranged to meet again in a couple of hours. When they did, Mulcahy handed Duffy a spare crash helmet, and the pair travelled by motorbike towards Epsom. They no longer needed a car stereo blaring out the *Thriller* cassette as an overture to rape and murder.

They rode around the area looking for a victim, then drove to a railway station. They parked in a side road, hid their crash helmets and gloves nearby, then took the southbound train deeper into the countryside. Two or three stops on, they came to Horsley. They walked down Station Approach, crossed the main road and, keeping alongside the railway line, soon saw that the road became a secluded path that was bordered by woodland on one side and the railway on the other. As they walked along the path, Maartje Tamboezer came into view cycling towards them.

Both looked around and decided the area wasn't clear, and so stepped aside to let her pass. They walked on, soon coming to a point where the path kinks. Seeing that there were no better ambush points up ahead, Mulcahy produced a reel of nylon cord from his pocket and said to Duffy, 'What goes up must come down.' Sensing that the girl was on her way to the parade of shops they had passed at East Horsley, and would soon be coming back, he tied one end of the cord around a post and the other through the chain link fence of the railway cutting, then they lay in wait on opposite sides of the path, Duffy nearest the railway line, Mulcahy hidden behind a tree.

Ten minutes later, they saw her returning. When she reached the tripwire, she stopped, and they sprung from their hiding places, Mulcahy pulling her off her bicycle and ordering her to be silent. Duffy held her by the collar and led her across the grass towards Lollesworth Wood, Mulcahy wheeling her bicycle behind them. When he flung it into the trees, Maartje screamed; Mulcahy then walked back to her and hit her across the face with the back of his hand. He told her again to be quiet and not to look at him, although neither man was making any effort to conceal his face. They walked her along the perimeter of the field (the longest route possible), then into the woods; through those, they then walked her around the edge of another field bordered by woodland, where Mulcahy decided 'this will do'. Mulcahy acted as lookout, but when Maartje tried to stop Duffy removing her trousers, he came back over enraged and threatened her. Then he left them. Moments later, a man walking the cinder path on his way to the station found the tripwire, untied it and walked on.

After raping Maartje, Duffy became alarmed that Mulcahy was nowhere to be seen. He eventually spotted him beckoning from the other side of the ploughed field. Duffy took Maartje by the arm and started to lead her across, but it was muddy owing to heavy rain the day before, so instead he walked her around the edge, following the line of the drainage ditch. Duffy challenged Mulcahy about having been left alone with her as both men forced the child into another wooded area. Mulcahy explained that he had gone back to hide the bicycle, and had been seen by a woman walking a dog. Maartje spoke again and Mulcahy went haywire. He said, 'You're looking at me again. I told you I was going to hurt you.' He told her to be quiet again, and then, without warning, struck her on the head with a large piece of flint he was holding. She was knocked unconscious.

Mulcahy pulled off her belt and put it around her neck, then placed a stick through it, saying to Duffy, 'That will make it easy for you.' Then he added, 'We're in this together. I did the other one, you do this one.'

Duffy used the stick as a tourniquet, and began to twist it, Mulcahy driving him on, murmuring, 'Yeah, yeah,' and, 'I done the last one, you done this one, we're in this together.' He told Duffy they had to take care of each other, then walked away, saying, 'I'm going to get the other bitch.' But he didn't seek out the woman who had seen him earlier. Instead, he hid behind a tree and watched Duffy carry out his orders. When Duffy retraced his steps around the field, Mulcahy ran up behind him and patted him on the back, like a school football captain championing a young hopeful. 'You done good,' he told him. Behind them in the spinney, amidst a dazzle of bluebells that were announcing the arrival of spring, Maartje Tamboezer lay dead.

Mulcahy handed Duffy a £10 note, half of the money he had found in Maartje's purse, then told him to go back to the station while he returned to the body to wipe away any fingerprints that might have been left on the belt and the rock. Once there, after cleaning up his prints, he used tissues and matches to set fire to parts of Maartje's body in an obscene attempt to destroy forensic evidence. Then he headed for home. Maartje's watch stopped at 5.35 p.m.

Just before 6 p.m., a resident saw a man in a dark blue jacket climb over a gate from the woods and enter Oakwood Close. Two other residents driving home together also noticed this man, and that he had mud on his right shoulder. He appeared out of place in an affluent cul-de-sac, and looked away as the car passed him.

As Duffy boarded the 18:07 train to Waterloo, Mulcahy was making his way past a sea of commuters coming out of Horsley station. A man in a car waiting for his wife was one of a considerable number of people who would later remember seeing a hurrying man first try to reach the platform via the ticket office, then, when he found that the door was locked, dash through the side gate and rush across the footbridge, colliding with two women as he did so. When the man reached the platform, the train was already moving off, but he frantically waved his arms about, and the kindly guard signalled for the driver to stop. Thanking him, the man boarded the train.

The carriage was empty except for two girls. The man sat down and began staring at one of them so intensely that she later said she would have moved carriages if her friend had not been with her. She looked out of the window but, because it was dusk, she could see his reflection as he continued to stare.[4] The two girls alighted at the next stop; Mulcahy and Duffy, travelling in separate carriages, got off a few stops later, returned to the motorbike and sped back to North London as fast as possible to try and establish alibis, Duffy calling in at a local video shop where he was known. When they next saw each other, Mulcahy talked about a God-like feeling when committing murder, and the feeling of having 'the power of life and death' over another person.*

When Maartje's mother returned home at 6.30 p.m., twenty minutes after the train carrying Duffy and Mulcahy back to London had left, she was alarmed by her daughter's absence. After telephoning friends, she contacted her husband, who was away on business, then called the police. A search of the area began, assisted by friends and neighbours.

---

* Peter Woodcock, who strangled three children during 1956 and 1957, similarly stated, 'I felt like God. It was the power of God over a human being.'

By nightfall, the family were frantic. At 10.30 p.m., Maartje's bicycle was found resting against a tree on the edge of the wood. The lock was not engaged and the keys were still in the mechanism. The surrounding area was taped off, but in the pitch dark, no other trace of her could be found.

At first light, the search continued. At 8.15 a.m., officers met two men ferreting for rabbits. When asked if they had seen anything suspicious, they mentioned what had looked from a distance like a green fertiliser bag in the woods. The search for Maartje was over. Surrey's biggest ever murder investigation, Operation Bluebell, had begun.

Detective Chief Superintendent Vincent McFadden and Detective Superintendent John Hurst arrived at the scene, and were confronted with what Hurst later called:

> [P]robably the worst murder I'd come across in my career. She had been savagely raped, subjected to brutal head injuries and strangled, and the killer had tried to destroy the body by burning. It was so horrendous, everybody was absolutely devastated by what they saw. I was of the view that there was no way we could ever give up until we'd caught whoever did this.[5]

At 10 a.m., Dr Roger Ainsworth, the pathologist, and a team of scientists from Aldermaston Forensic Science Lab arrived at Lollesworth Wood, along with Ken Williams,[*]

---

[*]   Ken Williams (1939–2009) introduced a wealth of processes that improved efficiency in the forensic photography field, and championed a system for the application of a physical developer, a chemical treatment used to reveal finger marking that would have been otherwise invisible to the naked eye. In addition, he developed a process for producing high-quality photographic prints from marks lifted from crime scenes using the specular reflection of light. Williams also introduced specialist light source and ultraviolet photography techniques to Surrey Police for the photographic recovery of injuries and evidence such as body fluids that may have escaped detection, and introduced equipment that used ultraviolet light sources to help identify marks from crime scenes. In addition to his forensic work, he also introduced video and video-stills technology to assist major investigations by making footage immediately available for investigation teams to use in briefings, and later, the introduction of digital cameras to the unit.

whom Hurst describes as 'a brilliant forensic photographer'.[6] Williams took stills and video of the murder scene, and the post-mortem was delayed to allow the deployment of the latest laser technology to detect fingerprints on the skin. String had been tied around Maartje's fingers and thumbs over her mitts, spent matches surrounded the body and a piece of stick was resting against her, but at first glance none of these items looked likely to offer much to the investigation.

The post-mortem revealed that although there were lacerations on the scalp caused by blows from a blunt instrument, Maartje had died from asphyxia due to strangulation by ligature. However, because the stick that had been used to create the tourniquet had fallen from the knot and was lying against the body, the distinctive murder method that had been identified in the Alison Day enquiry was not yet apparent to Surrey officers, and it was assumed that the stick had been placed beside the body merely as an accelerant to burning.

From semen stains on Maartje's clothing, forensic scientist Anne Davies* could determine the rapist was group 'A' and a secretor, but by measuring an enzyme in the blood called PGM, they could narrow it down further. Measuring PGM will divide people into ten categories. Davies' test revealed that the rapist was either PGM 1+, PGM 2+1+ or PGM 1+1-. This allowed the police to eliminate four out of every five suspects on the blood grouping alone.

John Hurst says that:

We didn't know at that point that there were two men, as the PGM evidence didn't divide any further than to tell us that

---

*   Anne Davies is today a distinguished behavioural and forensic scientist, and a pioneer in the prosecution of rapists. She also acted as technical advisor on the television series *Waking the Dead*.

there was a foreign PGM as well as the victim's; one alien PGM could mask another. Unlike DNA, which was still in the future,* a PGM result was a balance between percentages rather than a certainty.

Mulcahy appears not to have raped Maartje, however, by now being primarily interested in murder.

A major incident room was set up at Guildford Police Station, with 120 officers working on the case. Amazingly, the string contained a mine of information. It was a variety called Somyarn, spun from paper, and the only manufacturer was Somic, a firm based in Preston. It was, to be exact, Somcord b/24/K, made from 50 gram imported paper, which the company hadn't used since 1982. Somyarn wasn't sold in retail outlets, but was supplied solely for industrial use, chiefly to commercial laundries or for tying animal feed sacks. Untied, the amount used on Maartje ran to 9ft, and therefore the killer had surely been in possession of a full reel rather than having recycled a small amount. It had in fact come from Duffy's wife, who had acquired it while working at Sunlight Laundries.

The factory in Preston noted that the width of the string, between 17–18mm, meant it had come from an 'edge strip' (when the string is being cut, the pieces at each end of the block will always be slightly oversized or undersized). Far from being an indistinct ball of string, the combination of the unusual width and the age of the paper meant it was probably unique.

The following Wednesday evening, police officers stood at the entrance to Horsley station handing out copies of the *Guildford Times* in the hope that people would read

---

* The first person convicted of a crime based on DNA fingerprinting evidence, and the first to be caught as a result of mass DNA screening, was Colin Pitchfork, arrested in 1987 for the Leicestershire murders of Lynda Mann in 1983 and Dawn Ashworth in 1986.

the report of the case and answer their appeals for help. Thousands of commuters were questioned, and every man in the village was asked to account for his movements on the day of the murder. Already nearly 600 calls had been received by the incident room and hundreds of information forms had been submitted.

For the first time in a Guildford murder enquiry, computers were used to store every piece of information. John Hurst says, 'We were using a very early version of the HOLMES system, HOLMES being Home Office Large Major Enquiry System.' The system had been introduced in 1985, in the wake of the disastrous Yorkshire Ripper enquiry. In that case, the identity of the killer had been buried within a sea of paper which comprised over 150,000 statements and manual card indexes (the floor of the incident room at Wakefield had to be reinforced to take the weight of it, and there was a backlog of 36,000 documents still waiting to be filed when the killer was finally apprehended).[7] The subsequent Byford Report, which had identified failings in the £4 million Ripper Enquiry, wanted to ensure such mistakes would never happen again. The hunt for John Duffy and David Mulcahy had the potential to see history repeat itself. Any or all of the things that had let the Ripper enquiry down and cost a number of women their lives – namely shoddy detection, too much assumption, a lack of organisation, poor co-operation between different police forces and egotism – could all so easily have come into play here, but thankfully, they were eschewed.

Many lines of enquiry proved erroneous. A mysterious piece of metal found near the murder site puzzled police, but an appeal in the local press led to a British Rail guard identifying it as a tool used in the guard's van of special coaches.[8] There was also an appeal for a man who had placed a bag in a left-luggage locker at Guildford station on the morning of the murder and not returned to claim it, and another for an agitated man who had telephoned the British Transport Police that evening. The BTP number was the first number listed under 'police' in the Guildford telephone directory, and it was felt he may have mistakenly thought he was through to Guildford Police Station. The office was closed and the answerphone had recorded his distressed voice asking, 'Is that the police?', then a woman saying calmly, 'Now come on, you don't want the police, put your phone down,' and the man replying, 'Well what shall I do then?' before the call ended.

John Hurst told the *Surrey Advertiser*, 'We can't say this man is not going to strike again.'[9] He urged that no woman or child should walk out alone, particularly in more isolated areas. The same edition reported that the whole village was shattered by the tragedy, and that local schools had decreed that 'no child will be allowed to walk home unaccompanied'.

Scores of witnesses came forward, one or two reporting sightings of two men lurking on the footpath,[10] but the vast number repeatedly describing the same one man. The descriptions were impressively consistent, generally being: around 5ft 9in tall, with brown hair, blue jacket and blue trousers. One witness, who was waiting to turn on to the main road at the top of Kingston Avenue, the road that leads to the cinder path, had seen a man walk around the hedge and had been so disturbed by the way he had stared at her that she had missed a gap in the traffic. The man being described is clearly David Mulcahy, reinforcing Duffy's later recollection that he himself passed no one on his way back to the station.

A middle-aged woman reported to police a strange incident that had occurred on the cinder path three days before the murder. She had been walking from the

Medical Centre towards West Horsley when a man had jumped out in front of her and performed 'a war dance',[11] but he ran off when she called her dog. The woman described him as 5ft 8in tall, slim build, with collar-length dark hair, two or three days' growth of stubble, a mid-blue anorak and blue trousers. John Hurst recalls, 'We never got a lead on that. In the end, we could never find an actual connection with the murder.'*

Police initially felt that the crime was local, partly because of an apparent knowledge of the area. When I visited Horsley, I certainly found it hard to believe that Mulcahy could have found the route out of the woods at Oakwood Close so easily, and also have got his bearings quickly enough to walk so purposefully to the station, without any prior knowledge of the site. Although he and Duffy had initially been looking for a victim in the Epsom area, I believe that Mulcahy was the 'war dance' man from a few days earlier. The description is uncannily similar to those of the man seen on the day of the murder; additionally, he told Duffy that he had 'given someone a fright' a few days previously, and on every other occasion a reconnaissance had been carried out at the scene of their attacks.

The police soon realised they would have to cast the net wider, not least because of the number of witnesses who had seen the man running for the London train. This meant trying to trace every person who had been on that 18:07 between Horsley and Waterloo, and searching through 2 million rail tickets. They found dozens of tickets that could have been the one bought by the running man, but none with fingerprints that matched with criminal records.

---

* Another witness who lived near the railway bridge reported seeing a man of this description in the area twice before, once at the end of March and then again nine days before the murder. She described him as 28 years old, 5ft 11in, slim build, mid-brown hair brushed across his forehead, wearing a blue anorak and blue trousers.

John Hurst turned to *Crimewatch*, and was in time to secure a reconstruction and appeal in the next edition, broadcast just over a month after Maartje's death. The appeal focused on the sightings of the brown-haired man on the footpath a few days before the murder and on the day of the murder, including those in Oakwood Close and at the station. It also revealed the sighting of a man in a field close to the murder scene who had appeared to be peering into the adjacent field as if waiting for some people there to go away. This is likely to have been Mulcahy, either on his thwarted attempt to retrieve the bicycle or awaiting the opportunity of a clear escape route back to the station. Detective Chief Superintendent Vincent McFadden revealed that Maartje's Jordache purse was still missing, and that it had contained about £25, her door key and a Dutch bank card.

There were 156 calls from viewers, but little of the information led anywhere. A police constable from Cambridgeshire called to relate a report of string tied across a footpath beside a railway line recently, and a man of similar description being seen in that area, but this, along with claims by a few callers that they knew who the man in the videofit was, as well as a report of another attack on that path several years ago, all came to nothing.

By this point, my father had taken charge of the Alison Day case, and was about to make the breakthrough that would prompt John Hurst to write in his retirement book, 'Charles, I shall always remember the first time we met.'

The *Daily Mail* would later report that, because Charlie had suspected (wrongly, it would transpire) that Alison's killer had started stalking her at Stratford station, he had 'sent a message to police stations asking to be informed of any train or tube station incident'.[12] Brian Roberts explains, 'When Charlie took over the case, he immediately went out looking at any other murders or rapes that were unsolved, to consider whether they were linked or not, and combed the police gazettes for similar unsolved crimes.'[13] Barry Fyffe remembers, 'We were still in that portacabin at this stage, in the midst of the move to the Romford Incident Room, watching the telex and looking for any other attacks that may have had certain similarities.'[14] Then Charlie saw the report of the murder of Maartje Tamboezer, and telephoned Vincent McFadden.

The two men compared notes on how the two victims had died. As Charlie disclosed the details of Alison Day's death, he said to McFadden, 'She was strangled, but the strange part, and we've never let this out to anybody, is that a tourniquet was used.' McFadden asked what he meant by this. Charlie explained that this was a piece of wood put through the knot and twisted. Speaking about the case on television in 1988, he said of this moment, with a glint of professional pride, 'I can hear the silence now.'[15]

'Your dad and I got into the old Vauxhall Cavalier and drove down the M25 for the first of what would be many visits to Guildford,' continues Barry Fyffe:

> We met McFadden and John Hurst, and asked to look at the photographs of their victim. Then they went to get a cup of tea. We looked at the photographs and there, lying beside Maartje Tamboezer, was what looked like a burnt stick. They'd thought it was there to assist in burning the body. Charlie and I looked at each other and both knew exactly what it was. We had made enquiries with the Metropolitan Police Murder Index too, had gone back through the records and could find no previous killings that had involved a ligature of that type. We had always kept back that detail about the tourniquet; you do this in case someone for whatever reason tries to claim responsibility for the murder, so that you can test their story.

'This was crucial information,' says John Hurst. 'I was taken aback. Obviously we needed to sit down and talk immediately. And then, well, it really moved on. That turned everything around.'

On Wednesday, 4 June, the Senior Investigating Officers met at the Royal Surrey County Hospital mortuary. The two pathologists, Dr Ainsworth and Dr Vanezis, agreed that the two murders were connected pathologically, and declared that in all their experience neither had ever come across such a method of killing before.*

In looking at further possible links, both Charlie and John Hurst had studied the North London attacks. John Hurst was struck by similarities between the attack on the woman at West Hampstead station in June 1984 and the Maartje Tamboezer case. In both instances, clothing had been cut, hands tied and the blood group detected was A-secretor. Within a few days, liaison with Operation Hart, the investigation into the North London rapes which after a year without success was on the verge of closing down, led to this additional link being confirmed. The similarities in so many of the methods and the suspicion that there was a clear pattern of increasing violence which had ultimately led to murder resulted in McFadden holding a press conference on 13 June to announce the joint operation.

'We had one computer system linked to Surrey and then another to Hendon, where Operation Hart was based, but they were on two different formats: these were early days,' says Brian Roberts. All the same, he was still shocked at the resources available at Guildford:

---

*   Possibly the only other known use of the technique in a murder case occurred in Barnsley, South Yorkshire, in 2013, when Stephen Barnsdale-Quean murdered his wife using a Spanish windlass constructed with a chain, a hair bobble and a rolling pin. The forensic scientist on the case was Liz Harris, who will play a key role later in this story.

Not only were they not in a portacabin, but they had a computer system which you could type something into and it would find any occurrence of it. I mean that's now just the basic search function on a word document, but back then this was revolutionary.

'The Surrey team I had a lot of respect for,' says Barry Fyffe:

They were so committed to finding the people responsible for Maartje's death, and they put a vast amount of manpower and effort into it. John Hurst was very supportive towards us, and he made representation at the highest level to get more money allocated to our enquiry.

Hurst explains, 'You had to have a special formal arrangement to link murder inquiries between different forces, you had to write it all out, explaining what you saw as the links, in order to persuade the powers that be.' Vincent McFadden proved to be an excellent broker, allaying any fears the decision-makers harboured that linking the enquiry would result in an unending wild goose chase.

'Charlie made the crucial connection by old-fashioned detection and wearing out shoe leather,' says Brian Roberts. From being a seemingly unsolvable murder being run on a shoestring from a portacabin by an underfunded and poorly supported team, that link turned the enquiry into the biggest criminal manhunt since the aforementioned search for the Yorkshire Ripper, with three forces now pooling their resources for what came to be called Operation Trinity.

Their biggest hope was that the answer lay in Operation Hart's database of sexual offenders with an A-secretor blood group, the list termed 'The Z Men'. The twenty-officer team was currently interviewing every one of them, but John Duffy's name was still some way down the list.

The connections between the deaths of Alison Day and Maartje Tamboezer, and the rapes in North London, had been made just over a month after Maartje's death. But by then, Duffy and Mulcahy had already killed again.

Having walked from Maartje's house in Little Cranmore Lane – the windows of which are instantly recognisable as being the ones in the background of the photograph of her fifteenth birthday party, that image which was such a familiar sight on the television news in 1986 – before walking the cinder path and Lollesworth Wood, I stopped at the local pub. It was a Saturday afternoon in autumn, and the first log fire of the season was enchanting the room. A sixteenth-century inn, uncorrupted by gimmickry or kitsch, it was a charming place to spend an hour in the company of a circle of retired villagers. Soon I'd almost forgotten the reason for my visit, and the inconceivable events that once occurred here. But then, as I made to leave, music began to play in the bar. The track was Michael Jackson's 'Thriller'. An unpleasant coincidence, but one that haunted me as I took the way through the woods.

Those woods where Maartje was murdered are today part of the Horsley Jubilee Trail, a nature ramble that was completed in the year of the Golden Jubilee. This is a popular site for the local populace to take their children to share the simple pleasures of spotting the common blue and the clouded yellow butterfly, as well as the goldcrest and, much to my delight when I visited, the sparingly glimpsed green woodpecker.

And as I walk the cinder path, there ahead of me still stands the shabby post that Maartje's killers tied cord from and lay in wait beside. A few minutes earlier, I had reached the point by the railway bridge where one has the choice of taking the right fork and following that lonely path, or doing as Maartje's parents had advised her, and walking the main road to the sweet shop. It struck me that if Maartje had gone straight ahead, today she would be 44 years old.

5

ANNE

Two days after Maartje Tamboezer's death, on the day she had been due to go on that school trip back to her home country, a wedding took place in a small commuter town on the opposite side of London. The bride was 29-year-old Anne Lock. A week after she returned from honeymooning in the Seychelles, she vanished. The 'missing bride' story quickly became a media sensation, prompting wild speculation and fascination from a public in the grip of wedding fever following the announcement of the engagement of Prince Andrew and Sarah Ferguson, an event to which this story provided the perfect counterpoint in the press. Anne was the third woman to lose her life at the hands of John Duffy and David Mulcahy.

Anne Veronica Syniuk was born on 11 June 1956 in Barnet, North London. She left school at 18 to work as a secretary, first with the BBC, then for ATV* at their base in Elstree. She lived with her parents and grandmother, but by 1984 both her parents had died. By now she had fallen in love with 26-year-old Laurence Lock, who ran a meat-importing business locally. The couple had met through a passion for swimming, and married on 19 April 1986; at 29,

---

* Associated Television, an ITV powerhouse that broadcast in the London area at weekends between 1955 and 1968, and in the Midlands until 1982.

this would have been considered 'marrying late' in those times. Anne's 86-year-old grandmother moved into their marital home with them in Brookmans Park, a small and prosperous dormitory town midway between Potter's Bar and Hatfield, 19 miles north of central London.

By now Anne was working for London Weekend Television* as the secretary to Jeremy Bugler, editor of *The London Programme*, a commanding Friday-night series that explored 'the major stories in and around the capital' in an impressively tough fashion. In the mid-1980s, its growling theme music and putridly tinged opening footage of London life, from rioting to shabby casualty wards, most certainly painted the city as a dangerous place.

Anne had worked for Bugler for nearly three years. He remembers her as 'very conventional, quite reserved, and above all very proper':

> She was always on time, she did everything very correctly. You would never see her in the bar, and she never flirted with anybody. She was old-fashioned, shy in fact. She was a very good person who suffered the most dreadful misfortune.[1]

Anne and Laurence returned from their three-week honeymoon in the Seychelles on Thursday, 8 May, and she resumed work at Kent House, LWT's headquarters on the South Bank, the following Monday morning. The same day, John Duffy took a tube to the lonely station at North Weald in Essex, and loitered there waiting for a victim. PC Peter Basnett happened to be in the vicinity:

---

* The ITV franchise holder for the Greater London and Home Counties area at weekends between 1968 and 2004. After a rocky start, LWT became a fine broadcaster, in 1975 scooping more BAFTAs than the rest of the ITV network combined. Notable LWT successes included *Upstairs, Downstairs* and *The South Bank Show*.

I was in the company of DC Pat Blease, and driving past the station on a totally unrelated matter, when I saw Duffy, who I knew because I had interviewed him with Detective Inspector Tom Brazil for the rape of his wife. She had described that he had threatened her with a butterfly knife during that offence.

I knew that he lived in Kilburn, and so I was surprised to see him in North Weald. We stopped and searched him, and found the knife, plus a box of matches and some tissues, which at the time meant very little, but which were later important. He was arrested and taken into North Weald Police Station.

(When searched, Duffy claimed the knife was 'for cutting knots in his shoelaces'.) 'At the station, all the items seized were recorded on his custody sheet. He was then bailed to attend West Hendon Police Station at a later date and subsequently charged.'[2]

At West Hendon, he was charged with carrying an offensive weapon, and it was noted that he was already on bail for the charges against his wife; the trial for those charges had initially been set for 2 December 1985, delayed until 5 March 1986, and then delayed again. The police made a strong request to Recorder Peter Archer QC* at Acton Crown Court for bail to be denied on this occasion, but it was unsuccessful. Six days later, Duffy and Mulcahy murdered Anne Lock.

Although the station at Brookmans Park was busy at peak commuter times, it was otherwise a quiet place, isolated and bordered by woods and fields. The station was staffed by a single booking office clerk until 8 p.m.; after that, it was lawless. Mulcahy had been planning an attack there for some time; on several previous Sundays, he had noticed a

* Peter Kingsley Archer, Baron Archer of Sandwell (1926–2012), served as Solicitor General for England and Wales in the Labour government of 1974–79. He was an idealistic and frequently impressive politician, with an otherwise noble record of achievements.

woman alighting a train late in the evening carrying a white bag, and now told Duffy she should be their next victim.

Two twists of fate led to Anne Lock stepping off a train at Brookmans Park station on the evening of Sunday, 18 May. She would have accompanied Laurence on a weekend trip to Dorset, where he was planning a diving trip for his sub-aqua club, if she had not been on call as duty secretary that weekend. Bugler explains, 'It wasn't irregular for her to work on a Sunday. The programme was made on a fairly tight turnaround, and although it wasn't compulsory, people were grateful for the extra work when help was needed with transcripts.' Even so, she would normally have driven to work on a Sunday given the lighter traffic, but she had sold her car three days earlier, her husband having ordered her a new one as a present for her thirtieth birthday, which was three weeks away.[3]

She had spent that morning at home with her grandmother. At 1.30 p.m., the office had telephoned asking if she could come in to type up some scripts. She left the house, saying she wouldn't be late, and went to the station on a bicycle borrowed from her best friend, Lesley. The ticket office clerk, who knew her by name, told her the time of the next train to London and, after placing the bicycle in the cycle shed, which was generally left unlocked at weekends, she boarded the train at 3.43 p.m., arriving at Kent House an hour later.

Duffy had spent the early part of the day attending a martial arts class. He found Mulcahy waiting for him when he returned home to Barlow Road. The pair changed into darker clothing and, armed with knives, drove to Brookmans Park in Mulcahy's car, intending to lie in wait for the girl with the white bag. They arrived there at around 6 p.m., parked the car where it would be least conspicuous, at the cluster of shops close to the station, and wandered around, planning their attack. A police car passed them at one point, prompting Mulcahy to hide his knife on the ledge of the bridge on Station Road until it was needed. Prowling the narrow track leading from the railway line to the woods, they tried to appear as casual as possible when a man walking a dog passed them and said, 'Hello.'

Anne worked later than she had expected to, and at 8.30 p.m. handed the scripts to the drivers in reception who were waiting to ferry them to the producers' homes, said, 'Goodnight,' to the security staff and left Kent House. She walked to the York Road entrance of Waterloo station and took a Bakerloo Line train to Oxford Circus, then a Victoria Line train to Finsbury Park. There she waited for the train that would take her that short step from London to rural England. Another woman on the platform at that time was behaving strangely; seated on a bench, she was staring into space, cackling continuously. This rather eerie behaviour was referred to in subsequent appeals to try and jog fellow passengers' memories, but no one ever did come forward to say they remembered seeing Anne there.

Duffy and Mulcahy had by now returned to Brookmans Park station, and saw that the ticket office clerk had gone, leaving just the bicycle shed light on. The station lights came on automatically at 9 p.m. They went to the shed and saw what was clearly a ladies' bicycle, a red 'Londoner' with a wicker basket on the front. Thinking it might belong to the girl with the white bag, they decided to hide it, giving them the opportunity to grab her as she looked for it.

At about 9.40 p.m., a 16-year-old boy cycling through the station on his way home from a friend's house discovered a man loitering between the shed and the ticket office. A guilty thing surprised, the man asked, 'Have you seen anybody with an airgun? Somebody's been shooting at pedestrians with an airgun.' In the heat of the moment, Duffy had betrayed something of himself. It will be remembered that ten years earlier, he and Mulcahy had been convicted of shooting at pedestrians with an airgun, an activity they had continued to indulge in ever since.

Finally, they saw a train come in at 10.01 p.m., and one female passenger disembarked. It was not the woman with the bag, but they didn't care. As Anne crossed the footbridge, Duffy ran along the pathway beside the track to ensure there was no one else about, then joined Mulcahy on the platform. They talked casually, avoiding looking directly at Anne, then followed her to the bicycle shed. At 10.03 p.m., a nearby resident heard a scream coming from the direction of the station.

In her moment of confusion at not seeing the bike, Anne had been grabbed by Mulcahy, Duffy then telling her that he had a knife, and that they just wanted her money. Walking either side of her, they led her south along the footpath beside the railway line. Anne told them she had just got married and that her husband would be looking for her, but there was no humanity in them to appeal to.

They walked her nearly a mile down the footpath in the dark; while the psychological torture of a victim had always been part of their ritual, it had now reached its peak in terms of both the cruelty Duffy and Mulcahy were showing, and their confidence. The footpath at one point is interrupted by Hawkeshead Road; here, the lights of nearby Potter's Bar become visible. Having crossed the road, they led Anne through a copse and over a fence into a field. There, Duffy forced her to the ground, told her to remove her clothes and raped her while Mulcahy kept watch.

Mulcahy then threw Duffy his keys and told him to 'go and get the car' which was parked back at the station, adding, 'Take your time.' Duffy obeyed, taking Anne's handbag with him. He walked back to the car via a field on the opposite side of the railway line, searching the bag as he went. What happened while Mulcahy was left alone with Anne, we will never know.

Duffy waited in the car for over a quarter of an hour, becoming increasingly anxious. He was on the point of driving off to look for Mulcahy when he saw him jog into view, 'on a high and buzzing'. He ushered Duffy into the passenger seat, saying, 'I'll drive.' When Duffy asked about the risk of their victim recognising them, Mulcahy told him not to worry, as she would not be saying anything. As they drove off, Mulcahy, electrified, told him, 'Keep your eyes open for another one.'

Anne's grandmother had actually expected her home earlier than she would have arrived, and so by the time Laurence returned home, she was already distressed. He immediately unhooked the boat he had towed back from Dorset and drove to the station, arriving just as a train was coming in. Finding Anne was not on the train and that her bicycle was missing from the shed, he telephoned LWT to ascertain what time she had left, then drove to the next station down, Potter's Bar, which was manned. He enquired with staff there, telephoned friends and then called the police. A search began of the area around the station, and at dawn the bicycle was found, still padlocked, 75 yards north of the shed, leaning against a fence. Anne Lock was now officially a missing person.

The following morning, Detective Inspector Paul Dockley arrived on the scene. 'I was a young, thrusting DI,'[4] he says when recalling the case that he would play a crucial role in over the next fifteen years. 'I interviewed Laurence Lock, who was adamant he had met that train at Brookmans Park, but somehow the timings were slightly out. At first glance, one or two things didn't quite add up.'[*]

Two days later, the national press picked up the story. The media demand certain behaviours and so do the

---

[*]   The confusions were probably due to Mr Lock having miscalculated the time of his return, and maintenance work on the railway that weekend affecting some of the services.

public, and while Lock wasn't the victim of a campaign as severe as that suffered by Christopher Jefferies* many years later, there were certainly inferences and innuendos in the reporting of the story. As Dockley recalls:

> She loved her grandmother, who was living with them, so it seemed extremely unlikely that she would have vanished of her own accord. But the press went to town on the fact that a bride had vanished the weekend after returning from her honeymoon while her husband was away for the weekend, and that he was a butcher. You can imagine how the tabloids portrayed it.

Jeremy Bugler adds:

> It was very difficult for Mr Lock; he came under great strain, understandably, and it made the media decide that he was behaving like a suspect. There was speculation initially that she had run off too, but we all knew that whatever had happened to Anne, it wouldn't have been of her own accord or anything to do with him. She was such a straight up and down person, a woman of great regularity, and very happy. She couldn't wait to get back home every evening. There was a feeling from the beginning that if she hadn't been found in 24 hours then something horrible had happened.

The story broke in the national press on 21 May, with the headline 'Kidnap Fear For Vanished Bride',[5] a colleague

---

* Christopher Jefferies was neighbour and landlord of landscape architect Joanna Yeates, who disappeared from her Bristol home in December 2010 and was found murdered on Christmas Day. Jefferies was initially arrested on suspicion, and while held in police custody became the victim of a monstrous series of libels in the media. After another neighbour, Vincent Tabak, was found to be Joanna's killer, Jefferies won libel damages from eight publications. The Daily Mirror and *The Sun* were additionally found guilty of contempt of court.

saying, 'Anne is very much in love. For her not to have returned home, and still be missing forty-eight hours later, can only mean that someone has done something to her,' and Laurence saying, 'I have to believe she is still alive.' The BBC's regional news programme, *London Plus*, reported that police were 'completely baffled by the way a newly-wed woman seems to have, in their words, "vanished into thin air". Theories that she had been kidnapped remain just theories.'[6]

Laurence was convinced that she had been abducted, and determinedly said on the programme, 'If Anne is watching, we're looking for you Anne, we're going to find you, there's no doubt about that. Just hang on, we're coming.' He insisted that there was:

> no reason why she would have disappeared of her own free will. She was idyllically happy here and she just wouldn't leave her grandmother, me, the house or anything, she would have wanted to come home ... someone or something has detained her away from her home and the things she loves ... something is stopping her coming home because she'd come home if she could.

As with the disappearance of Alison Day, the police were unable to retrace Anne's journey that evening with certainty; as Paul Dockley points out, 'Whatever had happened to her could have happened at numerous places on her journey home.' Indeed, the *Daily Mail* were claiming a week later that the underpass leading towards Waterloo station that she would have taken was known by LWT staff as the 'Murder Mile' because of the number of muggings there, and that police at this point suspected that Anne had been 'abducted and possibly murdered somewhere between the studio and the station'.[7]

Even though it was surmised that if she had got that far, Anne would have taken the 9.38 p.m. train from Finsbury Park, which reached Brookmans Park at 10.01 p.m., a couple returning from a hiking trip were sure they were the only ones to alight from that train.[8] Furthermore, Laurence had arrived home just before 10 p.m., and said that when he arrived at the station to look for Anne, a train was just coming in. These discrepancies and confusions therefore spread the hunt for Anne over a wide area and a vague timescale.

At Brookmans Park, as well as the witness who reported hearing a scream and the teenager who encountered the 'airgun' man, someone reported a red car* at the bottom of Station Road that evening, possibly a 'Ford Escort or a Talbot Horizon, either a saloon or a hatchback, but not an estate', and another witness gave a strikingly good description of Mulcahy as:

> a man standing on the footbridge looking onto the road, a white male aged between 28 and 30, with a long face, prominent chin, mousey collar-length hair, straight at the sides and spiky on top, and wearing an army style jacket with no hood.

The next day, the local press issued a detailed description of Anne as:

> five foot six, with shoulder length blonde hair which she occasionally wears up, a deep sun tan, and wearing a Killy-make sleeveless white ski top with a navy blue back and red collar. Underneath she was wearing a pink wool top covered in small scotty dogs. She was also wearing blue jeans and grey Hi-Tec training shoes, a small pearl necklace and single pearl earrings.[9]

---

*   Mulcahy owned a Talbot Horizon, then a red Alfa Sud.

Paul Dockley managed with impressive speed to have the disappearance mentioned on that month's edition of *Crimewatch*, just four days after Anne's disappearance, making it probably the swiftest appeal in the programme's history.

'In those days, *Crimewatch* wouldn't deal with missing persons enquiries,' he points out, but they agreed to include the case in the 'Incident Desk' section of the programme, which consisted of brisk appeals without reconstructions. Coincidentally, the appeal for information on Anne's disappearance immediately followed the lead item: the murder of Maartje Tamboezer four weeks earlier.

The programme appealed in particular for two men the police wanted to trace. The first was 'probably a student', who had boarded a train at Potter's Bar at about 9 a.m. the Tuesday before Anne had disappeared, asked a woman on the train for a kiss, and got off the train at Brookmans Park.

The second sighting seemed more significant. The night before Anne's disappearance, at 11.45 p.m., a group of people returning to the station from a dinner party found that a bench had been positioned at an angle across the entrance to the platform. Having walked around it, they were then approached by a man who asked them what time the last train was, waited a few moments, then ran off.

The evening did lead to a breakthrough, though not via the public, as Dockley revealed to me:

I attended the studios on the afternoon of the broadcast, where each SIO would brief the phone teams on the jobs being broadcast that night. The first SIO was your father, who talked about the disappearance of Alison Day. I'm a North London boy so I knew the area and the River Lea in particular. I listened intently as he described the circumstances and the scene, which was alongside a railway station.

One of the next to speak was Vince McFadden, who spoke about the murder of Maartje Tamboezer, a young girl cycling alongside a railway line. By the time it was my turn to speak about the missing bride, my mind was working overtime about the similarities between the three cases. I could hardly contain myself after the briefing concluded and contacted my SIO, Detective Superintendent Ron Archer, and said I needed his permission to suggest what was going through my head: that these offences were linked.

I then spoke to your father and Vince. In those days young thrusting DIs were starting to be listened to, which was probably not always the case in your father's day. Both Charles and Vince questioned me at length about our missing bride. The conversation continued in the bar after the programme went out, and then, as I recall, we went to your dad's office, where Ron Archer met us and we talked. I said that although we hadn't got a body, the circumstances were incredibly similar. Vincent McFadden then made a phone call to his Chief Constable, and our incident room was moved from Welwyn Garden City to Hendon.

I was then made responsible for the outside teams, and I had a joint team of Hertfordshire, Met and BTP officers. There I was, surrounded by senior officers who had twenty years more experience. I had struggled in Hertfordshire to get this missing person enquiry ramped up; although Ron Archer had been behind me all the way, he'd been hampered a bit financially. Ron was a lovely man, just like your dad, a really nice genuine good quality copper. Ken Worker became SIO of the Anne Lock case as well as Operation Hart at this point. Ken was what I'd call a 'Steady Eddie' detective. It wasn't unusual to see him sat in his office with his jacket off, braces down and surrounded by clouds of smoke. I was blessed as a young DI. I learned a lot from these guys, from four really good detectives.

My father was fond of reflecting that 'most murders are solved on the back of an envelope', and Paul Dockley agrees:

> It's rarely one person solving a murder. It's a group of experienced detectives getting together, and those moments huddled around a bit of paper with a map sketched on it, and them all saying 'but what if it had been this?' A murder case is usually like a jigsaw puzzle. All you have at the start is a bit of blue sky, and you don't even know which way round it goes.

The publicity was by now generating an enormous response; the following day, the BBC reported that the police had received 'hundreds of telephone calls'.[10] On Sunday evening, exactly a week after the disappearance, police officers travelled Anne's route home, questioning passengers. Unbeknown to them, Laurence was also retracing his wife's footsteps. He went to the LWT offices, walked from the front door to the station, then recreated her train journey northwards. 'I found absolutely nothing,' he told the press:

> I just wanted to get the feel of what was going on. I have never been on that route before, but travelling it helped me to understand how my wife must have felt sitting on a lonely platform at night. I didn't find anything. All I got was a feeling of what it must have been like.[11]

The press implied there was some significance in the fact that Anne's best friend was staying at the house to help comfort her grandmother and that Laurence had been met by her when he arrived back at Brookmans Park after reconstructing Anne's journey. They went further the following day, deviously contriving a set of quotes purportedly from Laurence that read, 'I don't know how to look for people.

That's a police job. I'm just a butcher. I cut up meat for a living. All I want is my wife back.'[12]

The press also reported that Laurence had been questioned by police for several hours. 'I had to interview him as a suspect at one point just to put it to rest,' explains Paul Dockley. Tracker dogs, helicopters and vast numbers of officers were searching the area around the station, but in Dockley's words:

Operation Swallow, as it was called, began in mid-May, and with the search, as fast as we cut the undergrowth down, it grew again; that summer was very warm and very wet. At the same time we were still getting reports of sightings of Anne Lock all over the place. I'm not claiming I'm a super detective or anything, but after a while tied to a desk I decided I was going to go and walk the scene for myself. I'd already done it on my day off, but this time I walked the opposite side of the railway line, along a pathway that ran along the other side of the ditch. The search team were combing the ground with strimmers and scythes, all of them looking down, naturally. And as I looked up, there was Anne Lock's address book.

It was cradled in the branches of a hawthorn bush. 'Duffy had obviously flung it as he'd walked back to the car rifling through her bag. As soon as I saw it, I realised she was definitely here somewhere.'

Dockley's discovery gave the first real indication that Anne had actually reached Brookmans Park. Her diary was then found by another officer 700 yards away on the banks of a dry river bed, a few yards east of the bridge at Bluebridge Road, 250 yards south of the railway station and on the east side of the track. Anne's LWT identity card and her purse were found on the same footpath west of Bluebridge Road.

Laurence had made another appeal, this time on TV-am's *Good Morning Britain* programme, shortly before the items were found. But after identifying them at Hatfield Police Station, the press quoted him as saying, 'Now I know she's dead. I've got to accept the facts.'[13]

The police considered it a possibility that Anne's handbag could have been found by someone unconnected with her disappearance. After consulting with the Director of Public Prosecutions, they promised that there would be no prosecution if a person came forward admitting to having taken the bag, or who may have moved Anne's bicycle, provided they were not involved beyond that, but it was all to no avail.

Although they had always been careful not to spell out their speculation and risk, above all else, alienating their readers, the press did manage a few more days of insinuation either side of reporting on 6 June that Laurence Lock 'had now been eliminated from their enquiries'.[14] Having been unable to bear watching a *Police 5** reconstruction and appeal, he had mowed the lawn instead, 'because that is how we always spent Sundays. Anne would cook the lunch and I would mow the lawn. She's not here to make the lunch now but I must still cut the lawn. Life has to go on.'[15] Laurence had taken to wearing his wife's necklace on his wrist as a reminder, but the *Daily Mail* decided to claim he wore it around his neck.

The local press reported that the grounds and drains of the Locks' home had been searched by police, together with 'meat freezers used by Mr Lock in his butcher's business'.[16] The police maintained that they were 'carrying out a search of all manholes and drains in the area' and stressed that 'no great significance should be drawn from our visit to Mr Lock's home'.

*   Broadcast on 1 June 1986.

The previous day would have been Anne's thirtieth birthday. That week, police had been 'searching potholes and caves and sewers with the help of volunteers from local potholing clubs. Frogmen have also searched lakes, ponds and quarries.' They closed by saying, 'Mr Lock, who wears his wife's pearl necklace around his wrist as a constant reminder, spoke yesterday of the continued jibes that he is perhaps responsible for his wife's disappearance.' They quoted his dignified stance that, 'I try not to get upset about it. There is only one grief, the grief that my wife is missing and may be dead.'[17]

Although police could do nothing more that suspect a link, the continued publicity surrounding Anne Lock's disappearance was giving officers on both the Alison Day and the Maartje Tamboezer investigations serious cause for concern that this was a further connection. Brian Roberts, working with Charlie on the Alison Day enquiry, says that:

> When Anne Lock first disappeared, myself and Barry Fyffe had gone to Welwyn and said that we thought this was possibly connected. We had a Detective Constable from the British Transport Police who was my partner in the Incident Room, and he was actively involved in extending the search at Charlie's instigation.[18]

John Hurst also remembered taking officers from Operation Swallow around the scene of Maartje Tamboezer's death and them being 'very worried, but until Anne Lock's body was found, nothing was certain'.[19]

In reporting the link that had now been made between Operation Hart and the murders of Alison Day and Maartje Tamboezer, Peter Burden, writing on the front page of the *Daily Mail*, said, 'One of two rapists who may have attacked 23 women is also a multiple killer, police believe, and

they think his latest victim is vanished tv girl Anne Lock.'
Police said the link was 'purely speculative' at this point,
but that they were liaising with the twenty-strong team
at Operation Hart, 'an enquiry that has cost an estimated
£1 million', and which had been 'due to be wound up this
week. But now, because of the startling development linking it to the murders, the operation will continue for the
immediate future.'[20]

The press now began to speculate on a further possible link, when, on 9 June, another murder took place in
London with a tenuous railway connection. Helena Swann,
a 20-year-old Ministry of Defence clerk, was found dead
in her flat in Memorial Avenue, West Ham, having last
been seen on her way to buy a travel pass for her sister
at the nearby station. She was strangled with a wire flex
that was still plugged into the wall by her bed. An old
friend of Charlie's was in charge of the case, Detective
Superintendent Ron Chapman.* He confirmed that 'she
was sexually assaulted and did live near a railway station',[21]
but said it was too early to say that the cases were linked.
Although Helena's killer was never identified, no link with
this case ever emerged.

Fifty officers continued to comb the area between
Brookmans Park station and the Hertfordshire border

---

*   Ron Chapman had previously been attached to the Anti-Terrorist Squad and had investigated the assassination of Bulgarian dissident, novelist, playwright and broadcaster Georgi
Markov in 1978. Markov had been living in London and broadcasting on the BBC World
Service, the US-funded Radio Free Europe and Germany's Deutsche Welle, boldly criticising
the totalitarian regime that existed in his homeland under Communist Head of State Todor
Zhivkov. Waiting for a bus on Waterloo Bridge on the morning of 7 September 1978, he felt
a sting in the thigh. A suited man behind him picked up an umbrella and fled in a taxi. After
four days of horrific illness, Markov died of poisoning from a ricin-filled pellet that had been
fired from the umbrella. The James Bond flavour of the story captured the public imagina-
tion, with the Bulgarian Secret Police, assisted by the KGB, suspected of the killing. On 6 June
2005, *The Times* actually named a likely suspect, Francesco Gullino, codenamed 'Piccadilly'.
The date of the attack on Markov was the sixty-seventh birthday of Todor Zhivkov, for whom
perhaps the assassination was intended as a gift.

every day until finally, after seven weeks of searching and over 16,000 man hours, the *Welwyn & Hatfield Times* reported on 3 July that the police had called off the search for Anne Lock.

The speculative link between the previous two murders and the disappearance of Anne Lock was still not an established one, despite Paul Dockley's suspicions. But, he says, 'As a young DI, I pursued *Crimewatch* to do a proper appeal, and finally they allowed me on to the June edition, after filming the scene for a week.'

The appeal again yielded little; the videofit of the 'airgun' man that we now know to be Duffy, was unfortunately way off beam, describing him as 'about 35–40, 5ft 6in, medium build, receding collar-length dark brown hair, bomber jacket and dark jeans or trousers'.[22]

Monday, 21 July 1986 was my parents' silver wedding anniversary. They had planned to go out for dinner, but late in the afternoon, my mother came into my bedroom and said, 'We won't be going out tonight. Anne Lock's been found.'

Nine weeks after she had disappeared, and two days before the Royal Wedding, Anne was found at 3 p.m. by railway workers. Her dreadfully decomposed body was lying in thick undergrowth on the western embankment of the railway line, over 1,000 yards from where she had been abducted. Edward Stubbs was the Exhibits Officer on the case:

> She was found by the men that used to clean the drains by the track. When your dad arrived at the station, I drove him out there, and as soon as he saw what was left of her he said, 'That's the same bloke who's done this.' It was the way the hands were tied.[23]

Switching on the evening news, I saw my father and Barry Fyffe walking along the line path, and I remember it crossing my mind that they had clearly just had to look at something horrific. The following morning, I woke up and immediately noticed a stench in the house, and saw my father's blue pin-striped suit hanging off the back door. It wasn't wearing his usual scent of that time, woody Dunhill aftershave; instead it was fetid, virulent. My mother explained, 'He was at the post-mortem last night, and she'd been dead such a long time, lying in hot weather.' It strikes me now that my father, for whom discretion was a watchword, would never himself have shared such a detail with me.

For Edward Stubbs, this was the second horrific murder enquiry in recent memory; he had previously worked on the Dennis Nilsen* case for twelve months:

> That was an unusual case as normally you start with a victim, but there we started with a suspect. But you simply have to get used to it, seeing that kind of thing. I can't say any more than that, really.

Detective Sergeant Keith Hider joined the investigation at this point, and recalls, 'It was a horrendous discovery. Every piece of my clothing went to the cleaners, and I had about four showers.'[24] The effects of decomposition and of interference by animals meant that dental records were the only way to positively identify the body as that of Anne Lock.

---

* Dennis Nilsen, arrested in 1983, was one of the most prolific serial killers in British criminal history. He occupied a top-floor flat in a converted semi-detached house in Muswell Hill, North London; when his neighbours reported blocked drains to a plumber, the results were identified as human remains. The police immediately arrested Nilsen and asked him where the rest of the body was. He replied: 'In two plastic bags in the wardrobe.' Driving him back to the station, a police officer asked him if there had been one victim or two. Nilsen replied: 'Fifteen.'

Mulcahy had partially covered it in rubbish, twigs and branches, and had once again tried to destroy it by burning. Professor David Bowen,* a forensic pathologist who had also worked on the Nilsen case, pronounced the cause of death as asphyxial suffocation due to gagging; she had been suffocated by a foot-long sock being placed in her mouth. The other was tied across the front of the lower jawbone; Bowen's belief was that:

> The position of the second sock across the lower jaw could be either because she had successfully resisted an attempt at strangulation by flexing her head, so the material could not reach her neck, or, alternatively, that the sock had been placed in that position to force her mouth open.[25]

Again there had been an attempt to burn the body. Her hands were tied behind her back in the same way Maartje Tamboezer's had been, but this time with a length of tape.

The following morning, the *Daily Mail* crime correspondent Peter Burden defended the police search, saying, 'One has got to remember that it is summer. When she disappeared the vegetation was growing very prolifically. It's very easy to say in hindsight that she should have been found quicker.'[26] That evening, Vincent McFadden said of the nine-week hunt and of Anne's body being found 100 yards further on from where the search had ended:

---

* Professor David Bowen (1924–2011) was Head of Forensic Medicine at Charing Cross Hospital between 1973 and 1989, and Professor of Forensic Medicine at London University from 1977–89. He investigated some 500 cases of murder and suspicious death, including that of Ross McWhirter, co-founder of the *Guinness Book of Records*, assassinated by the IRA in 1975; teacher Blair Peach, killed at an anti-racism demonstration in 1979; PC Keith Blakelock at the Broadwater Farm riots in 1985; and Hitler's wartime deputy, Rudolf Hess, at Spandau prison in 1987. Bowen's autobiography, *Body of Evidence*, was published in 2003.

Hertfordshire police carried out a very extensive search over a very wide area. That search took six weeks. I would suggest they did all that could be expected of them. It's unfortunate the body was found just outside the area of the search, but where do you start and where do you stop with the resources that you've got?[27]

McFadden also said that:

The three murders in particular have occurred on a footpath near a railway line and not far from a railway station, and that must form part of any enquiry. We may be looking for someone who has knowledge of the railway, but we would want to keep all our options open.

Operation Trinity now publicly linked the three murders and three of the rapes, those at Barnes Common in November 1984, at Hadley Wood in February 1985 and at West Hampstead in August 1985, all of which were lone attacks.

Just over a week later, it was reported that 'a senior officer from another force is to investigate claims by the husband of murdered tv bride Anne Lock that Hertfordshire police bungled the hunt for her'.[28] Keith Hider says of the suspicion that fell on Laurence Lock:

You have to look at every line of enquiry. In any major enquiry the first suspects are always going to be the relatives. Yes, some of what Laurence Lock said was misinterpreted. But unfortunately, anybody who knew her was a suspect. It has to be that way.

Paul Dockley recalls that:

There was also another false line of enquiry, in that Anne Lock was actually found exactly where a previous rape had taken place, committed by the son of an RAF officer at Brookmans Park. He came into the frame and we did surveillance on him but it was just a coincidence.

There were further false leads too, as Ken Worker remembered in 1988:

> We had an awful lot of information come into the enquiry office, and a lot of it was anonymous, but all enquiries had to be followed up. And of course we had some people who wanted to confess to the murders; in point of fact we had one chap ring up and say that his son had confessed to him that he had thrown Anne Lock off the train. Well we knew at that stage really that that didn't occur; from the position of her body there was no way she had been pushed from a train. But of course we had to follow it up. This meant myself going down to the West Country and interviewing the man down there, and it would appear basically the father wanted to get the son out of the house, and the story about the confession was just not true.[29]

Bizarre as it sounds, Keith Hider says that:

> You get these sorts of things happening. I remember that incident particularly, it was on a Friday night and Ken had to rush down to either Devon or Dorset. Similarly, with any high profile murder case you have psychics turning up. I would always ask them, 'What other murders have you ever solved?'

My father's old pal Dave Cant, who lived in the area, remembers, 'Charlie always said there should be no professional jealousies in this job. Quite often there would be hostility from provincial forces who would refuse help from Scotland Yard, and he would get so angry about it.'[30]

I remember asking him many years later why it had taken so long to catch the Yorkshire Ripper. He had said that more than anything else, it was because, in his opinion, all the different forces that had been involved in that enquiry each wanted to be the one that solved it, and there was a clear lack of co-operation. I was reminded of this when watching a television documentary about the Yorkshire Ripper enquiry many years later, noticing that one of the officers from West Yorkshire Police, while conceding that the neighbouring force who actually captured Peter Sutcliffe had done a good job, said wistfully that 'it would have been nice to have nailed him in West Yorkshire'.[31] Thankfully, on Operation Trinity the forces mostly co-operated with one another without being proprietorial. They were now only a few weeks away from making arrests.

I arrive at Brookmans Park station on a cold, clear January morning, to be met by Paul Dockley. He shows me that the old cycle shed has long since been replaced by a transparent one. 'Crime prevention in action: with this you can see if someone is waiting behind it,' he says.[32]

Thousands of commuters stand in this mundane place bordered by tidy countryside every day, and yet surveying it at a quiet hour and with an awareness of its terrible history, it is impossible not to see how potentially dangerous it is. There is no distance between the platform and the path Anne was taken along; like all of the sites Duffy and Mulcahy chose, here one is only a short step from seclusion.

We walk the line path Anne Lock was led along thirty years ago, and as we do so, trains scream by. 'Imagine the terror of those trains rushing at you in the dark as you're being led along here,' he says. As we walk, we pass a couple of lone females, one jogging and one strolling. Being two males encountering a female on a lonely lane, one feels the need to apologise or reassure. With years of experience of what can happen anywhere at any time, Paul tells me, 'No way would I want my daughter walking along here.'

Retracing the steps Duffy and Mulcahy forced Anne to take that night takes us the best part of half an hour. Finally, after crossing a road and trudging beyond the Met boundary, a small copse to the right bordering a field suggests itself as the scene of her final moments of life. To the left is the railway embankment where she was discarded, and where her ghostly remains were finally found.

To Duffy and Mulcahy, afterwards their victims were no more than spent matches. Anne Lock was the last of them to lose her life. Although he wasn't involved in the case, as a decent copper and a decent human being, Dave Cant still mourns the tragic sequence of events:

> Anne Lock is buried at North Mymms, and her grave is always kept beautifully clean and smart. We had an old neighbour who is now buried up there, and whenever we visit, I always trot up to Anne Lock's grave and offer apologies on behalf of everybody that she was left to lie there for so long.

Walking this path, which I recognise from seeing my father walking down it on the evening news all those years ago, I half expect to find some improbable relic of it all still lying here undiscovered; a police ballpoint, an earring or something flung from her bag. But no. Thirty winters on, there is nothing.

CONVERGENCE

> London no longer seems to be a safe place for women. The
> fear now must be that so called serial crimes, that is, acts of
> violence carried out for no apparent reason by maniacs, are
> crossing the Atlantic to become commonplace here.[1]

So reported the television news one evening in the summer
of 1986, when reports of the disappearances of two more
women flooded the media. The first was estate agent Suzy
Lamplugh, who was last seen on the afternoon of Monday,
28 July, a week after Anne Lock's body had been discovered. The story immediately superseded that of the 'missing
bride'; Suzy too was a young, upwardly mobile and elegant
woman. She was never found.[*]

The second disappearance was that of 20-year-old Anglo-
Peruvian Anna Asheshov. She was in England studying for
A-levels, and the previous Sunday afternoon, while visiting
friends in Pimlico, had gone for a walk and not returned.
Her father later said that:

---

[*] Suzy Lamplugh was last seen leaving the Fulham estate agents where she worked
to go and show a property to a customer marked in her diary as 'Mr Kipper'. The obvious
echo of 'Ripper' by itself was intriguing enough for the story to continue to fascinate the
press and public to this day. Suzy's parents subsequently founded The Suzy Lamplugh
Trust, whose work is discussed later in this book. Suzy was officially declared dead in
1994. In 2002, Scotland Yard named convicted rapist and murderer John Cannan as the
man they believed was responsible.

England is a wonderful place to lose a child. Everyone cares, everyone helps. We wrote to hospitals, libraries, schools, British consulates in Europe, hotels, boarding houses. We wrote to every bus company in the British Isles, about sixty of them, and every one of them responded saying, 'We are doing all we can, we are pleased to help, send more copies of the poster.'

Amazingly, three months later, Anna was found living as a boarder at a convent where nuns had taken her in. 'Something nasty happened in London,' her father said. 'She can't remember.'[2]

And concurrent with the hunt for 'The Railway Killer', police were now also searching for 'The Stockwell Strangler', Kenneth Erskine, who killed seven elderly people in their homes; most of his victims were also sexually assaulted.

My father once quietly but assertively responded to that rather dubious suggestion that a certain crime had been a case of the victim being 'in the wrong place at the wrong time' by saying, 'There's always someone about. Whether they've gone out looking or it's opportunistic.' As elderly people often said when I was growing up, 'you never know who's about'.

As well as painting a picture of London as a city where 'no woman is now safe', the news that summer evening also announced a 'major breakthrough' in the Alison Day enquiry. As a result of the *Police 5* appeal, a witness had come forward to say she had seen Alison's abduction. She told detectives that from her flat near the printing works in Hackney Wick she had seen a young woman in the street looking as if she was unsure of her bearings, who had then been approached by two men who spoke to her, before one of the men took her arm and pointed up the road. The three then walked off. Both men wore sheepskin jackets and were described as being in their early twenties, with short dark hair. One was 'untidy looking, about 5' 7" tall and walked with a swagger'. Police now believed that 'one or both of the men was also responsible for the other two murders', which in itself was a huge step forward.

Barry Fyffe says, 'We were very cautious about it because she'd taken such a long time to come forward.'[3] However, after my mother had seen the report of the sighting on the news, she asked my father about it, and he described the witness as 'adamant' about what she'd seen, and when. Also, it is arresting that the witness was speaking independently of *two* men rather than one. The press reported that these two could be the men Operation Hart was hunting for in the London rapes enquiry, and a 'frightening sketch'[4] was circulated in the national press.

This sighting remains a puzzle. At this point, the police had no idea of the exact circumstances of Alison Day's death, but we now know that she was abducted on the platform at Hackney Wick station and never reached the street. The likely explanation is that this was a completely unrelated incident, probably on a different night, and presumably not one with a sinister conclusion, since no other attributable crimes were reported. Or it could be that Duffy and Mulcahy were the two men, but the girl was a different victim, who then managed to escape them before they found Alison. She could even have been the girl who telephoned the cab company.* This seems equally unlikely. Detective Sergeant Mick Freeman, who will come into the story later, says that:

* It may be worth noting that when they arrived at Hackney Wick, Duffy and Mulcahy parked their van at the Trowbridge Estate. Walking from there to the station would have meant walking past the bus stop where the sighting took place.

There are always coincidences on an enquiry, and if you're not careful, you can make them fit and they can lead you off in the wrong direction. But also, it's very easy to say, 'You've got to keep focused', but focused on what when you haven't got anything to start with? Very often in murder cases you can go down a particular line of enquiry and spend hours and hours on it only to find later that it's wrong. That's the danger.[5]

But fortuitously, the sighting did open the police up to the possibility that two men could have been involved in the murders as well as some of the rapes. Detective Sergeant Brian Roberts recalls that 'there was some consideration of it being two men, because of the distance that Alison Day had been taken and the control that would have to have been exerted'.[6]

Alison Day's inquest finally took place that September in Poplar; a local newspaper mentioned in the reporting of it that detectives would now be travelling to Shropshire 'to interview a man being quizzed in connection with the murder of 79-year-old peace campaigner Hilda Murrell.[7] The 32-year-old Scot, who is being questioned by West Mercia detectives in Shrewsbury, admitted to being a mass killer after he appeared in a London court. The man, a hotel worker, admitted to nine killings.'[8] Unlikely as a connection seemed, any such lead had to be followed up, although the description given of the suspect in custody bears no resemblance to the man now serving life for Murrell's murder.*

---

* Hilda Murrell was a 78-year-old rose grower, naturalist, diarist and campaigner against nuclear power. During the Second World War, she had undertaken voluntary work organising care and resettlement for Jewish refugee children in local foster homes and schools. By 1984 she was a prominent anti-nuclear activist, and was due to present a paper at the first public planning enquiry into a new British nuclear power plant (Sizewell B), when on 21 March 1984, her Shrewsbury home was burgled and she was abducted in her own car. She was beaten, repeatedly stabbed and left for dead in a field some miles away, finally dying of hypothermia. Her death inevitably spawned conspiracy theories, not all of them quelled by a 2003 cold case review which discovered DNA evidence that led to a labourer who had been 16 years old at the time of the murder being sentenced to life imprisonment.

'When you are on an enquiry like this, there is that constant dread that the person you're looking for has struck again,' says Keith Hider. It was a fear my father was surely experiencing when he told the BBC:

If we look at the dates of the rapes in North and North West London, it's a developing situation, and on the last three attacks that we know of he has killed the victims. And being a psychopath he won't stop until he's caught.[9]

He told the local press that:

The situation looks more hopeful now we have established some links but what we are dealing with here is a psychopath who is calm and collected. The first murder was difficult, the second easier and then after that it becomes a habit. He is a man entirely without feeling. There is no mental illness, just complete badness. I would say from what we know that he is London based and possibly a casual worker who knows the London train system very well. But the fact remains that he must be caught. He won't stop now. We must now just soldier on and hope for the best.[10]

However much compulsion was felt by Duffy and Mulcahy – and certainly as a pair their attacks were so obviously pre-mediated and so intricately planned that it's clear that self-gratification never overtook circumspection – the media attention and industrious detection must have had some effect on them. Two years earlier, they had seen their attacks as 'a game with the police ... we thought we'd never get caught'. Now they seemed to have gone to ground. As Paul Dockley says, 'When you see three murders that you've committed all featured on *Crimewatch* one after the other, if you were a criminal, what would you think?'[11] Indeed, on the next edition of *Crimewatch*, the definite connection between all three murders was reiterated at the top of the programme and a new artist's impression of the man who ran for the train at Horsley station shown. It was another reasonable likeness (although the hair was exaggerated as being permed) that yielded 250 calls.[12]

But heightened publicity alone could not be relied upon to dissuade the killer, so Detective Superintendent John Hurst, in charge of the Maartje Tamboezer enquiry, decided 'to take the attack to him'.[13] He mounted a huge surveillance operation every weekend at unmanned railway stations throughout the Home Counties, bussing hundreds of officers from the British Transport Police, the Metropolitan Police, Hertfordshire and Surrey to stations which had been identified as potential attack sites. Brian Roberts, working on the Alison Day enquiry, says:

> I remember the surveillance operation well. We had a briefing session at the Section House on Leabridge Road, as our team had responsibility for all the north-eastern stations out as far as Hertfordshire. The idea was to watch for any likely candidates hanging around.

The operation ran for a number of weeks, at great expense, using huge amounts of manpower. Suspects were noted and investigated. Sooner or later, it was quite likely that Duffy alone, or Duffy and Mulcahy, would be noticed.

But it was not to be. Because on 28 September, the *News of the World* decided to expose and sabotage the surveillance operation. Under the headline 'Guitar-String Maniac Strangled Three Girls: Rock Group Link To Railway Sex Beast', it claimed that, 'The evil railway sex killer is a musician, and could be in a rock group. All three of his victims were strangled with thick, bass-type guitar string.

My father, Detective Superintendent Charles Farquhar, outside Hackney Police Station in June 1986, having just taken over the hunt for the killers of Alison Day. (PA.25178280)

John Duffy (left) and David Mulcahy as teenagers. (PA.1390035. By kind permission of Hertfordshire Police)

Artist's impressions of the North London rapists.

Artist's impression of the man (Mulcahy) who boarded the train from East Horsley after the murder of Maartje Tamboezer.

Photofit issued by police in November 1976 in connection with a rape near Hampstead Heath. (Note the resemblance to David Mulcahy.)

John Duffy.

David Mulcahy, circa 1983. (PA.1390038. By kind permission of Hertfordshire Police)

Spaniard's Road, Hampstead, site of the attack on two Danish au pairs in July 1984. (Author's collection)

Footpath at Horsley, Surrey, site of the abduction of Maartje Tamboezer. Visible to the left as the path bends is the post to which a tripwire was tied. (Author's collection)

The path beside Brookman's Path railway station, site of the abduction of Anne Lock. (Author's collection)

The railway bridge at Hackney Wick, site of the murder of Alison Day, as it looked in 1985.

Artist's impression of two men a witness said she saw accost a girl on the night of the murder of Alison Day.

Alison Day. (PA.1344346. By kind permission of Hertfordshire Police)

Maartje Tamboezer. This picture was taken at her fifteenth birthday party, just days before her murder. (PA.1390095. By kind permission of Hertfordshire Police)

Anne Lock. (PA.1390030. By kind permission of Hertfordshire Police)

Tabloid coverage of the disappearance of Anne Lock in May 1986.

The Operation Lea team at the Romford Incident Room in November 1986, after the arrest of John Duffy. Far left is Brian Roberts, front centre is my father, and second from right is Barry Fyffe. David Mulcahy is listed as 'in custody' on the board behind them.

Detective Chief Superintendent John Hurst, of Surrey CID.

Detective Constable Caroline Murphy, whose detective skills triggered the remarkable Operation Marford. (PA.1390048)

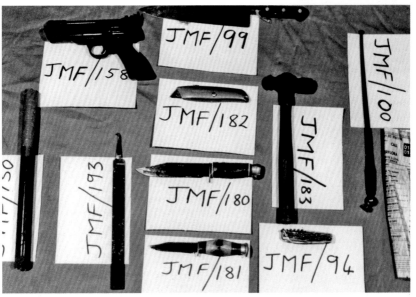

Weapons recovered from David Mulcahy's house following his arrest. JMF 181, owned by John Duffy, was used in the rape at Barnes Common, and was recovered from Mulcahy's home address when he was arrested in November 1986. (PA.1390041)

The Operation Marford team, receiving Commissioner's Commendations after the conviction of David Mulcahy in February 2001. Fourth from the right is Caroline Murphy, then Andy Murphy, Mick Freeman, Commissioner Sir John Stevens and Dave Cox.

My father and I, Cornwall, 1983.

One guitarist has already been questioned.' And then, fatally, it added a line of fact:

> The hunt for the triple killer now stretches across three counties and is being led by Detective Chief Superintendent Vince McFadden, Head of Surrey CID. He has set up special squads to keep watch on dozens of railway stations in the Home Counties late at night. The top secret exercise ... was ordered because detectives know the murderer likes to lurk around quiet stations.[14]

A vast amount of work and a good chance of making an arrest were wrecked. John Hurst said of the article, written by Alex Marunchak:*

> You never know with an operation of this magnitude when it is going to pay off, it could pay off at any moment on any day, and there we are, we've had this exposed by a Sunday newspaper and we have wasted a lot of the public's money.

But help did arrive from an unlikely realm: academia. Despite being a world traditionally viewed with cynicism by detectives, in November 1985, David Canter, Professor of Applied Psychology at the University of Surrey, had been invited to lunch at Scotland Yard. Senior police officers had grown curious about an arcane practice the Behavioural Science Unit of the FBI was championing though revealing little about: 'offender profiling', the practice of using information about an offence to draw conclusions about the offender.

---

*   Marunchak worked for the *News of the World* between 1981 and 2006. He was later arrested over allegations of computer hacking, but the charges were dropped when the Crown Prosecution Service decided that Scotland Yard had begun investigating the allegations too late, concluding that 'there is insufficient evidence to provide a realistic prospect of conviction'.

Canter had begun his career at the School of Architecture, and explains that:

As part of that research I studied human behaviour in emergencies, a fire for instance. If there has been a fatality in a fire, the investigation is carried out as if it's a murder enquiry, so the police interview lots of people about what exactly they did and so on; therefore I developed a way of working with police statements and witness statements, and it then turned out that when the police approached me about offender profiling, I had procedures in place for analysing statements, which are what most police enquiries are built around.[15]

Over lunch, the group discussed the possibility that Canter's research could be a tool in the detection process. A recent and prestigious project for United Biscuits, who had used Canter's skills as an aid to new product development,* had given him the funds to buy an Apricot** computer; with both this and his experience in two very different fields, he told police that he had a system which might be relevant to their needs. He was given one case to look at, a series of rapes (not the ones committed by Duffy and Mulcahy), and subsequently delivered a report of his theories. 'I became very interested in the concept and began to feel that psychology could contribute in some way.'

Then, fatefully, on 9 January 1986, travelling by train from London to Guildford, Canter picked up a copy of the London

---

*   Canter's research had broadly shown that consumers classified biscuits as being either unhealthy but enjoyable, or healthy but less enjoyable, so the conclusion was that a product that suggested it was both toothsome and healthy would capture both markets. Apparently, this led to the creation of Hobnobs.

**   Apricot was Britain's answer to Apple, and marketed itself heavily on the promise that it would supersede its rival. The machines were portable, attractive and competent, but the company was bought by Mitsubishi in the 1990s and the brand slowly laid to rest.

Standard. The front page was devoted to Operation Hart. The newspaper was offering a £5,000 reward for the North London rapists (Alison Day had been dead eleven days at this point, but her body had not yet been found, and it would be some time before her death was connected to the attacks). Inside was a breakdown of the attacks the police currently had linked, stipulating whether one or two men had been involved and listing the times and locations of the offences (with some inaccuracies). Canter spent the journey studying the article to see if any obvious patterns might emerge.

Working on the principles that people influence each other's actions (and therefore the difference between the two-man attacks and the one-man attacks might say something about both men), and also that human behaviour changes and develops over time (so therefore 'did time and partnership indicate anything about the character or lifestyle of these offenders?'[16]), he drew up a calendar of events that produced some tentative theories, and sent them to Scotland Yard. Several months later, after police had linked the first two murders with Operation Hart, he was invited to the Incident Room at Hendon.

> Your father was there, along with the other Senior Investigating Officers, and Vincent McFadden simply asked me if I could help catch this man before he kills again. I said I would try, but asked if anyone would be able to assist me, and he said, 'You'll have two police officers working with you from Monday morning.'[17]

This open-mindedness amazed Canter, and the work he was encouraged (though not paid) to do would make criminal history. John Hurst says, 'My philosophy was always that I would listen to anybody and see what they had to say. And a lot of what he said made sense.'[18]

One of the officers placed with Canter was Detective Constable Rupert Heritage and, although when told he would be working with a professor and a computer responded that he had never worked with either of those things before, the relationship worked splendidly. The pair took the information currently held about the attacks, such as the behaviour of the attacker before, during and after an attack and the sequence of the attacks, and systematised it to produce 'neat tables that would throw up any patterns that were in there'.[19]

A principle of modern offender profiling is that in the same way that any person's behaviour exhibits character-istics unique to that person, so a criminal leaves evidence of his personality through his criminal actions. An elemen-tary and oft-quoted example is that crimes committed by unemployed people are more likely to be during work-ing hours than those committed by people who have jobs. Canter also worked on 'the consistency principle', namely that an individual's behaviour in one aspect of their life reflects behaviour in other aspects of their lives, to a greater or lesser degree:

> An individual who goes off attacking women with an associate wouldn't be someone you'd expect to be caught up in a whole range of other social encounters. The behaviour shows some sort of disturbance in social relationships, and doesn't suggest an individual who has a lot of contact with others.[20]

This, and Canter's belief that the individual would be childless, a conclusion partly based on the fact that the viciousness of the attack on Maartje Tamboezer seemed difficult to associate with someone involved in bringing up children, fits Duffy neatly. It does not fit the gregari-ous husband and father Mulcahy. However, in his book

Criminal Shadows, Canter does add, 'At this stage I did not know of Colin Pitchfork for example, who killed two adolescent girls while he was married with young children.'[21]

These ideas, when superimposed over the recurrent behaviours displayed in the rapes, began to build up a profile. But the most significant discovery came when Canter asked Heritage to produce maps of where the attacks took place, with each year's crimes displayed on a separate transparent acetate sheet. They were placed chronologically on top of one another. When Heritage peeled away each layer, all the way back to 1982, what screamed out was that surely the killer lived within the area of the earliest offences in North London, an area Canter would later term 'a centre of gravity'.

The possibility of identifying an area where a killer might live from the locations of his crimes had been attempted before, though few people knew this at the time. In the final, desperate days of the Yorkshire Ripper enquiry, Professor Stuart Kind, Director of the Home Office Central Research Establishment, one of the members of a 'super squad' set up in November 1980, used his experience as a former RAF navigator to identify with astounding ease the area where the killer was likely to live. Kind had drawn a simple graph. On the left axis he placed times between 6 p.m. and 2 a.m. Allowing for the length of day on the bottom axis, he plotted the attacks and found that the 'late flyers'[22] were all in one particular area, which proved to be precisely where Peter Sutcliffe lived. It was stunning work after five years had yielded so little. But Canter points out that:

> The thing is, I didn't know anything about this, because it had so happened that Sutcliffe had been caught, by chance, so soon after that work had been done that more hadn't been made of it. If I'd known about that I'd have been much more confident when I presented my findings.[23]

On 28 July 1986, a week after Anne Lock's body had been found, the senior investigating officers gathered at the University of Surrey, and Canter gave a presentation of his findings: 'I presented my report as I would to students, and gave them my list of seventeen predictions about the killer.' Those predictions focused on only one of the two attackers, and suggested that he was childless, had a skilled or semi-skilled occupation that had involved weekend or casual work since June 1984, had lived in the area circumscribed by the first three attacks* since 1983, and had only one or two close male friends. Although Canter didn't know it at the time, police decided to cross reference the list of predictions with the 'Z Men' and see if this yielded any results.

Meanwhile, through his attendance of a martial arts club, Duffy had befriended a 20-year-old fellow enthusiast named Ross Mockeridge, an impressionable youth who came to view Duffy innocently as 'an older brother'. (Canter was quite correct in predicting that Duffy had only one or two close male friends.) Unlike Mulcahy, who had always been the dominant force in their relationship, Mockeridge was naïve and malleable; in him, Duffy saw the chance to become a leader himself. What Mockeridge didn't realise was that under the guise of a friendship, a kind of grooming was taking place. Duffy gradually exerted more and more influence over his protégé, until one evening, when the pair were standing outside the Royal Free Hospital, Duffy pointed out a girl and said, 'Come on, let's go and rape her.'

'Mockeridge thought he was joking at first,' says Keith Hider, 'but then when he realised Duffy was serious, he told him that he was in no way getting involved in anything like that.'[24] Duffy tried to persuade him that rape was 'a natural

---

* The first three attacks this prediction is based on were not in fact the first three committed by Duffy and Mulcahy, but despite this the result is accurate for Duffy's place of residence.

thing for a man to think about',[25] but to no avail. His psychological hold on Mockeridge was for a time a strong one, however, as shall be seen.

The Operation Hart team, meanwhile, had been ploughing through the list of 'Z Men', those with a history of sexual offences who had an A-secretor blood group. They had reached suspect number 1,594, but failed to get an answer every time they called to see him. His name was John Francis Duffy.

Detective Constable Peter Kelly finally put a note through the letterbox asking him to come in to West Hendon Police Station, which he did, on 17 July, accompanied by a solicitor. Kelly was immediately struck by Duffy's piercing blue eyes, his similarity to one of the photofits and the fact that he was the first of the 'Z Men' who refused to give body samples. Kelly and his colleague, DC Andrew Cody, made their apologies and left the room; outside, they both confided to each other that this could be their man.

Duffy raised their suspicions even further by the glibness of his answers, but there was not enough evidence at this point to charge him or to hold him in custody, so he was cautiously released. The two officers decided to escalate their suspicions.

Paul Dockley says:

> I was working out of one of the classrooms at Hendon when Peter and Andy came in and said they'd interviewed this guy the previous evening and hadn't liked him. As I recall, we went to see Ken Worker and told him that this guy, Duffy, had been charged with raping his estranged wife.

Worker felt that, on paper, Duffy wasn't a very exciting suspect, since he had ginger hair (witnesses had repeatedly described the shorter of the two attackers as fair-haired) and had only one previous conviction for a sexual offence, which was against his ex-wife rather than being a stranger attack. However, Worker later said, 'Nevertheless, I respected Cody and Kelly's feelings about him.'[26]

Dockley continues:

> He sent them to Duffy's local police station to make enquiries with the Collator there, the officer responsible for all the intelligence in that area, the card indexes and so on, to do some digging. They go up there and I get a phone call an hour later from them saying, 'You won't fucking believe this.'[27]

The previous evening, Duffy had left the interview with Kelly and Cody in a state of panic, having noticed the photofits on the table, and hatched an absurd, desperate plan. He found Ross Mockeridge and told him a *Boy's Own* story to hopefully appeal to his gullibility and loyalty. Duffy told him that he'd witnessed something that had put two mercenaries on his trail who were trying to frame him with the police, and that his only chance of survival was to fake that he'd been beaten up and lost his memory. Desperate, he hectored Mockeridge until finally the boy agreed to do as he asked: slash his chest with a razor and punch him in the face. Once it was done, Duffy made him swear an oath of allegiance, as he had once done with Mulcahy. Duffy then staggered into Hampstead Police Station, claiming he had been brutally mugged, had lost his memory and now could not even recall his name.

Duffy sought asylum in the psychiatric hospital at Friern Barnet. When Operation Hart officers arrived there, doctors informed them that their patient had been sectioned and was unfit to be interviewed.* Worker felt that although

---

* In fact, Duffy was not under very strict supervision at the hospital, and was frequently able to come and go without his absences being noted.

Duffy was a good suspect, there were other good suspects at this stage too, and so while Duffy remained confined they would concentrate elsewhere, and mount surveillance on him once he was released.

Worker's decision was as pivotal as Duffy's moronic reaction to his encounter with the police. Parallels with the Yorkshire Ripper enquiry are again essential at this point: during that enquiry, when Detective Constables Andrew Laptew and Graham Greenwood routinely questioned Peter Sutcliffe in July 1979, both officers were suspicious of him, and submitted a two-page report of their concerns to their superiors. Because Sutcliffe did not tally with presumptions made about the killer, which had no basis in fact, the report was filed, and Sutcliffe remained free to kill three more women and attack three others. Worker, however, respected the instincts of his officers, in the same way he and the other SIOs had respected Paul Dockley's instincts.

While Duffy submerged himself in faked amnesia at Friern Barnet (where the only patient he befriended was a man with strong delusions that he had murdered someone[28]), the legwork continued for all three police forces. In Surrey, John Hurst's teams of detectives were also tracing and interviewing known sex offenders:

> What we would be looking for in their homes would be Somyarn, nylon strimmer, knives, Swan Vesta matches, any weapons, and if we didn't know a person's blood group, blood and saliva samples would be taken, and alibis for the dates of the offences.

At the end of each day, Hurst would also compile what he called 'my five o'clock homework', going into the Incident Room and giving a list of any new lines of enquiry that had emerged that day that needed checking out. As part of one of these sessions, Hurst was sent a computer printout from Scotland Yard showing patterns of rape across London using a system called Crime Pattern Analysis. The report threw up forty attacks in addition to the twenty-seven which Operation Hart had identified. Hurst studied them carefully, and one stood out.

It was the attack the previous year which Duffy had carried out by himself at the back of the Copthall Sports Centre in Mill Hill. The victim had given a very good description of her attacker, and a vivid artist's impression had been shown on *Crimewatch*, although not as part of any larger enquiry. The rapist was described as 'only 5ft 3in tall, with light ginger hair and pock-marked skin'.[29] The attacker was believed to have had a dog with him too.

The similarity of the crime scenes and the methods to those in the murder of Maartje Tamboezer led Hurst to target the case with a squad of twelve officers, whom he sent to London armed with a good description of the attacker. Vets' records were checked in case the dog could be traced, dog-walking areas were patrolled and, because of the attacker's unusual stature, riding establishments were visited to check on jockeys. The team also liaised with local police stations. When one of the officers, Adrian Russell, visited the collator at West Hendon, he was shown Duffy's photograph. He immediately reported his findings to Hurst. The description instantly made Duffy their prime suspect.

Further checking on Duffy revealed that he had an interest in martial arts, had been unemployed, off sick or on leave on the dates of a number of the attacks and had been seen by Operation Hart officers because of his blood grouping and his arrest for the attack on his wife. The team also noted that he lived within the radius hypothesised by Professor Canter in his profile.

At 4.30 p.m. on Tuesday, 21 October, a 14-year-old schoolgirl making her way home close to the railway at Watford Junction was approached by a small, ginger-haired man who asked her the time. The man then forced her into a wooded area and told her, 'You have got to help me. The police are after me.' He used a knife to cut up her tights, then bound her wrists and covered her eyes with a blindfold, which slipped while he was raping her. Afterwards, he gave her tissues to wipe away forensic evidence and, after burning them, fled.

Hurst deployed a twelve-strong team to begin round-the-clock surveillance on Duffy on 11 November. There would only be one opportunity to apprehend and interview him, and so as much intelligence as possible needed to be gathered first. He was still attending the hospital at Friern Barnet as an outpatient two or three days a week. The team reported back to Hurst each morning on what had occurred, but after about a fortnight it became clear that Duffy had realised that he was under surveillance. His response would be to lose himself in the labyrinth of the London underground. His knowledge of the network allowed him to thwart the team; at one point, travelling on an overground train, he jumped from it while it was still in motion.

Fearing the police were closing in, he visited Ross Mockeridge again* and this time warned him that he could be found guilty of aiding and abetting, frightening him with talk of life imprisonment for both of them if his collusion with Duffy over the fake mugging was exposed. That night, 22 November, Duffy shaved off his moustache.**

---

* This incident may have occurred at any time after mid-July, but it seems to me most likely to have happened in the time between Duffy realising he was under surveillance and his arrest.

** Throughout the period of his offending, Duffy regularly switched between being clean-shaven and having a full beard or moustache.

The following night, Sunday, 23 November, he headed to Copthall Park, and loitered there looking for a victim. Before he could find one, at 11.30 p.m., the surveillance team he thought he had evaded swooped and placed him under arrest.

Duffy was taken to Guildford, and officers from all three forces gathered to question him. The police only had thirty-six hours to obtain some hard evidence before going before the magistrate to request he be further detained. Questioning him proved futile while he continued to protest that he was suffering from amnesia, but a search of his home quickly revealed an extensive arsenal, including knives, metal-loaded fighting sticks and Shinai (split bamboo canes) as well as hand strengtheners, a bull-worker, violent pornography and a copy of *The Anarchist's Cookbook*. This was a much-banned underground manual first published in 1971, which contained instructions on such activities as the manufacture of crude explosives and poisons, and, most significantly, techniques for overpowering victims using such methods as garrotting.* Police also found a box of Swan Vesta matches stuffed with blue tissue paper. When asked about this, Duffy claimed the tissue was to stop the matches from rattling in the box.

By 11.10 a.m. on Tuesday, the time was nearly up. Police applied for a custody order under the Criminal Evidence Act at a special hearing before magistrates at Guildford. Duffy sat quietly, 'wearing an open-necked white shirt and sweater, and carrying an overcoat', as John Hurst requested to the chairman of the bench, Lady Hemworth, that public and press leave the court so that he could inform her of matters which 'could be compromising in further

---

* *The Anarchist's Cookbook* was written by William Powell, who five years later converted to Anglicanism and so ever since has pleaded for its suppression.

investigations … if heard in public'.[30] Police were granted permission to hold Duffy for another two-and-a-half days without bringing charges; that evening's news reported this as 'one of the first uses of the new police powers on the extended questioning of suspects'.[31]

Charlie then interviewed Duffy. Barry Fyffe remembers that their suspect 'would talk at length about martial arts, but say nothing about anything relevant'. Duffy employed what the press would come to call his 'laser eyes' whenever he was asked a particularly searching question. John Hurst says that:

> His body language in itself certainly suggested guilt. And also, at no stage did he actually dispute or deny anything. He didn't say he did do these crimes, and he didn't say he didn't do them, he just insisted he couldn't remember anything.

Paul Dockley and Ken Worker also interviewed him, but Dockley says:

> He just made 'no comment' answers to anything relevant. He was happy to talk about his martial arts but he was making out he was away with the fairies, so didn't answer any of the questions we put to him, and believe me, we asked him everything. It was the most laborious interview I've ever known. It started off at four in the afternoon and finished off at two the next morning.

Talking to Duffy's ex-wife proved much more fruitful. As well as telling them of her ex-husband's obsession with violent films, she related a long history of abuse, telling how he had tied her hands during sex, how the more she had struggled the more he had enjoyed it, and of his boast one night that he had raped a girl and that it was 'her fault'. She hadn't believed him at the time, but this was enough now for police to be convinced of Duffy's guilt.

Police then visited Duffy's parents. Keith Hider describes them as 'the nicest people you could wish to meet'. Although they were incredulous, during a thorough search of the premises, in a pedal bin in the downstairs toilet police found a ball of familiar-looking string which was identified as being Somyarn. It was subjected to ruthless analysis in every aspect: its width and diameter, the thickness and weight of the paper it was formed from, the number of twists per inch, the direction of the twist and its colour. On every count it proved a perfect match to that used to tie Maartje Tamboezer.

Police also quickly ascertained from talking to Duffy's relatives that although he had a couple of acquaintances from martial arts clubs, including Ross Mockeridge (who was interviewed extensively by the Romford team), Duffy's only long-standing friend and probable accomplice was the person he had been inseparable from since he was an 11 year old. That man also shared his interest in martial arts, went jogging with him, had been convicted of petty offences with him ever since the pair were teenagers and fitted the description of the second attacker, a taller man with darker hair. And so, at 10.20 p.m. on Tuesday, 25 November 1986, police officers arrested David Mulcahy and took him to Guildford for questioning.

Innocent people tend to display a natural nervousness when being questioned by police, and despite the ingrained disdain for authority that those with a history of petty crime tend to possess, even they would be expected to show disquiet when being questioned about such frightening charges. The impervious Mulcahy, however, was cocksure in interrogation. He played down his association with Duffy, claiming the friendship had petered out years ago, and seemed unfazed by the seriousness of the offences he was being questioned over. He provided alibis for the murders, saying he was sick and bedbound on the night of Alison Day's death, working on the afternoon Maartje Tamboezer was killed, and with his family on the night of Anne Lock's murder. He did admit to having been with Duffy on various occasions but denied any crimes had occurred. However, there were some telling remarks:

> OFFICER 1: While you were out with John …
> MULCAHY: Yeah …
> OFFICER 1: … have you ever – think about it …
> MULCAHY: Yeah …
> OFFICER 1: … ever had any encounters? With a girl.
> MULCAHY: What d'you mean 'encounters', what you mean a whistle across the road or something, or like an actual like grabbin' 'old …
> OFFICER 1: A confrontation with a girl.
> MULCAHY: No.
> OFFICER 2: Ah, well you look away, are you certain?
> MULCAHY: Absolutely a hundred per cent positive. It's not my style I'm afraid. I'm married.

The second officer then pressed him:

> OFFICER 2: Raping women?
> MULCAHY: *(in mock disbelief)* Oh no, I wouldn't do that.
> OFFICER 2: Raping women?
> MULCAHY: No. It's not me, I don't need to rape women, I've got a nice wife at home, I get all the sex I can handle. Plus sex and violence to me don't mix.[32]

However unenlightened some male attitudes still were in the mid-1980s, the proffering of 'I've got a nice wife at home' as the first reason why you don't commit rape is incriminatory behaviour. His remark that to him 'sex and violence don't mix' sounds like a hasty afterthought.

A search of Mulcahy's home and of his two vehicles revealed masking tape, tissues, Swan Vesta matches (he was a non-smoker) and various weapons, including a considerable number of knives. Some of these items were found in the cab of his van.

The announcement of a second arrest made the front page of the *Daily Mirror* as well as the evening news; it was reported that police had 'thrown a news blackout over their hunt for the killer ... the hush up operation was imposed as a number of women arrived at Guildford Police Station. The women, believed to be rape victims, looked tense as they got out of unmarked police cars.'[33]

Ken Worker, running Operation Hart, tried to get as many as possible of the twenty-seven victims they felt sure had been attacked to attend the identity parades, but found that 'there were some that were too frightened to come'. Some victims had left the country: the two Danish au pairs, for instance, had returned to their homeland soon after the attack on Hampstead Heath in July 1984. John Hurst remembers well the courage of the women who did attend, however:

> It was the opinion of myself and most of the other officers that the rapes committed by Duffy and Mulcahy numbered way beyond twenty-seven, and were more likely to be forty or more. One girl told me of being dragged into an alleyway by them which stank of urine, the whole experience was utterly vile. The little girl attacked at Watford, who was only 14, crying her eyes out, walked straight up to Duffy and picked him out, it was incredible.[34]

Similarly, the woman who had been trapped in the waiting room at West Hampstead railway station by Duffy and Mulcahy in June 1984 took less than a minute to pick Duffy out of a lineup.

Five girls in all positively identified Duffy, strengthening the evidence against him. Even the victim of the rape near the Copthall Sports Centre, who had failed to pick him out the previous year, did on this occasion identify him. Although her trauma had subsided enough to allow her to identify Duffy, some victims were still not in a fit state, and those asked failed to identify Mulcahy. John Hurst says, 'They were petrified. In those days victims had to walk along a line and point out or touch the person. Anyone, especially a young girl, would find this terrifying.' It should also be remembered that Mulcahy was always the more violent of the two and the more physically imposing; he was also the one who made threats to the victims, after searching their handbags often warning them that 'we know where you live'.

Sifting through souvenirs from the time of my father's retirement from the police, which took place four months later, I find a photograph of the Operation Lea team at the Romford Incident Room, taken after Duffy had been charged with the murder of Alison Day. Behind Charlie on the wall is a list of Duffy's known associates, including the name David John Mulcahy. Next to that name are the words 'in custody'. It looked promising for the police at this point, and they were granted a further twenty-four hours to question Mulcahy, but when that time was up, with no forensic evidence and no identifications, he was released from custody.

They continued to build up a case against him, and at a further identification parade four months later, the arts student who had been attacked in South London in July 1983 did pick him out. Checking his alibi for the Alison Day murder, namely that he was signed off work suffering from bronchial pneumonia, Mulcahy's GP in fact revealed that he had actually been signed off work with catarrh and asthma at the start of December, and that she had declared him fit for work again on the 23rd. Alison was killed on the 29th. But this and one identification were simply not enough for him to be charged with the sheer volume of offences police were convinced he was guilty of.

It was a devastating blow to the enquiry. Keith Hider was the officer who had the thankless task of returning Mulcahy's clothing to him after he was released from custody, and confesses, 'I said to him, face-to-face on the doorstep of his property, "One day I'll be knocking on your door again." He just laughed at me.' Paul Dockley was similarly dispirited:

> At the time I was looking at the evidence of linkage between Duffy and Mulcahy, and to me it was strong. I think we had an eyewitness who had sighted two men on a motorbike at a station near where Maartje Tamboezer was murdered that hinted at Mulcahy's involvement too. I was saying to your dad and Vince McFadden that we just needed to charge him and get it into a court, saying that the courts would have to believe that the childhood association between them, the descriptions the victims had given and so on would all count for something, but we didn't really have any formal concrete evidence, they were right. And your dad then gave me the best piece of advice. He simply said to 'be patient. He'll come in time. We'll get him, something will happen.' And of course, he was right.

With Duffy formally charged on 30 November, the task now for all three forces in Operation Trinity was to prepare the case to put before the Director of Public Prosecutions. The evidence in the Maartje Tamboezer case and in five of the rapes was strong, thanks to a combination of forensic and other evidence, but John Hurst was worried by Duffy's continual assertion that he was suffering from amnesia, despite the team challenging him that when he been released from Friern Barnet, he had visited a video shop where he held a membership under a false name, and had clearly had no difficulty in recalling it. Then came what Hurst called 'a great breakthrough from the Romford Incident Room'.

Operation Lea officers had initially considered that Ross Mockeridge, as a friend of Duffy's, could have been the second man, but it quickly became clear that this wasn't the case. However, Barry Fyffe says:

> We looked upon Ross Mockeridge as being a bit like a dripping tap. He potentially held valuable information about Duffy. He was a young man with a strong sense of loyalty and friendship. Initially he had clammed up, but he came from a very good family, so we felt that perhaps it was simply that he needed time to work things out in his own way and in his own time. We didn't pressurise him. Two officers kept in contact with him, and eventually he opened up.

Mockeridge confessed that Duffy had made suggestions to him about them committing a crime together, and also, vitally, he made a sworn statement telling the truth about Duffy's amnesia claim. Duffy's defence was in ruins.

Alongside the Maartje Tamboezer case, the evidence for five of the rapes looked equally strong, but despite exhaustive work, the other two charges of murder looked more vulnerable. In the Anne Lock case, there was no forensic evidence to call on. In the Alison Day case, forensics were the only hope, although it will be remembered that because of so much evidence having been destroyed by the body being in the canal for so long, the only hope was that the five sets of alien fibres lifted from Alison's sheepskin coat could be matched. Over seventy different items of clothing from Duffy were examined, but more than half of them were made of fabrics unsuitable for shedding fibres. About thirty samples were lifted from the remainder of the clothes, however, which Dr Geoffrey Roe and his team began to try and match with those found on Alison's coat. There were roughly 2,000 fibres in total which had to be tested.

Charlie told the BBC in 1988:

> It's a long and tedious task for the scientists to find comparisons with fibre evidence, and often with no good result. But I realised that the evidence in the Alison Day case was weak. So I thought that we'd ask for the fibre evidence, to give us strength to the case if it does turn up. And I thank my lucky stars that I did because just a few weeks before the trial, the results came through, and we found that we had thirteen separate identifications of fibres found on Alison Day from clothing of Duffy.

Speaking with that tone of magnetic professionalism that he always used on the rare occasions that he talked about his work, he concluded by saying, 'Those fibres were the single most significant piece of evidence in the Alison Day enquiry.' He added, resolutely, 'In fact, it was virtually, a *fingerprint*.'[35]

Watching that interview again, it remains for me the perfect expression of his combination of determination and solicitude. This book has brought me into contact with so many detectives, and they all have possessed that combination of a firm handshake, a sharp mind and a compassionate soul. I find nowadays that I tell people my father was a *detective* rather than simply a policeman, having noted the respect that the other officers I've interviewed have both for him and for that word.

Four months later, at the age of 55, Charlie retired after twenty-eight years of service and nine commendations, having solved twenty-two murder inquiries. There was a memorable send-off at the Metropolitan Police Sports Club in Chigwell, heralded by a piper and attended by over 300 friends and colleagues. He certainly exited the police force via the gift shop, being presented with a small fortune in gardening tools. Flicking through the autograph book he was given that night, I notice a sweet comment from Eric Brown, originally in charge of the Alison Day enquiry, 'Was it my groundwork or your detective ability, Charlie? Anyway, you ensured a superb result.' Another reads, 'Great days at Finchley were enjoyed under your command. An education under Farquhar is second to none.' And another, 'I've been told a nerk demands respect and a man earns it. No one has earned it more than you as a fellow officer.'

Dr Geoffrey Roe, whose painstaking work on the fibre evidence meant there was now a very strong chance of a conviction for Duffy in the Alison Day case, wrote modestly, 'Glad to have been of some assistance.'

'I'll always remember that night,' says John Hurst, adding:

Not least because my team and I turned up and we were all standing listening to the speeches with drinks in our hand, then we put them down on the table behind us to applaud, and when we turned around again, a load of boys from the Flying Squad had walked off with them!'[36]

The cake presented to Charlie was emblazoned with both the traditional motifs of a detective – a Sherlock Holmes pipe and violin – and the words 'The Man's A F★★★★★★ Diamond'. And among the artefacts I have unearthed in my excavations for this book is Charlie's leaving certificate, signed by then-Commissioner Kenneth Newman. It describes my father's conduct as 'exemplary'.

In the increasingly dehumanised and unstable world of work, fewer and fewer of us are able to make a vivid impression and devote our whole working lives to a craft. The days of the majority of people defining themselves by their occupation are no more; today, people can spend their entire career in a call centre, working from a script. Even the police force, like the teaching profession, through damaging interference as much as corrective regulation, is being robbed of the merits of individuality. The evening of my father's retirement party and the mood of that room stands in my memory as the perfect summation of a successful career, one few today have the opportunity for, and even fewer achieve.

Free of the constraints that come with being a serving officer, he took the opportunity to speak out publicly about what he saw as the serious deficiencies which nearly sabotaged Operation Lea, in the hope that somebody would take notice. The local press reported that he had 'spoken out sharply over the way budget restrictions are hampering murder investigations'. He blamed government restrictions on the police budget for extreme pressure on manpower and finances, saying:

> We've become so money-orientated that it seems to take priority over everything. It's not right to be told how much you can spend on a murder investigation. You've got to have some limits, but there are a lot of murder enquiries where there are leads to go on but investigations have to stop because of a shortage of manpower and money.[37]

Another newspaper reported, 'When he first joined as a young PC, the pressure came from the public. Now he claims the pressure is far worse from inside the force than from outside.' It quoted him as revealing that:

The Keighley Barton enquiry cost a quarter of a million, while the Alison Day enquiry has cost about £1.3 million at Guildford, half a million at Romford and three-quarters of a million at Hendon, where the three computer-linked cases were set up. You have got to keep the normal functions going at the station and if you take people away from one job to do another then something has to suffer. You can't take a quart out of a pint pot. In the last year the force and Romford has suffered because of the Wapping dispute[,] which demanded a lot of man hours that all had to be paid for.[38]

A third local newspaper reported him as saying:

Some senior people fly over from force to force looking for promotions. They change so often you never know who they are. The exercise is to become Chief Constable, but they can't all be Chief Constables, and this lack of loyalty does no good.[39]

He told my mother that 'to do thirty years in a job you love is something not everybody is lucky enough to have done', but personally I think that although he was a professional who knew how to get the best out of himself and his troops, and was fearless in challenging authority in the interests of justice, the internal politics of Operation Lea left him with few regrets about retiring. All the same, I don't think such a person ever truly stops being a policeman; it is an attitude as much as an occupation. The one benefit of inevitable withdrawal symptoms after such a career, though, was that in the years that followed he was more easily tempted out of his usual reticence to discuss his work. That has been, I hope, to this book's advantage.

Barry Fyffe oversaw the remaining duties at the Romford Incident Room, and Duffy was committed for trial at the Old Bailey on 24 June 1987, the trial set to start at the beginning of 1988. My father began work as a security consultant at Federal Express, pausing only to take us on a Whitsun week holiday to Cornwall.

In May, David Mulcahy was one of a group of roller-skating enthusiasts to take part in a thirty-six-hour marathon up and down the 5-mile long promenade at Southend-on-Sea in order to raise money for Guide Dogs for the Blind (as they had done the previous year, when Mulcahy had featured on *Blue Peter*) and for the local St John's Ambulance Brigade. Charity work is a readily available veneer of respectability for such a man.

A television documentary crew covered the event, and in November, a half-hour programme celebrating the spectacle was broadcast.* Hiding in plain sight, unable to resist the glare of attention, there was David Mulcahy, swaggering, jocular and cocky, happily being interviewed at length about his innocent hobby.

Watching the man I have spent a chilling winter researching and trying to understand, I search vainly for something in this bizarre fifteen minutes of fame that hints at his true nature. He comes across as hyperactive, incessant, a show-off. He clearly loves the fact that skating through the centre of London attracts crowds of onlookers, despite it also attracting unwanted attention from the police. But ultimately, there is nothing I can draw from it, except to note the resemblance to so many of the witnesses' descriptions (particularly those of the man leaving the scene of the murder of Maartje Tamboezer) and tell-tale features some of the rape victims reported, such as the mole on his chin.

This is a man who had come too close to being caught perhaps, who had been frightened back to everyday life. There are no answers on this cassette as to how he man-

---

* *Open Space: Southenders,* BBC2, 9 November 1987.

aged that so easily, nor are there any answers elsewhere. To be able to compartmentalise your evil, to be able to consciously choose when to pursue it and when to retire it: that is as inexplicable as the evil itself.

SEPARATION

I could tell at breakfast if my father was going to court that day, by his choice of suit. As I recall, if it was a navy blue affair with a narrow pinstripe, adorned by his Flying Squad tie, he was probably 'at the Bailey'. His best suits perfectly expressed his modest command.

My father once described the judicial system to me as a game played out by two very skilful teams, which, if both do their jobs to the best of their abilities, should yield the right result. From the point of view of the police, a trial might also resemble a theatrical event, and not just in the obvious sense. Courtrooms are indeed places of drama, but although the stakes are much higher, like a play a trial is the moment when many months of work are presented in public to be judged. All that labour could result in a unanimous affirmation but it might simply fail to persuade those 'twelve good men and true' (or in the case of the trial of John Francis Duffy, six men and six women).

The Ladybird Book of London did very well as a guide in the days when this chaotic, hurry-scurry city still had a kind of order to it. Newspapers were printed in Fleet Street, everyone in the City sported a bowler and brolly, fruit was bought in Covent Garden, jewellery was bought in Hatton Garden, health was put right in Harley Street and the world was put to rights at Speakers' Corner. Even the tragic seemed a

regimented breed, tramps haunting the Embankment and
addicts clustering in Piccadilly Circus, where they awaited
the stroke of midnight that allowed the all-night chemist to
provide them with tomorrow's prescription.

The law was similarly compartmentalised; The Wig and
Pen pub opposite the Civil Courts gaggled with the sound
of the law at lunch and with the gossip of journalists from
neighbouring Fleet Street.* The Magpie and Stump, opposite the Old Bailey and still doing business today, was once
known as 'Courtroom Number 10', brimming as it was
with detectives and crime reporters. In the days when the
Old Bailey was still Newgate Prison, it had been a favourite
place for watching public executions.

The Old Bailey has the grandeur, the smell and the
menace that minor public schools still possessed in those
days. The smell is of dusty books and dusty regulations.
The barristers who pad the corridors, robed and bewigged,
resemble brusque teachers in gowns and mortarboards. The
stained glass and the oak panelling suggest stern religiosity.
The status of the red-robed judges of the High Court is
protected by one of the only written parts of the British
Constitution, the 1707 Act of Settlement, from which time
their unchanging attire also dates, a time when horsehair
wigs, silver-buckled shoes and stockings for men were quite
the fashion.

Everywhere within the Central Criminal Court one
is aware of the fierce gap in confidence between those
who command here and so many of those who are reluctant visitors. This building and its terrible history dwarfs

* The Wig and Pen, said to be the only structure in the Strand to have survived the
Great Fire of London, was originally built as the home of the gatekeeper of Temple
Bar, and from 1908 was the sanctum of thirsty lawyers and journalists. The defection
of newspapers from Fleet Street to Wapping and ultimately to the internet, as well as
increasing sobriety, led to its closure in 2003.

the spirits of even the innocent. Here the diminutive John Duffy, away from the alleyways and footpaths of his crimes, was rendered insignificant. There were speculations in the press by some police officers that he enjoyed the attention of his trial, but if that was the case, even that attention was diminished somewhat by the fact that the trial of 'The Stockwell Strangler', Kenneth Erskine, was beginning on the same day as Duffy's, and in the neighbouring courtroom.*

Standing in the dock and flanked by three prison officers, Duffy, dressed in a dark blue suit and tie, stared blankly ahead as the case opened, occasionally glancing at the jury. He appeared 'an unlikely culprit, who gave an appearance of insipid youth, emphasized by his soft, nasal voice'.[1]

He was charged with three murders, seven rapes, a buggery, two common assaults and a malicious wounding. The rapes included two that were committed with another man, on 3 June 1984 at West Hampstead station and in Kentish Town on 14 July 1985 (the night that three attacks occurred). The others were the rape of the nurse at Hadley Wood in February 1985, the rape near the Copthall Sports Centre in November 1985 (the attack that John Hurst had connected with the murders and which had led the police to target him), the rape of the 14-year-old schoolgirl in Watford in October 1986, the physical and sexual attacks Duffy carried out on his wife and the attack on her boyfriend. When asked how he pleaded to each of the fourteen charges, in a clear voice he replied, 'Not guilty.'

The trial began on Tuesday, 12 January 1988, and would last six weeks. The press made an application at the outset for permission to name Duffy as the accused, despite the

---

* Erskine was found guilty of seven murders and ordered to serve at least forty years, at the time the longest minimum sentence ever imposed.

fact that a defendant accused of rape usually remains anonymous until a guilty verdict is reached. Mr David Farrington, defending Duffy, protested that naming him would bring suffering to his family, arguing that 'these highly emotive offences have attracted very large amounts of publicity, the sort likely to lead to revulsion in the minds of ordinary members of the public. If his name is published, then his family will suffer greatly.' But the judge permitted naming him on the grounds that Duffy's alleged involvement 'in three murders which had gripped the public interest, cast a very different light on the matter'.[2]

Mr Justice Farquharson (no relation), who had earned a reputation as 'a matter-of-fact, yet at the same time crisp and highly persuasive'[3] advocate, brought to the bench the same scrupulously fair style which had made him so esteemed a prosecutor. By coincidence, the following summer he was the guest at my school Speech Day and handed me the English prize. I remember him as a kindly man with a hint of Mr Pickwick about him.*

Anthony Hooper QC, prosecuting, had taken silk the previous year, and would go on to become a Lord Justice of Appeal and a Privy Councillor. He stressed at the start of the trial that the evidence in the Maartje Tamboezer enquiry was the core of the matter; his mission was to prove a direct link between Duffy and that crime, and then apply the similarities to the other two murders, which would hopefully, coupled with other evidence, demonstrate Duffy's guilt in all three cases.

* Sir Donald Farquharson (1928–2011) was widely predicted to become Lord Chief Justice, but the onset of Parkinson's Disease forced him to retire in 1995. He prosecuted brothel madam Cynthia Payne, as a judge he jailed jockey Lester Piggot for a £3 million tax fraud, and at the Court of Appeal he helped quash the convictions of the Guildford Four, the Birmingham Six and three men who had been jailed for the murder of PC Keith Blakelock. In 1986, the 'Farquharson Guidelines' for prosecution advocates were incorporated into *Archbold*, the bible of criminal law.

Keith Hider points out that, 'For any case to get in front of a jury, it has gone through so many stages; it could have been dropped by the magistrates or the Crown Prosecution Service. But having said that, even once it's got to court it can still get kicked out.'[4] Brian Roberts also asserts:

> However strong the evidence is, you can always get a jury who don't want to convict, and if you've not got an absolute 'knife-in-the-hand' moment anything can happen. Thankfully, it became apparent to me very quickly when I was giving evidence that we had a very attentive jury on this one.[5]

In his opening speech, Hooper described Duffy as 'a shrewd, sharp, calculating man' with a stare as unflinching and direct as a pair of laser beams, who 'drills with his eyes'. The remark was instantly seized upon by the press and crystallised the sentiments of many of the victims, who had described the smaller of the two attackers as having piercing blue eyes. Hooper built up a picture of Duffy as 'a ruthless operator who planned his crimes with militaristic precision', telling the jury, 'Faced with crimes as horrible as these, perhaps some of you think that he wouldn't do it unless he was sick. But he knows what he is doing. He is certainly not inadequate, nor backward. He is not sick.'

It was only when the jury was handed photographs of the massive array of weapons and body-building equipment found at Duffy's home that the accused appeared to show a flicker of emotion. Hooper then presented to the court the copy of *The Anarchist's Cookbook* found with the weapons, and read the jury passages detailing how to dominate prey, how to use a garrotte and on the importance of planning an escape route. The jury was also shown the strangulation scene from *Jaws of the Dragon*, a video cassette of which was found in Duffy's home.

Duffy's obsession with martial arts and his perverted interpretation of the accompanying philosophies was described in detail. It was revealed that Duffy, who neither drank nor smoked, attended a karate club in Judd Street, King's Cross, and bought much of his weaponry from the Cobra 2000 shop in Malden Road, Kentish Town. The owner of that shop would later call him 'a quiet, undistinguished person. He didn't strike me as an oddball. I think he turned to martial arts and violence because he was so inadequate.'[6] Duffy had studied 'Zen-Budo', an ancient martial art; his tutor confirmed that he was taught 'a number of lethal skills including the "crab claw" hold, used to cause severe pain or death'.[7] Hooper then turned the jury's attention to another exhibit: a collection of thirty-seven keys found in Duffy's home, each of them alleged to have belonged to a victim.

When considering the murder of Maartje Tamboezer, Hooper revealed that she had been beaten about the head, strangled on a second attempt and her body set on fire. He also declared that blood and semen samples were all consistent with Duffy being the rapist, but because of the conditions of the samples, the genetic evidence alone was not conclusive. In addition to the forensic evidence, he mentioned the unusually small footprint (250mm long) found at the scene that exactly matched one of Duffy's shoes, and the Swan Vesta matches and tissues found at his house, asking, 'What could this be other than this man's rape kit? It was ready for another rape or another murder.' Of Duffy's claim that the tissues were stuffed inside the box to stop the matches from rattling about, he said, 'That must rank as one of the most ridiculous excuses ever heard.'

Turning to Duffy's amnesia, Hooper described how after his release from hospital, Duffy returned to a video club where he held a membership in a false name and was able to remember that name without any hesitation. He insisted that 'the amnesia is a total sham. He is pulling the wool over everyone's eyes. It is made up so that he doesn't have to answer the numerous questions police put to him.'

Duffy's ex-wife, Margaret, was a key witness for the prosecution. Speaking softly, the 25-year-old former nursery nurse was asked in detail about her marriage to the man she said had changed from 'a nice person to a raving madman'. She said that 'it got to the situation where I couldn't stand looking at him or touching him', and that her husband once stuffed a handkerchief in her mouth, and on another occasion put his hands around her throat. She told how Duffy had practised martial arts moves at home three or four times a week, had perfected flicking a knife open and had regularly been out jogging for up to four hours on an evening.

Hooper pointed out that no attacks seemed to have occurred during the period in 1983 when Duffy and Margaret were trying for a child, and contrasted this with the period when Duffy's masculinity came under threat due to him discovering that he had a low sperm count. Margaret told the court how he had shown her a personal stereo he claimed had belonged to a girl he had raped, that he had said she was to blame for the attack, and how he had frequently beaten and gagged her, as well as how he had ceased looking for work and stayed at home watching violent films instead. While his wife gave her evidence, Duffy sat listening intently, occasionally flashing glances at her. Margaret stood leaning forward, resting her hands on the edge of the witness box throughout.

Hooper then turned to the period when Duffy saw his masculinity as being challenged again, by Margaret leaving him and finding happiness with someone else. She confirmed that two months after she had left Duffy, he had found out she had a new boyfriend, and when Duffy had threatened to go and see him, she had agreed to meet him in a park. Once there, he had punched her in the eye, then raped her at knifepoint. Hooper then asked about the assaults on Margaret and her new boyfriend, which had seen the couple require hospital treatment for head wounds that had been caused by a telescopic cosh, and finally about Duffy's amnesia claim, of which she said, 'I never believed John had amnesia. I still don't believe he's got amnesia. John is a very clever man.'

Margaret was now to face aggressive cross-examination on her ordeal from the defence. But that was not all. A tabloid newspaper decided to present the evidence she had given to the court as if it was an exclusive interview. The full-page article the following day was headlined 'My Kinky Sex Ordeal'[8], and was accompanied by a photograph of Margaret leaving the Old Bailey, for which there was subsequently a charge for Contempt of Court.*

David Farrington's cross-examination of Margaret was driven by the fact that at one point she had broken the injunction that she had taken out forbidding contact between her and her husband. She admitted this, but said it had only been done in an attempt to stop him pestering her. Farrington then claimed she was lying to provide the media with 'a juicy story', and suggested that she had visited Duffy two or three times a week since she had left him, and had made love to him four or five times in that period, suggesting:

> It was a case of absence makes the heart grow fonder. This man, who you cannot stand to touch, the man with the scary eyes, the man who had tied you up, put a handkerchief in your mouth, you are going back on a regular basis to visit.

* At a subsequent hearing on 5 February 1988, the photographer apologised and blamed the night sub-editor for printing the photograph. He was bound over for twelve months and fined £500.

She repeatedly replied, 'That is not true, it's nonsense,' and said she had only ever returned to their flat to collect important mail.

'Mrs Duffy came across as a truthful and sympathetic witness,' remembers Keith Hider. So too did the prosecution's next witness, Ross Mockeridge, who confessed, 'It was difficult to come to terms with what John was accused of. Because of my great friendship and feelings for him, I tried to protect him at first.' When he was asked why he only gave police details of what he knew in stages, he said that because of his friendship with Duffy, 'it would have been extremely difficult to give all my evidence about him to the police in one go'.[9]

Mockeridge told the court how on several occasions Duffy had referred to rape as 'a natural thing for a man to think about', and said that he had personally felt depressed after Duffy's arrest, had contemplated suicide and had seen a psychiatrist. Farrington seized on this and accused him of living in 'a lonely, introverted world of fantasy' and of making his story up. It was a scattergun defence; Farrington had little to challenge these witnesses with other than to suggest that they were lying, although what motivation Mockeridge in particular would have for doing so wasn't made clear.

Hooper then turned to the rapes. He began by showing the jury that Duffy's home was within walking distance of five different railway stations. The court was then shown a video of the identity parade in which the woman cornered in the station waiting room at West Hampstead had taken less than a minute to pick Duffy out of the line-up. Now 26, the victim proceeded to give her evidence 'in a whisper'.[10]

Video footage was then shown of a second identity parade, in which the woman who had been dragged off the street and into an alleyway by two men on the night that there were three attacks had also picked out Duffy. She had been walking home from a dance after Live Aid when the two men threw her to the ground and raped her. 'I did not scream because I was terrified,' she told the court.

> They had told me not to make a sound or they would cut me with the knives. I believed it. I was frightened I was not going to get away. I remember a feeling of horror when I realised what was going on.[11]

The red-haired attacker had told the other one, 'This is a good one,' as he raped her, and the victim told the court, 'It was something which made me think it had happened before.' Before the two men had fled, the red-haired man had put a cigarette in her mouth, saying, 'She needs one,' and adding, 'See you again.' The woman told the court that she was still suffering from the effects of the attack two years later. Once she had completed giving her evidence, the court adjourned for lunch; when they returned, it was announced that a female juror had been taken ill and sent home.

The woman raped behind the Copthall Sports Centre was challenged by David Farrington about the fact that she had failed to identify Duffy a month after the attack took place, but then had done so a year later. Medical evidence presented to the court explained that the victim had been suffering from Rape Trauma Syndrome, a symptom of which can be that a victim's experience vanishes from the memory, often to return in detail some time later.[12]

After the rape victims had given their evidence, two of them having broken down in tears while doing so, the woman who had been travelling on the North London Line on Christmas Eve 1985, five days before Alison Day was murdered, told how she had been so intimidated by the man staring at her she had rushed off the train at Homerton, pretending that a man on the platform was her husband. She said she had not reported the incident initially, but after seeing appeals on television about the case she had then contacted the police at both Notting Hill and West Hampstead, but no action had been taken. After the three murders had been featured on *Crimewatch*, she had contacted police again and made a statement, and the following March had picked out Duffy at an identity parade.

The court then turned to the three murders, first considering that of Alison Day. Dr Roe's fibre evidence was presented to the jury, as were Dr Vanezis' findings on the manner of strangulation, Hooper explaining the specifics of the tourniquet to the court and asserting, 'With this extraordinary manner of strangulation, you can imagine that you can get a tremendous amount of pressure.' Dr Vanezis confirmed that there had been sexual interference but said that rape was difficult to prove because the body had been submerged in water for so long. Charlie and the rest of the Operation Lea team gave their evidence, no doubt aware that when they had been lodged in a portacabin at Hackney, the idea of the enquiry reaching the Old Bailey would have seemed fantastical. Barry Fyffe says:

> We were a very thorough team. Everybody did sterling work. Quite a few people were very surprised at how well we did when we got to the Bailey. Although we'd started off with next to nothing, some of the evidence in the Alison Day enquiry that was put before the court had a huge impact. We weren't being carried by the other forces, we were there in our own right. Dare I say it, we felt very proud of our work, considering we were such a small team.[13]

Huge amounts of evidence were presented from Operation Bluebell; Hooper even produced a leaflet found in Duffy's home that came from the manufacturers of a West German nylon gut, of the type used to ambush Maartje Tamboezer. There seemed little to challenge; the horror of the offences and the excellent detection of them quelled any reasonable doubt.

The court now turned to the murder of Anne Lock. With no forensic evidence to link Duffy to the murder, Hooper's strategy was to make a connection between Anne's death and the two deaths Duffy was so heavily incriminated in. There cannot have been anyone in the courtroom unfamiliar with the 'missing bride' case, and few who had not been aware as his name was called that Laurence Lock had once been the subject of suspicion and insinuation.

Laurence arrived at the court to give his evidence accompanied by his 66-year-old father, Alfred, who was advised not to sit in the public gallery to watch the proceedings due to their distressing nature. Alfred Lock instead sat in the gallery of Court Number Two while his son was subjected to an hour of cross-examination. Laurence frequently glanced across at Duffy while giving evidence; one newspaper reported that, 'He appeared distressed and strained as he relived the desperate search for his bride. He seemed to resent the questioning of the Defence, and blew out his cheeks several times at the questions.'[14]

A clerk then entered the court with a note for the judge. After reading it, Mr Justice Farquharson halted proceedings and told Laurence that his father had been taken to Bart's Hospital, saying, 'I think you should go there straight away. He is very grave.' Laurence exclaimed, 'Oh, God,' slammed down the papers he was clutching and rushed from the witness box to the door.

Alfred Lock had come out of Court Number Two complaining to a police constable of feeling unwell and saying, 'My family has been under a lot of stress', before collapsing. The officer had given him the kiss of life, and a WPC had performed a heart massage while they awaited an ambulance, but by the time Laurence arrived at the hospital, his father was dead.

Keith Hider was at the hospital with him:

> We then rushed him to his mother's house so that he could inform her of what had happened before the press got there. Although he'd had problems with the police earlier on, I think he was grateful for the effort we put in to try to assist in what was a truly tragic situation.[15]

The ordeal for Laurence Lock was still not over, however. Back at the Old Bailey, the case had proceeded, with Hooper apologetically asking the jury to look at the photographs of Anne's body and warning them, 'They are terrible pictures I am afraid.' But after presenting the prosecution's case on Anne Lock's murder, the judge paused proceedings and sent the jury out. After ninety minutes of reviewing the evidence and listening to legal submission, he told the returning jury, 'I've come to the conclusion as a matter of law that there is insufficient evidence for you to bring a verdict of guilty in relation to the charge of murdering Anne Lock.' He rejected the prosecution's suggestion that the killing was so similar to the others that the same man must have been responsible, and directed the jury to return a verdict of 'not guilty' on that count.*

---

* The previous year, in the extraordinary trial of a transport worker who confessed to killing his brother in a scuffle but who denied murder, Farquharson instructed the sympathetic jury to find the man guilty of manslaughter rather than murder. The jury defied him, returning a verdict of not guilty three times, until finally he informed them that although he understood their strength of feeling, as a matter of law he could not accept their verdict. He then discharged them, and the Defence altered the man's plea to one of manslaughter to avoid a retrial. Farquharson then sentenced him to two years' imprisonment, suspended. It was believed to have been the first time since 1670 that there had been such defiance of a judge's ruling, and ironic since both judge and jury shared the same desire for clemency regarding the defendant.

It was a regrettable turn of events, not least because it prevented Laurence Lock from fully clearing his name, but in legal terms it was not entirely unexpected. Ken Worker had felt that:

> We were relying on the evidence of the other two murders, as we had no forensic evidence. Although we charged him, which we did because we felt it was in the public interest, we often felt that we would lose that part of the case against Duffy.[16]

Paul Dockley remembers:

> We'd held an identity parade at Hertford in the big parade room there, and the boy who'd had the encounter with the man loitering at the station talking about an incident with an airgun did pick Duffy out. But to be honest, we had very little else.

However, Keith Hider does point out:

> Having been alerted to the possibility of this happening, discussions were held, and in a way it did add strength to the other two counts of murder, because rather than the jury then having doubts about all three counts, dropping this one for lack of evidence reinforced the fact that there was strong evidence for the other two.[17]

The defence did not call Duffy to give evidence. After six weeks of trying to make bricks without straw, in his closing speech to the jury David Farrington offered no mitigating circumstances, instead saying, 'I throw this man at your mercy.' After more than seven hours, late in the day on Thursday, 25 February, a verdict of guilty was returned on the rapes at Watford and Hadley Wood. The jury were then sent to a hotel for the night, and the following day continued considering the other eleven charges. After a total of fourteen hours of deliberation, they found John Francis Duffy guilty of a total of five counts of rape and two charges of murder. They were discharged from giving verdicts on the charges of malicious wounding of Margaret's boyfriend, the two charges of assault on Margaret herself and two further rape charges, having been unable to reach a decision; these charges were ordered to remain on the files. During the final day of the trial, a female juror was taken ill, and at the conclusion of the proceedings was led away by a nurse. The judge said that the details of the offences had obviously affected the jurors, and excused them from any further service for the rest of their lives.

Mr Justice Farquharson described Duffy as 'a predatory animal'. He said, 'The wickedness and beastliness of the murders committed on those two very young girls hardly bears description,' and described them as being 'as appalling as anything I have come across'. He said that Duffy had attacked 'in a degrading and disgusting way', telling him, 'You cut short those two young lives and blighted the lives of all the families of those young girls.'

The judge, who said he had never seen one man accused of so many rapes and murders, then sentenced Duffy to seven life sentences, with a recommendation that he serve no less than thirty years, and added that having regard for the nature of the crimes, Duffy should not depend on that being the total amount of time he would be serving.

As Duffy was led away to begin his life sentence in an isolation cell at Wormwood Scrubs, he gestured to his mother, Philomena, who collapsed, sobbing hysterically. She was helped away by her husband and daughter. Frank Duffy was close to tears outside the court as he told the press:

My heart goes out to those women and to the parents of the two dead girls. I could picture what it could be like if it was my girl. I know how I would feel. I am terribly sorry, I would like to say that to them, but I still don't believe it was my lad.

Philomena said she was 'so sorry' for the rape victims but desperately maintained, 'My son did not do it. If we can, we will appeal against this decision. I will never believe he did it.' She said that he had been 'a good son', her husband adding, 'To do these things he must have been sick because he would not do them with a sane mind. He is a god-fearing man.'[18] Duffy's 90-year-old grandmother, who still lived in the house Duffy spent his first five years at in Dundalk, said, 'My Johnny is a good, good boy. They must have the wrong person.'[19]

Keith Hider says:

Having heard the stories from his ex-wife, I think they eventually accepted the truth. But having dealt with a lot of criminals, and a lot of their families, I have to say that Duffy's parents were without doubt the nicest and most decent people you could have wished to meet. When Duffy was on remand, when they came in to see him, his mother would say to me, 'Thank you for looking after my son.' After he was sentenced, one of the barristers came out into the foyer of the Old Bailey and said to them both firmly, 'You must understand that you will never see your son again outside of prison.' It was heartbreaking really. They hadn't comprehended it fully until that moment.[20]

Alison Day's parents were interviewed by a local newspaper. Alison's mother, Barbara, described the night her daughter went missing as 'the coldest of the winter, and the longest one for us'. She went on:

In the days that followed I kept myself occupied washing and ironing all Alison's clothes, cleaning her room and keeping busy, hoping against hope she would come through the front door. Ken, I knew, was convinced she wouldn't be coming home to us and tried to prepare me for the shock that was to come. But how can anyone be prepared for the loss of a lovely girl in such horrific circumstances? She was always laughing, and would do anything to help anyone. I miss her so much.

Alison's father said:

We visit her grave once a week to put fresh flowers on it. I think sometimes of Duffy when I am there and what he has done to Alison and to us. He has robbed us of a lovely daughter, robbed Alison of life, of marrying and having children, he has robbed us of grandchildren and I will never forgive him. I would like to see capital punishment restored, a life for a life. I wouldn't need five minutes in a room to take revenge. I would like to line him up against a wall and shoot him.[21]

Laurence Lock told the press, 'I know some people will still point the finger at me, but I know and the police know that I am innocent.'[22] (The police made it clear to the press that the file on the murder of Anne Lock would be closed.) Laurence did not attend the inquest on Anne that was finally held five months later, but angrily said that the police had 'heaped blunder upon blunder and made my life a nightmare. The finger was pointed at me.'[23]

In the wake of the trial there was, however, great praise for how a killer had been caught by 'intuition, science and sheer hard work'.[24] It was reported that Operation Hart officers had worked an average of eighteen hours a day; at one point, after a televised appeal, there had been eighty new reports of sexual assaults to consider.

Detective Inspector James Blann of the team said, 'By the end we were researching 400 to 600 cases of indecent assault from 1982 onwards.'[25]

There was fascination and praise also for the work of Professor Canter. *The Times* reported, 'The Home Office is considering training police in the technique,'[26] and that Rupert Heritage had been awarded a Bramshill Fellowship to train in Canter's department at the University of Surrey. It also claimed that a special committee was being set up by the Association of Chief Police Officers, and that recommendations would be made to the Home Office and to forces across Britain to consider employing Canter's techniques. Although Canter himself had heard little from the police after presenting the profile to them, after Duffy was charged Vincent McFadden did telephone him to say, 'I don't know how you did it, or if it was all flannel, but that profile you gave us was very accurate and very useful to the investigation.'[27] The Surrey team had a tie designed in memory of Maartje Tamboezer and to commemorate the case, with a small image of a bluebell woven into it; they presented one to Professor Canter as a token of their appreciation.

There were some accusatory noises in some of the press about aspects of the enquiry, in particular that Duffy had been allowed to be bailed on two occasions despite police objections, and on the fact that some information had not been centralised along the way. The *Daily Mail* pointed out that Charlie had specifically requested that he be informed of any suspicious incident on the railways, and yet the complaint from the woman who felt sure she had been intimidated by Duffy on Christmas Eve 1985 had not been passed on to him.

For the most part, however, criticisms were made with the vast benefit of hindsight. Mr John Bennion, Deputy Chief Constable of Hertfordshire Police, said an enquiry by Sussex Police had cleared his men of everything except one or two small points regarding Operation Swallow, and Vincent McFadden said of the entire four-and-a-half year investigation, which had cost £3 million in total, that he was satisfied everything was done as quickly as possible to identity Duffy from 4,900 suspects, calling it 'a very professional job'. He added, 'The right man was put into the system. It was picked through and it was shaken until he came out. I would attack anyone who said there was a little bright reflective arrow pointing in Duffy's direction.'[28]

Both Charlie and John Hurst were singled out for praise in the press; Hurst for his brilliant and methodical detective work and the importance of his intuitive linking of one of the rapes with the murders, Charlie for his dogged determination to keep the case going in its impoverished early stages and for making the crucial connection between the murders of Alison Day and Maartje Tamboezer. As well as some thoughtful appreciation in *The Times*, John Hurst was also the subject of what he calls 'a hilarious piece in the *News of the World* about how I defeated the "laser-eyed killer". It was written by Charles Sandell, known to everybody as Charlie Scandal.'

Charlie was dubbed 'the remorseless hunter'[29] in a similarly sensational piece by the local press. Speaking of the pressure to close the case down, he said:

> When you are told to give up, it does make you more determined. People have always said I was stubborn, but that's what detective work is really all about. I never like to admit defeat, especially when people's lives are involved. It was satisfying to have Duffy in custody by the time I retired and to know that he won't be able to kill or rape again.

He added:

The Days will never get over what happened. Their lives have been shattered forever. The Tamboezers and the rape victims will never get over it. Their lives have been ruined. If there had been a death penalty, I doubt if anyone would mourn John Duffy.

The quote surprises me in its candour, until I remember that he was a civilian by this time, and could speak freely. He and I never agreed on the death penalty; police officers are as biased by their experience as the idealists are biased by their innocence.* All the same, with a new understanding of the crimes of Duffy and Mulcahy, I can well understand such strength of feeling.

The two detectives both shared interesting reflections on Duffy. Charlie said:

You could see the evil in that man's eyes. I asked Duffy how he felt about poor Alison, strangled and thrown into a freezing river. He said, 'It's fate. If she was meant to die at that moment then she had to die. If I'd killed these women, then it was pre-determined from the day I was born.'[30]

Hurst said of Duffy:

In my twenty-two years' experience with crime, I have never found a man so calculating and cunning. He is very intelligent and alert. He gave me the impression of being able to react to any type of situation in which he found himself.[31]

He added, 'Duffy has told me he is quite happy to do thirty years. He is able to shut himself off from the real world.'[32]

---

* The restoration of the death penalty was debated in Parliament four months later, in June 1988.

When asked by ITN if the case was now closed, he responded carefully, saying, 'I would say it's closed, but I'm not satisfied that we have cleared up everything that should be cleared up as far as John Francis Duffy is concerned.' He said he was certain there were further rapes that remained undetected, and added:

> As a detective I have a desire to finalise the whole thing and know the whole picture, but I don't think we ever will. He's not said a great deal from beginning to end, and I do not believe we ever will know exactly what he's responsible for.

That evening's news report concluded by reminding viewers that Duffy had acted with an accomplice, at least in some of the rapes, and that 'tonight, that man is still at large'.[33]

Brian Roberts calls it 'the most significant case I ever worked on':

> I returned to the Murder Squad in the late Nineties; when I totted it up, I had worked on twenty-three murders. But this case was so significant for me because of Charlie. It was one of the finest pieces of detective work I was ever involved in. It exemplified to me that, more than anything else, wearing out shoe leather and talking to people is the way you solve a murder.[34]

Ken Worker retired shortly after Duffy's conviction, and died soon afterwards. Keith Hider calls him 'a true gentleman. He died far too young; flying back from visiting his son overseas he suffered deep vein thrombosis.'[35]

John Hurst retired in 1993. He had joined the police as a cadet in 1957, and went on to work in the fingerprint department and as a Scenes of Crime Officer before joining the CID. He describes detection as 'a craft':

Men like your dad had such expertise. I worked on a lot of murders in particular over the years; years before Operation Bluebell I had worked on what was known as the 'Red Riding Hood murder', in which a girl walking to her grandmother's house in the snow on Christmas Eve to deliver presents had been killed by two dreadful men.* Certain cases stick in your mind; I have two daughters, but when they were growing up they didn't really know much about my work, I was the person who left home at half-seven in the morning and came in at eleven at night. And of course when you're exhausted, the last thing you want to do is talk about it all.[36]

There were two further questions the press raised in the wake of Duffy's sentencing. The first was regarding the martial arts training that Duffy had been so obsessed by. Experts at the clubs he attended were, however, very quick to dismiss any idea of him being a brilliant fighter as the fantasies of an inadequate coward. One instructor called him 'well below average as a martial artist. I think he only trained on and off for about two or three months, so he was quite a bad student really. He didn't have a determination to carry

---

* Fifteen-year-old Janet Stevens left her home in the Surrey village of Pirbright at 2.15 p.m. on Christmas Eve 1970 to buy chocolate at the local post office to give to her father for Christmas, and to deliver presents to her grandmother. She never reached either destination. On Christmas Day, police officers and members of the public searched the snowy countryside; a local bakery and an off-licence opened up to provide chicken pies and brandy in plastic cups to the search teams. Janet was found in a shallow grave on the army ranges that afternoon, having been strangled. Chief Superintendent Maurice Jackman was, according to one officer, crying and in a violent rage at the sight. A few days later, children playing ball against a garage door saw a red plastic bag in the snow which contained wrapping paper, as did the car parked inside. David Smith, a 21-year-old driver, and Peter Baker, a 17-year-old Royal Navy cook, were later arrested. On the day of the crime, they had been drinking, when Smith decided they should rob somebody. They had driven past Janet, bundled her into the car, drove her into a wooded area and killed her. The younger man claimed that he hadn't intervened because he was frightened of Smith, who had a knife. There was no robbery or sexual assault; in that sense there is perhaps an echo of Mulcahy in his later stages. At Smith's trial, a prisoner who had shared a cell with him and who had himself just been convicted of murder, said Smith told him he did it simply because 'he liked strangling people'.

on his training. Really just a coward in my eyes.'[37] Another instructor said, 'The man was insignificant. He was nothing. Things like Ninjutsu and these sorts of things do unfortunately attract some people with a bit of a fairy-tale element in their lives, but usually they don't last long.' He made the sound point that, 'The discipline that's required in martial arts works against the lack of discipline the uncontrolled maniac might have.'[38]

The second question was over the now apparent dangers to lone women using the railway network. Despite police reassurances that in the last year there had been a 34 per cent decrease in rapes and sexual assaults on the network in the London area, there was now a serious demand for British Rail to increase staffing levels at potentially dangerous stations. British Rail turned down a BBC interview that had intended to discuss the fears of female passengers, but claimed that lighting was being improved at stations and that transparent shelters were being introduced at platforms; there were also plans to install CCTV at stations between Euston and Watford and in Network South-East car parks.[39]

Ruth Bashall of the Campaign to Improve London Transport identified stations such as Hackney Wick, which had been built only eight years previously, as having a number of obviously unsafe areas cloaked from staff, where 'the lighting is not very good and the possibilities of dark corners where someone could hide and attack are endless'.[40]

In fact, the previous year the *Daily Mail* had reported that British Rail was now designing stations with women in mind, and that, 'No longer will they be the dark and dismal places where women fear to tread. The stations of the future will be exciting places where women want to be.' The promise came from Alan Etherington, a project director who was masterminding a £100 million development plan for Liverpool Street station that was due for completion in 1991. He was determined that the new station would be 'lively, colourful, light and bright'.[41] One of his three daughters had been a friend and colleague of Anne Lock.

But despite these concerns, by 1989, London Transport was removing guards from underground trains, something which Paul Boateng MP called 'a major dereliction of duty'. May of that year saw the arrival in London of the rather bombastic 'Guardian Angels', a volunteer crime-prevention group from New York who patrolled the tube network for a number of years to less than universal approval. (Membership had dropped to only twelve people by 2007.) The same month that Duffy was starting his trial, London Transport also admitted that the side panels on all seventy-five wooden escalators on the tube were being cleaned, according to some workers for the first time in fifty-six years.[42] Despite the fast-multiplying computers, this was still a scruffy, dank city, much of which was conducive to the activities of Duffy and Mulcahy.

This was a less empathetic society than we live in today, and just as frightening. The Cold War often felt to be warming up for a nuclear winter, there was a new ruthlessness in the attitudes and behaviours of the government of the day, and the Minister for Housing and Planning, George Young, allegedly described homeless people, who were rapidly growing in number, as 'what you step over when you come out of the opera'.

The seventies and eighties could be merciless times, and the people could be bovine. Combing through the tabloid press of the era in researching this book, one can't help but notice that amidst the de rigueur homophobia and chauvinism – all written in that unique tone that demands obedience and allegiance and tries to legitimise prejudice – there also lurks a bullying attitude to sex that doesn't say pleasant things about the society that spawned a pair like

Duffy and Mulcahy. In a double-page spread the weekend
after Duffy was sentenced, the *News of the World* boomed,
'Rail Monster Couldn't Make Love Says his Girl.' The
piece, which had clearly involved duping a female acquaint-
ance of Duffy, opened by announcing, 'Railway sex fiend
John Duffy, claimed by police to have raped as many as 50
women, was a wimp as a lover.'[43]

Yet in the same edition of the *News of the World* as a report
on Duffy's trial was an article describing the sexual prowess of Jimmy Savile. Savile's brother, who the article failed
to mention had been dismissed from his job at a South
London hospital after allegations of abuse, said of the girls
Savile has sex with:

> He checks them out thoroughly so that he knows they aren't
> going to spill the beans. He has his group of 'specials' scat-
> tered around the country. He says he likes having two in
> every port, so to speak, in case one is sick when he arrives in
> town. If a 'straight' lady came along and genuinely cared for
> him he wouldn't recognise her. He doesn't trust a soul. He
> doesn't even like children, though he spends so much time
> with them.[44]

As well as the work being done to make train travel a safer
and more pleasant experience for women, the day after
the verdict on Duffy, the National Association of Victim
Support Schemes launched a two-year project that aimed
to ensure that bereaved friends and relatives in Essex,
Merseyside, Sheffield and South London would be referred
by police to specially trained counsellors. In addition to this,
the disappearance of Suzy Lamplugh had prompted Suzy's
mother, Diana Lamplugh, to set up The Suzy Lamplugh
Trust, a charity which began by raising money for workplace self-awareness courses, but which broadened its

mission over the years to campaign for everybody to be able to enjoy life to the full while remaining safe. Triumphs included measures to combat harassment, for stalking to be recognised as a criminal offence, the registration of minicabs, safer car parks, train and tube stations and the registration of sex offenders.*

The day after Duffy began his life sentence, the *Daily Mail* printed a story with the headline, 'Police Thought I Was a Rapist, Too: Duffy's Best Friend Tells of Ordeal as the "Second Man".' Pictured cuddling his wife, with staggering hubris, David Mulcahy said, 'The last 16 months have been a nightmare for me and my family. I just want to clear my name.' The article reported that, 'Mr Mulcahy … plans to sue the police for wrongful arrest and for destroying his reputation.'[45] He didn't.

Mulcahy said that his wife had miscarried their fourth child during his arrest, that he had lost his job and that 'some of the mud always sticks'. He trotted out an already dented alibi:

> On the date the police said I was involved in one of the murders I was in bed with pneumonia. They were round to my work place, my friends, and my neighbours. They even questioned my parents who are both very ill.

His wife added, 'I never doubted him. He is a good husband and father.'

However, after all this indignation, Mulcahy made a telling remark when asked why he thought Duffy was innocent,

---

* Diana Lamplugh was appointed OBE and awarded four honorary doctorates for her work on The Suzy Lamplugh Trust, and, with her husband Paul (later also appointed OBE), the Beacon Prize for leadership in personal safety. She wrote many books, training manuals and articles in a magnificent endeavour which was cut short by a severe stroke and the onset of Alzheimer's disease. She died in 2011, but the work of The Suzy Lamplugh Trust lives on.

'I don't think John was capable of doing all these things. He has always been a mummy's boy. He's a born coward.' The inadvertent revelation that to him, rape and murder signify masculinity and strength, gives one the measure of the man.

Confident as this performance may have been, he failed to beguile a different daily newspaper. A *Daily Mirror* journalist doorstepped him the same day, and was told, 'Do you think I am going to talk to you about being a rapist? If the police thought I did these things they should have charged me.' The subsequent article named Mulcahy, and immediately under his remarks added:

> Police say they know who one of the accomplices is but have failed to get enough evidence to charge him and bring him to justice. The police bid to arrest a second man was wrecked because two men were involved in some of the crimes causing the forensic evidence to get confused.[46]

This was far bolder insinuation than that which had been used in relation to Laurence Lock, though again Mulcahy took no action.

Instead, he returned to life as a family man. It was as if his rape and murder spree was just another one of the many passing phases this Jack the Lad and Jack of all trades went through, now filed away in his past along with other short-lived pastimes and occupations such as roller-skating, soul music weekends and cab-driving. It appears almost inconceivable that a man who was the driving force behind so much evil could simply 'give it up'. Perhaps he needed Duffy. Perhaps the police had simply gotten too close. Or maybe his true equivalent is some Nazi war criminal, once capable of unleashing the darkest, most depraved evil imaginable and yet in full control of himself, able to then shrink back into society, seemingly out of reach of that obscene past. Not a serial killer,* but a multiple murderer, acting not through compulsion, but simply through choice.

Sacked from Westminster Council (this may have been partly due to his uncooperative response to any task he was ever given), Mulcahy worked as a freelance plasterer. His wife was working as a part-time carer in the evenings, leaving him to look after the children. In 1989, both his parents died and he had a brief affair with a young girl who was lodging with the family. His wife forgave him, saying, 'She threw herself at him, but David told me it was only canoodling.'[47]

In 1990, Mulcahy lashed out at his 9-year-old son Christopher, beating him with a stick. The child was made a ward of court and taken into foster care for two years. The other children were put on the 'at risk' register. Mulcahy was found guilty of assaulting the child and fined.

The psychiatrist James Gilligan has said that, 'The most dangerous men on earth are those who are afraid they are wimps.' Isaac Asimov called violence 'the last refuge of the incompetent'. There perhaps lies something, just something, of a clue. And probably as much of one as we will ever have.

* My father once remarked in a television interview that psychopathic serial killers generally don't stop until they are caught or they die.

SEVERANCE

If the seventies and eighties, for all their novelty value and colour, were still dark days for Britain with regard to certain attitudes and behaviours, the nineties were a time of quiet revolution. The decade began with the exit of Margaret Thatcher from Downing Street and ended in a flurry of impetuous optimism for the new millennium, albeit an optimism soon to be deadened by disillusionment and by new breeds of terrorism.

While it wasn't the most exciting decade to live through, the nineties was a time of increasing tolerance, democratisation and compassion, even if these were behaviours that needed laws put in place in order for some people to acclimatise. By the end of the decade, the explosion of the internet and the conception of social media heralded a more communicative, if still deeply troubled society. That new communicativeness would be intensified by the events of 11 September 2001.

The new demands of a changing Britain were reflected in the triumphs and controversies of the decade's policing. The Policing Diversity Strategy, set up in response to issues raised by the enquiry into the death of Stephen Lawrence,[*] aimed to provide better protection to ethnic communities from racial and violent crime. That case had suggested serious failings in aspects of policing in Britain. The investigation that the final chapter of this book is devoted to, however, was very different.

Professor David Bowen, who had been the pathologist on the Anne Lock enquiry, said of the team who were determined to see justice done in the case of David Mulcahy: 'Their work was a masterpiece of forensic detection.'[1] The enquiry, which came to be called Operation Marford, is one of the most remarkable stories in British criminal history.

Throughout the nineties, David Mulcahy, declared bankrupt, had worked on building sites, as a minicab driver, as a motorcycle courier and as a chauffeur. His son Christopher died of leukaemia in 1997. Presumably frightened by how close he came to being caught in 1986, Mulcahy sunk himself into family life, perhaps this being a rare instance of detection working as a deterrent. Murderers are rarely deterred (after all, if capital punishment worked as a deterrent it would never have had to be implemented). But some murderers do appear capable of being 'scared off', at least temporarily, by run-ins with the law. Christie, the Notting Hill murderer of the forties and fifties, had two significant

[*]   Eighteen-year-old Stephen Lawrence was murdered at a bus stop in Eltham, in a racist attack which took place in April 1993. The day after the attack, a letter giving the names of five suspects was left in a telephone box. Two weeks later, Stephen's family publicly complained that the police were not doing enough to catch the killers. The suspects were subsequently arrested and charged, but the charges were then dropped when the Crown Prosecution Service decided certain eyewitness evidence was unreliable. Stephen's parents then took out a private prosecution against the suspects, which collapsed when the judge ruled that same eyewitness evidence inadmissible. The case was reopened in 2011, and new forensic evidence led to two of the suspects being found guilty of murder in January 2012. Serious accusations were made about police attitudes; the ensuing Macpherson Report judged the Metropolitan Police 'institutionally racist' and made seventy recommendations aimed at improving attitudes. Ten years on, another report said that significant progress was now being made in this regard.

gaps in his offending, one of which was probably the result of having been a suspect in a murder case which led to one of his fellow tenants being hanged.*

Perhaps Mulcahy needed Duffy, since there is no evidence that he ever offended alone. Perhaps their evil was a case of *folie à deux*, the condition in which a person with severe personality disturbances forms an intensely close relationship with another person and infects that person with his or her condition, but when the pair are then separated that infection vanishes.

The shutters came down in Duffy's mind after he was separated from Mulcahy. He never attempted to appeal. He was well behaved in prison, quiet and polite, but still claimed to have no memory of the offences he had carried out. Certain police officers, however, did not forget so easily.

Les Bolland had been the office manager on the Anne Lock enquiry. When he reached the rank of detective superintendent in the mid-1990s, he no longer needed permission to initiate an enquiry and decided to visit Duffy, who was by then serving his sentence at Whitemoor Prison in Cambridgeshire. Brian Roberts says, 'We were always of a mind to see what a few years in prison might do to Duffy.'[2]

Bolland found Duffy to be approachable but apprehensive about unlocking the memories of his past, fearful that confronting them could trigger a breakdown. Bolland decided to wait a little, but had a note added to Duffy's prison file, requesting that if Duffy ever began to talk about his crimes, Hertfordshire Police would like to be informed.

---

* John Reginald Halliday Christie and his wife occupied the ground-floor flat at 10 Rillington Place, an address that would become one of the most fearsome in criminal history after police discovered the remains of six woman concealed there in 1953. It was then remembered that four years earlier, Christie had been the key witness in the trial of Timothy John Evans, who had occupied the top-floor flat and been accused of murdering his wife and daughter and subsequently hanged. Several enquiries into the case finally led to a posthumous pardon for Evans, although the full facts of the case remain a mystery.

The meeting between the two men set a chain of events in motion. Over the next few months, Duffy began suffering violent nightmares, many of which, he claimed, involved a girl being pursued along a towpath. He was therefore visited by the Head of Forensic Psychology at Whitemoor Prison, Dr Jenny Cutler. Their first meeting took place in November 1997.

Duffy confessed to her that his initial amnesia had been faked, but Dr Cutler decided that after his arrest, once Duffy's parents had been informed of his crimes, the psychological stress had genuinely triggered a mental shutdown. She would later say, 'I think at that point he became genuinely disassociated from what he'd done … in my experience if a memory is being suppressed it's because it is unpalatable.'[3] She assured him things could go at his own pace, and over the next few months Duffy came to trust her (some suggest he became infatuated with her), and he began to journey back into his past. At this point, knowing nothing of the details of his crimes, Cutler thought that a matter of repressed memories was all she would be dealing with, completely unaware of what the implications of liberating those memories might be.

Duffy's recollections to her reached his first day at secondary school, at which point he began referring to 'another kid'. At one point he said 'the other kid's a friend'. As he unburdened himself about the 'friend', she realised that he was referring to someone he had committed his offences with. When she innocently asked which prison his accomplice was in, Duffy told her that he wasn't in prison, that he was still free.

Astounded, she told Duffy that she would have to inform the police of the revelation. She then checked Duffy's prison file and there found the note from Les Bolland asking to be informed if Duffy should ever start talking about his crimes.

She telephoned him, asking for material that would assist with her counselling. Making a decision that would prove crucial to the events that ensued, Bolland shrewdly refused, aware that if Duffy's confessions ever resulted in a prosecution for his accomplice, a defence lawyer could accuse the police of having schooled him on the details. And so instead, the confessions that followed were received by Cutler with a lack of foreknowledge on her part.

Duffy spoke of the intense loyalty between him and David Mulcahy, of how they had responded to the bullying they suffered at Haverstock by finding inspiration in martial arts philosophy, immersing themselves in a deeply perverted interpretation of it. He recalled their nocturnal drives around North London, how he had found the risk-taking David 'exciting' to be with. He seemed troubled at reneging on the childhood truce the pair had made to protect each other, and said he had sworn to protect Mulcahy's family in the event Mulcahy had been caught and he hadn't,[4] but Dr Cutler also recorded in her notes that he 'has mixed feelings about David. It worries him he might still be offending, thinks he should pay for what he's done.'

Jenny Cutler would later describe Duffy's confessions as 'very flowing'[5] and felt that he was looking to ease his conscience, having finally got back to a state where he was capable of comprehending what he had done. Some are more cynical of the notion that Duffy was suddenly developing a conscience. David Canter speculates that he might have simply 'got a bit bored'.[6] Paul Dockley says, 'Many of us thought it more likely that in reliving his offences he was, in his own perverted way, bragging to his psychologist, boasting to her of his sexual prowess.'[7]

It is certainly the case that Duffy's memories were swarming back with chilling vividity. But crucially, he was now also confessing not just to the crimes he had been convicted of, but many that he had not previously been charged with, such as the rape of the two Danish au pairs on Hampstead Heath in 1984.

Perhaps there was also scorn in Duffy's confessions. Mulcahy had never visited him throughout the ten years of his incarceration. One wonders if there had been a rift between the pair prior to this; as far as we know, Duffy never asked Mulcahy for an alibi in 1986 after being questioned by police (although this may have been to try to avoid the police establishing a link between the pair). Perhaps Mulcahy had been unaware that Duffy had been offending alone, and was furious at how his reckless behaviour had nearly led to both of them being imprisoned. Whatever the case, Duffy must have known that the bond he had once honoured no longer held any advantage to him, and that to forcefully sever it might for him yield psychological benefits.

While Duffy journeyed back into his past, Hertfordshire Police waited patiently, unaware that in that very area of North London which a decade ago had been Duffy and Mulcahy's hunting ground, a series of virtually identical rapes was now taking place. They were being investigating by the Metropolitan Police at Hendon, in an enquiry named Operation Loudwater,* which was housed in the same building that had once been home to Operation Hart. Detective Constable Caroline Murphy had recently joined the Area Major Investigation Team, and had expressed a particular interest in cases of serial sexual offences. She recalls:

> The four rapes that had occurred had been linked by their characteristics and by DNA, but when the DNA was checked against the database there were no hits. I was having a drink with a fellow officer, John Haye, and telling him how frustrated

---

* By this point, names for police operations were being generated from a central computer.

I was that we couldn't find a DNA match. I told him they were stranger rapes, all at knifepoint, and that the attacker came up behind the victims, on isolated pathways or in wooded areas, sometimes close to railway stations. It so happened that he had been on Operation Hart all those years before, a case which I knew a little about because since then it had been used in training presentations.

He told me about John Duffy, and said it was worth checking to make sure he hadn't been released or let out on a work party. He also said that there had been a second man involved in some of the offences, who had been questioned at the time but released through lack of evidence, though he couldn't recall that man's name.[8]

Caroline Murphy located Duffy at Whitemoor, and telephoned the prison to check he hadn't been released. The Police Liaison Officer who spoke to her confirmed that Duffy had never been out of the prison, and also that he was one of twenty-three prisoners now serving an irrevocable 'whole-life tariff' on the orders of the Home Secretary, Michael Howard.* DC Murphy says:

I was assured he was never going to be released and would never set foot outside of prison on a work party. But on that first call, the officer also told me that for the first time Duffy had actually started talking about his crimes to the prison's Forensic Psychologist, and that she might be worth speaking to. He put me through to her and she said, 'Yes, he's been confessing that he committed his crimes with someone called David Mulcahy.' I said, 'I'll get back to you!'

---

* The decision to impose a 'whole-life tariff' on Duffy may have been an additional factor in his deciding to confess to further crimes; my father certainly thought so.

While she awaited the arrival of her new boss, Detective Superintendent Andy Murphy ('The best boss you could ever wish for,' she says), and his right-hand, Detective Sergeant Mick Freeman, Caroline spent a week feverishly typing out a forty-page report with which to greet them when they arrived:

> I laid out what I'd done to date on Operation Loudwater, and also detailed the offences and their similarities to those carried out in the 1980s. It was also chilling that David Mulcahy actually lived precisely in the vicinity of two of the current rapes. Then when Andy arrived, I sent him an email asking to speak to him, with my report attached. Within an hour he replied asking me to come and see him. Then he, Mick and myself had a coffee in the canteen and he simply said, 'Tell me more, I'm intrigued, this is fascinating.'

Fearful that Mulcahy had become active again, Andy Murphy immediately put him under surveillance, and sent Caroline Murphy and Mick Freeman to the Metropolitan Police Property Stores to investigate whether there were any exhibits still in existence from the eighties offences which might establish a connection forensically.

Meanwhile, Paul Dockley, now a detective chief superintendent in Hertfordshire, remembers that, 'Les Bolland was contacted by Operation Loudwater about this series of rapes, and he said to me, "Would you believe it, they're talking about Mulcahy." We said that whatever assistance we could give, we would. It sounded remarkable.'

As well as searching the vaults in the faint hope of old exhibits, the team also needed a sample of Mulcahy's DNA to see if it matched with the current spate of attacks, and so brought their suspect in for questioning. He proved to be, in Mick Freeman's words, 'as arrogant as they come',[9] asking for a bacon sandwich and treating the whole situation as something of a joke. Sat in an interview room with him, Caroline Murphy recalls, 'He wouldn't make eye contact with me, only with Mick. He couldn't handle me at all.' He mostly gave 'no comment' answers, until he was asked if he was prepared to provide a sample for DNA testing. Mulcahy was brash and playful with them, until Caroline suggested that if he wasn't prepared to provide a blood sample, some hair would suffice.

'It was at this point that his macho arrogance ... really came through,' she says. 'It was the only time he ever made eye contact with me.' Staring at her, Mulcahy said, 'D'you want some hair?', then savagely ripped a tuft from his head. 'You could hear it coming out by the roots, the sound was revolting. But I was adamant I wasn't going to give him the satisfaction of reacting the way he wanted me to.'

The sample was sent to forensic scientist Liz Harris for testing, but the result was disappointing. It was not a match with the current attacks. As had been the case in 1986 and 1987, Mulcahy was released. However, his DNA was now on file.

Operation Loudwater did have a breakthrough some time later, as Caroline Murphy explains:

We had briefings every night and sent out teams and decoys. And at one of these briefings, an officer who had studied the description of the attacker said, 'You know, this may be nothing, but it reminds me of a man I dealt with who grabbed a woman in a lane. A nearby resident had heard her and called the police.' There had been officers in the vicinity and he'd been arrested, but he was only charged with attempted robbery, and that's why he had slipped through the net. The officer went away and checked his notebooks, and gave us the name Edward Biggs. We arrested him, took a DNA sample, and got a match.

It had actually been six years earlier that PC Stephen Chappell had arrested Biggs. He had always suspected the real motive for the attack had been rape, and he was proved right. After three years of carrying out attacks in North London, Biggs was sentenced to life for two rapes, one attempted rape and four indecent assaults.*

Then came what Caroline Murphy calls 'a day I'll never forget'. Mick Freeman says:

> When we had been hunting for exhibits, we never thought for a minute that anything would still be around. And anything which might have been relevant turned out to be on the top shelves, in bags which were inches thick in soot, bird droppings and so on. A lot of the stuff was in the wrong place or had been moved to long-term storage, and was very hard to find. We searched and searched. And then suddenly, there it was.

What Caroline had found, amidst thousands of relics of historic crimes committed in the capital, was a small collection of exhibits from a case of rape in 1984. Specifically, the rape of two 18-year-old Danish au pairs by two men on Hampstead Heath on 15 July 1984, at 2.30 a.m.

The exhibits, consisting of the trousers and underwear from the two girls, had then been sent to the lab for testing. Caroline continues, 'I was in the office with Mick and Andy, when the telephone rang. And it was Liz Harris, phoning to say that she had been testing the exhibits for DNA, and had come up with a positive match.' Fourteen years after the crime, traces of semen found on the underwear and the

---

* Edward Biggs, 37 when he came to trial, was a bed salesman from Clapton, East London, who had spent ten years from 1982 living in America, where he had at one point been arrested under the country's anti-stalking laws. Female blood found on a knife after his arrest did not match that of any of his known victims; his DNA profile was subsequently sent to the FBI to be checked against scores of unsolved rapes across the USA.

trousers of one of the Danish au pairs had been analysed. They contained the DNA profile of one David John Mulcahy.

The likelihood of another random person having the same DNA profile was one in 51 million. 'Andy went and got a bottle of whisky. I'd never even drunk whisky before,' Caroline says.

DNA had proved Mulcahy's innocence with regard to Operation Loudwater, but it had now also proved his guilt in an offence from his past he thought he had escaped justice for. Also, crucially, with Duffy's DNA being found on the items belonging to the second victim, these tests were corroborating the version of events Duffy was giving. A further test upgraded the findings to SGM+ in ten areas, raising the odds of another person having the same profile to one in a billion.*

Andy Murphy later said that if they had arrested Mulcahy at that point, 'while it may have been possible to sustain a charge of rape, there would have been no opportunity to gather evidence to charge him with the full list of offences for which he was believed responsible, including murder'.[10] Paul Dockley told me:

> The executive team, which was myself, Dave Cox, who was the Chief Superintendent in overall charge, and the guy from the British Transport Police, were faced with a situation where we needed to make a policy decision: do we nick Mulcahy for this one offence, or do we reinvestigate the whole shooting match and put a proper case together? We realised we could nick him for that attack and he could admit to it and claim it was the only offence he ever carried out with Duffy. So we decided we were going to call in all the past SIOs, your dad and all the others, to garner their knowledge and thoughts.

* This was an exceptional result even by DNA standards. When the forensic evidence in the Maartje Tamboezer case was tested again in March 1999, it identified Duffy's DNA with a statistic of one to 104 million.

As a result, Andy Murphy decided to launch a complete reinvestigation. Operation Marford would prove to be the first time in Britain that a cold case team investigated a serial killer enquiry. The enormity of their task was daunting, especially when it was discovered that a vast amount of material from the original enquiry had been destroyed. Operation Marford would mean analysing 4,000 exhibits and 6,000 statements, locating witnesses and, without being able to guarantee a conviction, contacting victims who had spent years trying to destroy their memories of the attacks. It was an investigation which would climax at the Old Bailey two-and-a-half years later in the longest murder trial in British criminal history: the Crown versus David John Mulcahy.

The team had three months in which to build their case, as they could not risk leaving Mulcahy at liberty any longer than that. During that time, he was kept under round-the-clock surveillance. Officers were aghast at witnessing a man who they now had proof had committed violent rapes now living the life of a family man, still an attention-seeker and an extrovert, and still fond of extremely dangerous driving, but a man whose daily routine was now little more than taking his children to school and going to wherever in the capital he had work.

Until Mulcahy was arrested, the operation needed to remain highly secret, but, echoing an incident from the original enquiry, somehow information was leaked to the press. Caroline Murphy says:

> Andy had a call from a newspaper who asked if it was true that we were reinvestigating the case. He had a meeting with the journalist concerned and thankfully managed to get him to agree to keep a lid on it in return for an exclusive when it was over. If that hadn't happened, it could have been disastrous.

Now came the matter of approaching the surviving victims of Duffy and Mulcahy. Andy Murphy appointed Mick Freeman and Caroline Murphy to deal with many of the women, and speaking to them both it is easy to see why. Mick has that aforementioned combination of the firm handshake and the compassionate soul, a professional, fatherly and steadfast man. Caroline is determined, vigilant and sympathetic. The fact that all but one of the victims eventually gave evidence against David Mulcahy is testament to those qualities and skills as much as it is testament to the courage of those women.

Mick Freeman says:

> Many of the victims were now abroad, several of them having been working over here as au pairs at the time of the attacks. We had to contact the police in a number of different countries and explain the situation to them, and say, 'For God's sake be tactful, but could you make contact with these people and say we are reopening this investigation, would they be willing to speak to us?' and so on. Then the replies would come back from the police, and if it was a 'yes', we would then arrange a visit. With the women overseas we also had to explain to them the British judiciary system, how it works and so on, and having gone out there and explained it all, the crunch then came when we had to say, 'Would you be prepared to come back to the UK for a possible trial?'

The evidence relating to the Danish au pairs meant that their co-operation was vital. Nearly twenty years on, Caroline Murphy still finds recalling the experience of dealing with the two women extremely emotive:

> I contacted the police in Denmark and dealt with a detective there. She was amazing. The Danish system is very different to

ours, they can access everything about their citizens and it's compulsory to report a crime over there. I explained how delicate the situation was, and she was able to tell us where both of the women were currently living, and that both of them were now married. Mick and I then flew over to meet her and discuss the circumstances of the case and how we needed to approach these women in the most delicate way possible. We decided it would be better if she made the initial contact.

One of the women had gone on to marry her childhood sweetheart, and had told him what had happened to her. When the attack had happened, she said that she felt she had been dealt with by the officers at the time in a very caring manner, they had really looked after her. But since that time she said she would never walk alone at night, and that so many areas of her life had never been normal again. But she felt that the way she had been dealt with had helped her a little, and she was therefore quite prepared to speak to us. And she wanted to help for the sake of the other victims too.

However, the other victim, who was also now married with children, had never told her husband or her family. Her experience with the police at the time had been the exact opposite of her friend's, she had felt quite abandoned. She was, quite understandably, undecided about helping us. We said that we would leave her to think about it, and then the following day she said that she had decided to support us. Both women wanted this man off the streets. It was always on their minds that he was still out there, and if anyone ever walked a little too close to them on the street they were frightened.

Mick Freeman continues:

The German au pair, who was raped at Brent Cross, had returned to Germany, and despite having been a fluent English speaker, she had never spoken a word of English since the attack. She was simply unable to do so anymore. I went out to see her with one of the chaperones. Now, Germany has a very weird system to say the least. To my mind, interviewing a victim over such a matter, you would ideally want to do it in the comfort of the person's home, where they feel secure. But in Germany it has to be done at a police station. We also had to do it through an interpreter. So we arranged to meet the woman at her local police station, and it transpired that she was now married and her husband, who she had never told about the attack, was actually a police officer who was on duty at the time. We were interviewing her on the third floor and he was on the ground floor, completely unaware of all this.

The woman was interviewed accompanied by her lawyer and a psychiatrist. 'In the end, she was just unable to come back to England. We had a statement from her which was introduced into the evidence but it was accepted that it was just too traumatic for her to come back.'

This was an enquiry like no other. And not only regarding the worldwide operation to contact the victims. For by now, Duffy's counselling sessions with Jenny Cutler had reached a point where he felt able to speak to the police, unaware that they had already begun an investigation into Mulcahy via a quite different route. From the outset, it was made clear to Duffy that nothing could be offered to him as an incentive, that no deals could be struck. Duffy was a whole-life prisoner, and the notion of him ever being released was ludicrous. Duffy understood this, and said he was still prepared to testify if the case did come to court. To do so, he would first have to be tried for the additional crimes he was now confessing to, which would mean exacerbating what was already an unending sentence. Duffy testifying against Mulcahy would also be the first time that a highest category prisoner had given evidence against an accomplice. And so, in December 1998, a series of taped interviews conducted by Les Bolland began. They would result in sixty-five hours of confessions by John Francis Duffy.

Every day, Duffy was brought from Whitemoor to Royston, a high-security police station in Hertfordshire. Bolland used completely open questions throughout the interviews, aware again of how any leading question would inevitably be seized upon by a defence counsel in the future. Every detail in Duffy's mind was voiced. The confessions were exhaustive; frequently, they were nightmarish. Duffy's manner was generally quite clinical and emotionally sparse, with no attempt being made to minimise his involvement in the offences. The pleasure both men had taken in the planning of their crimes was calmly admitted. There were so many offences of rape that Duffy admitted he could not remember every one of them. He eventually confessed to twenty-two separate attacks, seventeen more than he was found guilty of in 1988.

When it came to talking about the murder of Alison Day, Duffy began to show signs of emotion, and the interview was suspended. When it resumed, finally, after thirteen years, the full horror of what had occurred that night in Hackney Wick was laid bare for the first time. And although it became clear that Mulcahy had been the one who had first turned to murder, equally clear was Duffy's complicity.

When Duffy described the killing of Maartje Tamboezer, Bolland said:

> He actually virtually murdered her all over again, right in front of my eyes. His face screwed up and he started twisting his hand and twisting the tourniquet; he killed her again in front of me. It's the most chilling, frightening thing I've ever come across in twenty-eight years, which in this line of work takes a bit of doing.[11]

And finally, Duffy also confessed his part in the death of Anne Lock.

The confessions suggested to the Operation Marford team that for Mulcahy, the sexual element of the crimes gradually lost its appeal as he became more interested in increasing the violence and prolonging the terrorising of a victim. The fact that it was Mulcahy who had initiated murder was maybe another clue to the factors behind Duffy's confession; perhaps he felt a bitterness at having taken all the blame for something he felt he had been lured into. It is interesting that when Duffy had been on remand at Brixton Prison in 1988, he befriended one Russell Bishop,* himself awaiting trial for murder. After he was acquitted, Bishop told the *Daily Express* that Duffy 'reckoned he was being made a scapegoat for the murders, like I was'.[12] What Duffy was saying at that time must count for little given the circumstances, but it is interesting when placed in context.

The legwork in London continued. Mick Freeman says:

Westminster Council dug out Mulcahy's worksheets for the period when he was employed by them, and on the relevant days you'd usually find that he'd say he'd been somewhere all day but in fact he'd finished the job earlier than he claimed and had then gone off with Duffy. Where he'd been booked from say 9 until 5 to retile a porch or whatever, we went back to some of these people and they could actually remember that he'd been gone by lunchtime. We were shooting down his alibis all the time.

We did enquiries with the cab office in Kilburn where he'd worked too, run by a lovely guy. We asked to see his records

* Russell Bishop was arrested in October 1986 and charged with the murders of two 9-year-old girls in Brighton, in a case known as the 'Babes in the Wood' murders. He was cleared of the charges at his trial in December 1987, but is now serving life for the attempted murder of a 7-year-old girl in Brighton in 1990.

and he'd kept them all, which was fantastic. Unfortunately they were all stored in an old shed which was infested with rats. But it was the same story when we eventually accessed those as well.

Another forensic breakthrough was made when Mulcahy's fingerprints were found on two more exhibits from the 1980s, pieces of tape that had been put over victims' mouths. 'I don't think it had been possible to take prints off sticky tape in the eighties,' says Paul Dockley. 'One of these prints was on the inside of it as I recall. But five years before Operation Marford I had been able to lift a print from an artexed wall, so things had advanced considerably by then.'

The one thing the team could not find was any evidence that Mulcahy had offended since Duffy had been put away. 'We dug and dug and dug,' says Mick Freeman:

We asked ourselves why he should suddenly stop, having been so prolific for so long. But we couldn't find anything. To all intents and purposes he had just reverted to being a married man. I think he did need Duffy.

Caroline Murphy remembers:

There was an offence that had occurred, I think in Buckinghamshire, which I located. A woman had been raped and murdered and was found in a lake. She was tied up in a not dissimilar way to the three murder victims we knew of, but we could never link it forensically. The most we could assume was that things had simply got too hot for him when Duffy was arrested.

When one considers the years that Mulcahy spent driving a minicab, years when he would have been alone with vulnerable females countless times and had by sheer stealth managed to supress whatever urges he may have had, one realises again that his offending was not a compulsion, but merely a recreation.

During the three months that Mulcahy had been under surveillance, Operation Marford had seen detectives travel to Germany, Denmark, Canada and America, not to mention Scotland, where two officers interviewed my father about the Alison Day enquiry. Colossal amounts of evidence had been amassed; the documentation for the case would eventually take up an entire office from floor to ceiling, and take the junior barristers soon to be employed on the case over a year to work through. Now the time had come to arrest David Mulcahy.

The arrest took place in the early morning of Wednesday, 3 February 1999, at his home in Chalk Farm. Andy Murphy later said that Mulcahy 'didn't seem bothered when we came to arrest him. He answered the door with a towel around his waist saying, "What do you want?"'[13] Keith Hider remembers, 'He said that it wasn't convenient as he had to go and lay a floor somewhere.'[14] As he was being led to the car, he told his wife he would telephone her later to let her know what time to come and collect him.[15]

'We told him that he was now being rearrested for committing offences in the company of John Duffy,' says Mick Freeman:

> When we'd brought him in for questioning over the Operation Loudwater rapes, he'd known damned well that he wasn't involved in that, so he was very cocksure. And this time I think he assumed we were just clutching at straws.

The questioning of Mulcahy focused first on the attack on the Danish au pairs, since this was the strongest piece of forensic evidence police had.

His solicitor wasn't the most amiable person but we did the preliminary first interview, in which he said 'no comment' to everything. Then, just as I finished the interview, I asked him if he understood what DNA was. Again he replied 'no comment'. Then I informed him that we had found his DNA on the clothing of one of the victims. I stopped the tape and I wish I'd kept it running. Because suddenly I looked at him and realised what was about to happen. I grabbed the waste paper bin, held it up, and he was violently sick into it.

This expression of physical shock was the most emotion Mulcahy ever allowed himself to show to the police.

A mouth swab was taken to acquire his DNA as evidence in the case (Mick Freeman explains that, 'You can't use DNA that has been acquired in a different enquiry, it has to be taken again'), and on the Friday morning Mulcahy appeared before magistrates at Tottenham, charged with rape and possession of a firearm which had been found in his home.

A thorough search of his home was now carried out. In addition to the vast amount of knives and weaponry, there were also a number of fascinating tangential items. A grey zip-up jacket was subsequently identified by both the victim and a witness to the rape on Barnes Common in January 1984, and by the witness who disturbed the attempted rape on Highgate West Hill in July of that year. And crucially, Mick Freeman found the cassette which Duffy had referred to throughout his confessions: Michael Jackson's *Thriller*.

Among the family snaps in the house, as well as pictures of Mulcahy from the mid-1980s in which his hairstyle, earring and so on tally with the descriptions of Duffy's accomplice given at the time, there was also a curious and sinister find. A series of photographs of a young boy, fully clothed and placed in a bath full of water, his wrists and ankles tied up in a manner disturbingly reminiscent of that used on the murder victims. The child was subsequently identified as a nephew of Mulcahy's who, when questioned, downplayed the incident as being merely horseplay, although the pictures themselves throw severe doubt on the credibility of that claim.

Throughout the enquiry, Mulcahy was, in Caroline Murphy's words, 'very belligerent and extremely arrogant':

> Initially he was dismissive, saying it was all rubbish and that we would never prove it. He made a lot of allegations, of which I was always his target because I was the officer he felt had instigated the whole thing, but actually he had serious issues with all three of the key female officers on the case.

Mick Freeman embarked on a marathon run of interviews with him, questioning him first about the other rapes Duffy had confessed to. Mulcahy read a prepared statement at the beginning of each interview, denying any involvement in the offences being put to him, and from then on answered 'no comment' to every question. Freeman recalls:

> As the interviews continued, probably as a result of what he'd been told by his solicitor, he seemed more and more confident that we'd got nothing whatsoever on him. And now when I think back, I think, 'My God, didn't I ask some stupid questions', but I worked on the principle that you have to cover every single angle, so that at any subsequent trial he couldn't suddenly say, 'I was never asked that question; if I had been, I would have answered it.' So it was just a matter of closing down every escape route.

On Monday, 15 February, Mulcahy was charged with ten more offences of rape and again remanded in custody for fur-

ther questioning. Keith Hider accompanied him to court and
experienced 'a few threats here and there in the back of the
van'.[16] Exhaustive questioning then took place on the three
murders, and on Wednesday, 31 March, he was finally charged
with the murders of Alison Jane Day, Maartje Tamboezer and
Anne Veronica Lock. He protested his innocence, telling his
wife and friends that Duffy was lying, that the police had
fitted him up and that the 1 in 1,000,000,000,000 DNA
match was either faked or erroneous.

Little did Mulcahy realise that everything Duffy said was
being tested exhaustively. A vast security operation was put
in place so that Duffy could be taken back to the scenes of
his crimes to give police further recollections of the events
that had occurred. Andy Murphy gave the officers the
instruction to constantly try and disprove everything that
Duffy told them, because if so much as one claim by him
turned out to be a lie, it would throw doubt on everything.
And in fact, Mick Freeman says, 'It quickly became apparent that he was telling the truth.' Furthermore, for someone
who had once claimed amnesia, Duffy's recollections were
remarkably detailed. Freeman adds:

> His recall was astounding; one of the attacks on the Heath had
> taken place on a park bench, and when we found it, he said,
> 'No, it's not this one, it was further over that way', and sure
> enough, 25 yards away, there it was. He never played down his
> part in it at all. He was told from day one no deals would be
> made. And anyway, he was a full-term lifer anyway, so what
> deals can you offer?

When confessing to the murder of Alison Day, Duffy had
insisted that the initial assault had taken place under the railway bridge, but when officers led him there, they found that
the bridge was in fact a solid mass with no walkway running

under it. Photographs of the site from 1986, however, would reveal that in those days the bridge did in fact have a walkway under it which had been bricked up in the intervening years. Similarly, when describing in detail the events of the afternoon Maartje Tamboezer was murdered, Duffy said that as he marched his victim across the field to where Mulcahy was beckoning him, at one point he lost sight of his accomplice. Sure enough, visiting the location revealed that there is indeed a dip in the field which one would only be aware of if one was looking for someone on the opposite side.

Retracing the events of that afternoon, and also the events regarding the death of Anne Lock, officers realised the full extent of the protracted psychological torture that had been inflicted on these women. Caroline Murphy says, 'When we visited the place where Maartje was killed, we kept thinking we must have misunderstood at first, we couldn't believe the distances the victims had been taken, it was so frightening.'

For Mulcahy, this undoubtedly became the greater source of pleasure. Caroline continues:

> To walk these murder sites and to hear what these men had done in these places was deeply shocking. Not many detectives ever have the opportunity to visit the scenes of three murders with one of the perpetrators and walk through exactly what took place. With Alison's murder, she had also been so close to getting away, she had come so close to escaping them. My dealings with Duffy overall were limited, I only had very brief dealings with him at some of the scene visits. I can't say I ever got to speak to him directly, but every officer who was there found it chilling to say the least. Listening to him talk about the crimes on tape and at the scenes and knowing in detail what he had done … I remember Mick saying to me, 'You'll never be involved in anything quite like this ever again.'

Mick Freeman feels that:

> If Duffy hadn't been arrested when he was, the pair of them
> would have just gone on and on. You look at the murders
> and each one has got that greater element of force than the
> previous one, there's more and more brutality and persecu-
> tion. Mulcahy clearly needed that extra buzz since he wasn't
> getting sexual gratification from the rapes any more. In the
> earlier rapes, you can see this sadism increasing; the girl at West
> Hampstead station for instance was forced to walk beyond the
> edge of the platform and along the embankment. She eventu-
> ally came up on the next bridge, and as she did so they were
> driving past and that's when they saw her and joked about
> offering her a lift.

Before Duffy could give evidence against Mulcahy, he
first had to be tried for the seventeen additional crimes he
had now confessed to. On Wednesday, 24 March 1999, he
pleaded guilty at the Old Bailey to nine rapes, six conspiracies to rape and two burglaries with intent to rape (those
which took place with Mulcahy in the mid-1970s). He also
pleaded guilty to the rape of Anne Lock, although he could
not be retried for her murder under the 'double jeopardy'
rule.* He was remanded in custody, with sentencing to take
place after psychiatric reports had been completed and the
trial of Mulcahy had taken place. Over the months that
followed, the knowledge that he would soon be exposed
to his victims, his former accomplice and to fierce cross-
examination meant Jenny Cutler needed to do enormous
amounts of work counselling him to avoid him attempting suicide or suffering a complete mental collapse. He was

---

* A legal principle which prevented people being tried for the same crime twice. It was
finally scrapped in England and Wales in 2005, after nearly 800 years.

aware of the fact that no one apart from his family cared for his well-being and that if he took his own life, he would not be mourned.*

Over the drizzly winter of 1999, while the country was planning its celebration of a new millennium (and panicking about the Millennium Bug), the case against Mulcahy was being prepared for the Crown Prosecution Service, who would then decide whether or not there was enough likelihood of a successful prosecution for it to be sent to trial.** Leading the case for the prosecution was Senior Treasury Counsel Mark Dennis QC. Mick Freeman says:

> I've got nothing but the greatest admiration for the Prosecution team. Mark Dennis was a fantastic man. The only phrase that didn't feature in his vocabulary was 'it can't be done'. A hard taskmaster but absolutely brilliant, as was his number two.

Junior defence counsel in court was Brian Altman QC, who took over several months into the preparations due to the previous junior, Jonathan Laidlaw, being required on another case. Laidlaw himself said at the time of the prosecution's case, 'Usually the word of a man like Duffy would count for very little, but it is very hard to think what reason he has to lie.'[17]

Assessing the evidence, the prosecution had on its side the fact that the scientific and circumstantial evidence all supported Duffy's accounts of the crimes. When assessing evidence other than Duffy's, they decided that the strongest evidence came from the Maartje Tamboezer case. The sheer volume of eyewitnesses who reported a muddied man

---

* Duffy's father died during this period.

** The CPS lawyer on the case was future Director of Public Prosecutions Alison Saunders.

either in Lollesworth Wood or making his escape from the village was huge, and it was clear that the man they were describing could not be John Duffy. The descriptions were arrestingly accurate for David Mulcahy and, in addition, now that the police knew the full protracted geography of the crime, it was indisputable that it must have been a two-man attack.

With the CPS confirming that there would be a trial, there were now 344 possible witnesses to assemble, and six months to wait while the defence considered the evidence. During this time, police chaperones kept in constant contact with the rape victims. One of them, the woman attacked on Barnes Common in January 1984, was now living in America. There was a point before the trial when she had felt unable to proceed; the team then discovered that she felt she needed to confide in her daughter, which finally she did. Amazingly, the teenager responded by telling her, 'I knew there was always something you were holding back from me,' an admission which led to a blossoming of what had hitherto been a difficult relationship.

As the trial drew nearer, the second of the Danish au pairs also felt unable to go ahead, until Caroline Murphy flew out to see her, and was told, 'I can't let you down.' Before the victim came to Britain, however, she made the decision to tell her husband, who was 'simply incredible. He supported her all the way.'

A date for the beginning of the trial was now circulated: Monday, 11 September 2000. Andy Murphy, sensing what the nature of the defence would be, warned his team that they were beginning what was probably going to be 'quite a long trial and quite a dirty trial'.[18]

After several weeks of legal argument, proceedings got underway on 3 October. The judge was Mr Michael Hyam,[*] the Recorder of London and therefore the most senior judge at the Old Bailey. Mr George Carter-Stephenson QC's defence of Mulcahy would be a straightforward one, 'Mr Mulcahy maintains, as he has done since his arrest in February 1999, that he is innocent of all these matters.'[19]

Mark Dennis meticulously depicted to the jury the world that Duffy and Mulcahy had created for themselves over their sixteen-year friendship, a friendship that had seen them descend from being unhappy children to becoming first the most prolific serial rapists this country has ever known, and ultimately to becoming killers. In his opening speech, Dennis described theirs as a 'unique and wicked bond', and assured the jury that however much Mulcahy's defence team might attempt to underplay their relationship, a mass of evidence would be brought before them to prove that the pair had in fact been inseparable; everyone from Duffy's ex-wife to the superintendent who oversaw their work at Westminster Council would confirm this fact.

At the outset, Dennis felt it was vital to preclude any suspicions that Duffy had been offered any incentives to give evidence against Mulcahy. A letter from the Home Secretary was produced confirming that the length and the conditions of Duffy's sentence were irrevocable, and that he was now also awaiting sentence on the additional offences he had recently pleaded guilty to.

---

[*] His Honour Michael Hyam was a popular and scrupulous judge, whose dispensation of justice always blended jurisprudence with considerations of the specifics of the case in question. He could be severe in his punishments but just as often compassionate. In 2001, he told a 19 year old who had killed the baby she had conceived when she was raped, 'This is on any view a tragic case. You have already suffered a great deal.' He placed her on an eighteen-month community rehabilitation order. Hyam died in 2004, having collapsed at the annual dinner of the Institute of Barristers' Clerks. He was 66.

After presenting maps to the jury showing the frequency and geography of the rapes, the prosecution began to call the victims to give evidence. Mick Freeman says, 'Each of the victims had a specific woman police officer dealing with her. I look back on it now and I think of how absolutely brilliant these officers were in how they went about it.' It had been entirely the job of the female officers to record the specific details of the attacks, but now the women had to speak of their experiences in public and withstand fierce challenges from the defence.

The victim attacked in Burton Road in October 1982, who had been walking home holding a teddy bear, clutched a handkerchief and looked to her husband in the public gallery as she gave her evidence. After being marched down Burton Road, Duffy and Mulcahy had flung her over a 4ft-high wall and on to a pile of rubble when they had heard a car approaching. They had then gagged her with Elastoplast and raped her. The victim said that after they had both run off, the shorter man had returned, dragged her back over the wall and then vanished again. Ever since that night, she had never worn anything around her neck because it would remind her of the feeling of that knife pressing against her. The next morning, she had returned to the scene and found her bag and the teddy bear still lying there. She had burned the clothes she had worn in revulsion, but had determinedly returned to Burton Road again one night several weeks later, and forced herself to walk down it again to prove to herself that she could.

The legal secretary raped in March 1985 told of how that Sunday evening she had been listening to music on a Walkman* at about 7 p.m., on her way home from working

---

* This may have been the Walkman that Duffy later showed to his wife and which he boasted he had stolen from a girl he had raped.

overtime, and had taken a steep downhill path off North End Way when she had been grabbed and dragged on to the Heath, then raped on a bench. The taller man had ordered her to remove all of her clothes, but he had then been unable to achieve an erection, which had enraged him. He had forced her to perform oral sex on him instead; the shorter man had then raped her too. Afterwards, she had telephoned her flatmate from a callbox. The flatmate informed the police; returning to the scene with them, she had found her bag, but items such as a library card containing her address were missing, which had made her terrified that the men now knew where she lived.

At the beginning of 1985, the woman had been studying law part-time and had been happy and ambitious. But after the attack, too ashamed to tell her boss what had happened to her, after taking a week off she had left her job and all the prospects it was offering, and taken a low-paid temping position because everything in her life at that point had now become associated with the rape. Before coming to court, she had told her husband about the attack; she later told a newspaper that she had been worried that he would leave her, but he had assured her that 'there was absolutely no chance of that'.[20]

This was a magnificent recurring theme with regard to the victims. The support they received not just from the police but from their partners was quite remarkable. Now, two years on from their first meeting, Caroline Murphy flew out to Denmark with two police chaperones to bring the Danish au pairs back to Britain for the first time since 1984. Their husbands both attended court with them, unfaltering in their support. Caroline says:

> The victims faced very tough cross-examination. Mulcahy's defence team never even acknowledged any of our team if you

shared a lift in the morning, and usually you all appreciate that whichever side you are on, you are all there trying to do a professional job.

It was a thuggish defence, which tried to suggest that the victims were lying on behalf of the police, or that the police had put words in their mouths. Professor David Bowen would later say of this idea, 'Nothing could have been further from the truth, as witnessed by [the victims'] courage to come forward to be interviewed and give evidence.'[21]

The jury were visibly unconvinced by the behaviour of the defence. The victims were unshakeable, many of them now admitting that they had recognised Mulcahy at identity parades in 1986 but had simply been too scared to pick him out. Paul Dockley says:

The victims remembered quite a lot. I remember sitting with Andy Murphy at the bi-weekly briefings we had and he kept us informed of what was coming out evidentially, and I think they brought out some really interesting points, and even, with the passage of time, now actually remembered more sometimes than they had done in the initial aftermath of the attacks.

The social worker attacked on Barnes Common, who had flown over from America with her daughter, 'gave her evidence very well, she wouldn't be swayed,' remembers Mick Freeman:

She was gripping the rail in the witness box so tightly. After she'd finished and left the courtroom, I went out into the foyer to her and she just broke down, sobbing, hanging on to me like grim death. This went on for about 10 minutes, and in the end she let out this deep sigh and said, 'I'm so glad I did that. I can now start a whole new chapter in my life.'

The judge allowed a statement to be read out from the German au pair attacked in January 1985 at Brent Cross, accepting that she was unable to face the pressure of the trial. It detailed how she had been walking home from a disco when she had been accosted by two men, and had tried to defend herself with an umbrella. They had then frogmarched her to a stream under a bridge and used her scarf to blindfold her. The taller man had asked her name and address as he had raped her, and said they would both find her if she told anyone. The woman had only been in the UK for two months when the attack took place; the court heard that now, as a 35-year-old mother of three, every day she has to walk past a park where she lives and every day it reminds her of the attack.

'When it came to evidence about the murders and the box the rape victims had testified in was empty, I felt desperately sad.'[22] These were the words of the arts student raped by Duffy and Mulcahy in July 1983, who was now seated in the public gallery watching the proceedings. Mulcahy was not charged with the attack on her because the Crown Prosecution Service felt there was insufficient evidence for a realistic prospect of conviction (which could have in turn had a damaging effect on the rest of the case). 'So many of the details of the rapes were identical to mine,' she said. 'When the woman in the witness box began to cry, I cried too, because I felt totally empathetic with her, even physically.'

The court now turned to the murders, beginning with that of Alison Day.

Telephoning my parents one evening that autumn, my father answered. How I regret now the paltry amount of time we ever spent talking. However, I clearly remember on this occasion him saying to me, 'Do you want to meet me for lunch next week?' He told me he was coming down to London to give evidence at the Old Bailey. I took a day off work, fascinated and baffled by it all, and hopeful I would get to see him in the witness box. The following Monday morning, I walked across what Horace Rumpole* called 'dear old Ludgate Circus', and outside the Central Criminal Court read the noticeboard informing me that Trial 19990900, 'R v Mulcahy', was taking place in Court Number One.

Sitting in the public gallery, I was reminded of how small a space the most famous courtroom in the land is. So small, in fact, that peering down at the mass of paperwork the prosecution and the defence were consulting, I was close enough to gradually realise that – although thankfully blurred a little by distance – the photographs currently staring up at me were of the canal at Hackney Wick and of the body of Alison Day.

Gazing journalistically around the chamber, I remember first settling on the judge, his attire bringing a splash of majesty and colour to the room. In the witness box stood Dr Peter Vanezis, pathologist on the Alison Day enquiry, whom I recognised from a documentary about the case my father had appeared on some years previously. Being above the barristers, I could not see their faces, but I quickly became familiar with their personas while watching their wigs bobble as they questioned. The defence, referring (much to my fascination) to 'Superintendent Farquhar' while cross-examining Dr Vanezis, was bovine and stony. The prosecution was sharp and deliberate.

Beside me in the public gallery were an elderly couple, clutching hands. I wondered if perhaps they were Mr and Mrs Day, looking, as they did, as if they had lived with their tragedy for a century and yet were still reeling from the shock.

---

* Fictional barrister of television, radio and books, created by Sir John Mortimer.

My eyes then wandered back over the proceedings, and I looked to a rather anonymous man seated on the left of the room, a man whom my gaze hadn't paused on before. He was ten years or so older than me, wearing a cheap dark suit, had neat brown hair and rather resembled the downmarket estate agent I was renting from at the time. He was taking furious notes of everything that was being said in an A4 notepad that was resting on his knees; at first I assumed that he was a court reporter. Then, gradually, I realised that I was looking at the man who was here today accused of rape and murder: David John Mulcahy.

The octagonal dock in Court Number One takes up a tenth of the room; it is disproportionately large because it may need to accommodate up to twenty prisoners at a time. It occurred to me that not only had John Duffy once occupied it, but so had so many of the other mass-murderers of history whose infamy makes them now seem more like characters from penny-dreadfuls than beings who once lived and performed terrible crimes against real people. For most of us, names like Christie, Crippen and Haigh denote waxworks in the Chamber of Horrors more than they represent real human suffering. But looking down at that space on that damp morning, I realised that in this room, the room such wicked acts lead to, there is no sensationalising of crime, no mythologising of crime, and there are no fanciful ghosts. Seated there, that man was merely the latest in that grim parade of those failed and unremarkable people who have sought to establish themselves in this world through violence and cruelty.

He looked rather innocuous; in fact I could not imagine at first glance any woman feeling uneasy if he was sitting across from her on a train. But as the day went on, I began to notice certain habits in him. He would occasionally desist from scribbling and sit back, watching the proceedings.

Then, after a witness answered a question, he would instantly and exaggeratedly bolt forward and be hunched over his pad again, scribbling urgently. The effect was clearly to try and suggest that something had been said that was easily disprovable, that an obvious mistake had been made. It didn't work. On other occasions, he would roll his eyes at the evidence, or gesture with his arms in disbelief. When Keith Hider was in the witness box, 'after about 15 minutes of all that, I protested, and the judge acknowledged it. Mulcahy treated the whole thing as a game.'

I met my father in the foyer at the end of the morning session, catching traces of the hushed chatter that was all about the place. He was in conversation with a forensic scientist he had known years ago about the forthcoming trial of Barry George for the murder of television presenter Jill Dando, the scientist saying that in his opinion there was no way it could lead to a conviction, since there was simply no forensic evidence.* He would, of course, ultimately be proved right. My father and I lunched at Ye Olde London on Ludgate Hill, where he told me with disappointment that at the court he had also encountered two former Flying Squad colleagues who were now standing trial for corruption.

Despite having been retired for more than ten years, he took the whole day in his stride, compared to my amazement when beholding the unremarkable David Mulcahy. I remember wondering if in some way these proceedings were going to undermine the work that had been done by him and his colleagues in the eighties, but as Caroline Murphy told me, 'That was never going to be the case. We couldn't

---

* Jill Dando, BBC Personality of the Year in 1997, was, with horrid coincidence, co-presenter of *Crimewatch* at the time of her death. She was shot outside her house in Fulham at 11.30 a.m. on 26 April 1999. After a year of fruitless enquiries, police investigated local man Barry George, who had a history of stalking and sexual offending. He was convicted of the murder on 2 July 2001 but his conviction was quashed on its third appeal in November 2007, and he was acquitted after a second trial in August 2008.

have done what we did without their work.' I asked him if the revelations about David Mulcahy had come as a surprise to him, and he said, 'We were always sure it was him.' I suppose it demonstrated what he had told Paul Dockley all those years earlier, 'Be patient. He'll come in time.'

Matters moved sluggishly in the courtroom that afternoon, meaning I never got to see him in the witness box. But a few days later, eight weeks into the trial, the time came for the prosecution's major witness to give evidence. Before that witness was called, Dennis warned the jury that what followed would be 'the most chilling evidence you are likely to hear, but also the most compelling'. He then called John Francis Duffy.

The jury's opinion on Duffy as a witness of truth would be crucial. He would either be the case's strongest witness or its weakest link, the defence determined to prove him 'a manipulator and a liar'. Brian Altman said after Duffy's first day in the witness box, 'It's got to be one of the most extraordinary days I've had in getting on for twenty years of practice at the bar. The seconds became minutes and the minutes became hours, and you could have cut the atmosphere with a knife. And suddenly there he was.' All eyes fell on Duffy as he stood looking at the dock he himself had once stood in, and which was now occupied by the man whose bond with him had only finally been severed after a decade of separation. They had once been, in Duffy's words, 'like brothers'. Now they were enemies. The pair had seen each other briefly at committal proceedings some months earlier, but now Duffy was to spend eleven days only a few feet away from him.

This was the first time Duffy had spoken of his crimes publicly. Paul Dockley says, 'At first he was very nervous but he gave his evidence with certainty, him and Mulcahy looking at each other throughout. You could see the animosity between them.' Mick Freeman said Duffy was mostly 'calm and collected, and very matter-of-fact':

> He was unshakable, this is what I did, this is what happened and so on. Mulcahy was sitting there glaring daggers at him.

Indeed, at one point the impotent Mulcahy erupted from the box, 'Why don't you tell the truth and get it over with?' To the allegation that he was trying to shift the blame for his crimes elsewhere, Duffy said:

> There is a lot of self-hate for what I have done. I feel a lot of guilt. I raped and killed innocent young ladies. I accept that. I am not trying to shift the blame. I did what I did. It became too much for me, the realisation of what a disgusting person I was. There's no excuse. No promises have been held out. I've no hope that by giving evidence, one day I'll be a free man. I expect to die in prison.

Duffy claimed that the offending became 'part of life'. Professor David Canter says:

> I often quote that in lectures. He was unable to give it up, which is what I inferred from the patterns of behaviour and the geography of the offences, that they had started out as being opportunistic and showed a sort of developing commitment.[23]

Duffy told the court, 'We would get excited by talking about what we did to the victims, and we got bolder as we progressed.' He said that Mulcahy considered himself 'an immortal warrior' who liked the idea of 'playing God with his victims'. Rather more prosaically, he said of his own motivation, 'I was having problems at home and I just wanted to strike back at my wife.'

In describing the rapes, Duffy revealed how several times in the early rapes they had intended to kidnap a victim and hold her hostage: count number one in this trial, the rape of the woman holding the teddy bear, had been one such occasion. They had even laid a mattress out on the floor in Duffy's flat beforehand, but when they did trap the woman, neither man wanted to be left alone with her while the other was fetching the car.

Duffy only really showed emotion when describing the full details of the murder of Alison Day. After reliving her pleas of 'it's only the moustache I have seen, I will not tell anyone, don't hurt me', he appeared to falter and gulp in air. The court was adjourned briefly while he composed himself and while the jury had a break from the relentless, harrowing details.

When detailing the murder of Maartje Tamboezer, he said that as they marched her across the fields, Mulcahy 'was becoming very aggressive, hyper, shouting at the girl':

> Then he raised his fists and hit her. She crumpled to the floor. She was struck on the head, at the side. It was a swinging blow. I noticed he had a rock in his hand, or a stone. She just crumpled up and fell to the floor. I believe she was unconscious.

He then told how Mulcahy had ripped off her belt and handed it to Duffy with a piece of stick through it, and told him to kill her. Duffy said, 'I actually started twisting it while David turned away. I think I just got caught up in it. It is very difficult to explain. I just continued twisting until she was dead.'

The specifics of Anne Lock's death differed from the others, a factor which had led to Duffy being found not guilty of her death in 1988. Rather than strangulation with a tourniquet, she had been suffocated, her mouth deliberately forced open. Duffy's story, that this time Mulcahy had acted alone and had hinted afterwards that he had done something different to the victim on this occasion, would corroborate this to some degree, but this part of the case was the most difficult for the prosecution. It relied almost entirely on Duffy's word. When relating his account, Duffy also revealed that when the pair had first been looking for a victim at Brookmans Park, they had planned to grab a young woman they had seen outside the station, but her mother had appeared and called her name. He also confessed that they had practically given up when they saw Anne Lock step from the train. When accused of trying to shift the blame for the murder of Anne Lock by claiming that he wasn't involved, Duffy said, 'I still have a responsibility. I walked away and turned my back. If I could stand trial for it now, I would.'

When reviewing Duffy's time giving evidence, Mark Dennis called it 'a tough old war of attrition', but felt that he had been 'a very compelling witness, and the more the cross-examination went on the more of the human being seemed to become visible, after initially it being an almost inhuman being standing there'. Brian Altman reflected that, bafflingly, 'at the end, he almost evoked sympathy'.[24]

Perhaps there was a touch of revenge in Duffy's performance too. It became clear to the court throughout the trial that his primary motivation was always rape, whereas with Mulcahy it became murder, and that telling Duffy to murder Maartje Tamboezer was in some ways Mulcahy testing Duffy's commitment, since he may have felt Duffy had become uneasy and troubled after the first killing. Caroline Murphy suspects that some of the reasons behind Duffy's confessions were connected with his family too:

His grandmother had died, and his mother hadn't visited him for a while I seem to recall. Whether it was out of remorse, or even because of jealousy at Mulcahy being free while he was in prison, who knows? Who knows what goes through the mind of a man like that?

Also giving evidence was a woman who had befriended Mulcahy in the eighties when they had both regularly gone on weekend trips to soul music concerts. As she would later tell *The Times*, on one occasion, at Bognor Regis, they were walking along the beach arm in arm when:

> He became very distant and stared out to sea … It was the first time we had talked to each other. It started off about his family and he said that they had been subject to racist attacks. I asked him how could he protect them when he was working day and night. He suddenly stopped and looked out to sea.

Mulcahy had then said to her, 'I have done something which could put me away for a long time.' The woman's first reaction was 'that he had robbed a bank, but then I dismissed that':

> I did not have the chance to pursue it. The friends behind us caught up and we went on. I saw two sides of him. The playful side; you would never realise he was married with children. And suddenly I saw this serious side of him. He did not frighten me. I saw a sensitive side. I did not feel threatened or vulnerable.

Mulcahy did not look up throughout her evidence. She would later recall:

> On the way down to one of the weekends he drove his car madly. He took roundabouts on two wheels and had mock

fights with his passenger who was a friend. He did not seem like
a man with any responsibilities. He just wanted to have fun.[25]

Mark Dennis ended the case for the prosecution by showing the jury some photographs of Duffy and Mulcahy as
children, which had been provided by Duffy's father. There
were fears that showing the jury images of Mulcahy as an
innocent child could have a detrimental effect on the case,
but these were quickly dispelled. The pictures did what
they were intended to do: demonstrate once again the
'unique and wicked bond' between the pair, a bond which
the defence, by underplaying their friendship, had tried to
claim was fantasy.

'After the prosecution case was completed, I turned
to Mark Dennis and said, "… and?"' remembers Mick
Freeman. 'Because the evidence was overwhelming. Of
course, there's always that doubt at a trial, because anything's
possible with a jury, but the whole thing was clutching at
straws from the side of the defence.'

The defence's case was simply to claim that Duffy was a
liar and Mulcahy was a family man. The defence wanted the
transcripts of the police interviews with Mulcahy in 1986
to be read out in court, but Mark Dennis also arranged for
the tape recordings of them to be played, to allow the jury to
hear the character of the man at that time, in all his arrogance.

There was a shocking development when the defence
insisted on calling Laurence Lock to give evidence.
Presumably the tactic was to reignite old suspicions.
Laurence stood in the dock for just three minutes, revealing to the court that fourteen years on from the death of
his wife, he had no memory of the events of that summer.
Close to tears, he said there was 'a gap in his life' and that he
had 'no direct memory' of that time, just the image of the
beauty of his wife's smile. He said:

I have memories of the funeral. My father died as a result of those events and my mother grieved for him and I had to care for her for ten years. There is a gap in my memory from before we were married. I don't have any clear memory of the night she disappeared but I have memories of her smile. I remember that vividly.

It was a shattering revelation. Both the prosecution and the defence counsels then apologised for calling him to give evidence, and the judge told him, 'I am sorry you have had to come here.'

Now came the moment when David Mulcahy stepped into the witness box. His performance there would be as crucial to the defence as Duffy's was to the prosecution. Initially he seemed credible, blending lies and truth as he had done in questioning many times before, saying that Duffy had indeed been 'a good friend' when they were at school, but that they had drifted apart after Mulcahy had met his wife (which was in 1977), and following a 'pub fracas'. However, under cross-examination, the court saw in him both anger and absurdity. His explanations on more than one occasion prompted laughter from the jury, as he insisted that if Duffy did have an accomplice, it could not have been him, and must have been another friend of Duffy's who fitted his description. He also accused the police of fabricating the DNA by somehow obtaining his semen and planting it on the clothing of the Danish au pair.

Mark Dennis had an ace up his sleeve, but before playing it, he first asked the usher to hand Mulcahy a piece of paper, and instructed him to read the words on it to the court. The words were the lyrics of Michael Jackson's 'Thriller', the words that he and Duffy had chanted again and again on their hunting expeditions. Stripped of their musical camouflage, those demonic verses describing something evil lurking in the dark, the lines about trying to scream, about how 'no one's gonna save you from the beast about to strike' and about how 'you're fighting for your life inside a killer' simplistically told the story of how rape turned to murder. The more matter-of-factly the words were read, the less expression Mulcahy tried to put into them, the more unpleasant they sounded. Everyone in the room was hearing what was essentially a transcript of what had passed between those two men on so many occasions in the build-up to another life being disfigured or destroyed.

When questioned about the night of the murder of Alison Day, despite Duffy's mother having confirmed that there had indeed been a telephone call from Mulcahy that had prompted her son to change his plans and go out, Mulcahy once again claimed he had been suffering from bronchial pneumonia at the time and that he had been bedridden. This was then crushed by a statement police had taken from his GP in 1987, which revealed that he had in fact been seen by her earlier that month and found to be suffering from catarrh and asthma, and also that when she saw him again, six days before the murder, 'by that time, he had recovered'.[26]

At the end of his cross-examination, Mark Dennis played his ace. When Duffy had been brought in for questioning by Operation Hart in July 1986 and suspicions had been raised, police had actually questioned Mulcahy too, having made the association based on the pair's previous joint convictions for petty crime. At the time, Mulcahy had only been questioned about two murders, those of Alison Day and Maartje Tamboezer. (Anne Lock's body was actually found the following day.) Dennis revealed to the court what he suggested had been 'a fatal slip' on Mulcahy's part: Mulcahy had, without prompting, denied *three* killings, not two, and had actually mentioned Anne Lock's name during the interview. Dennis finished his questioning of Mulcahy decisively by asserting that the reason he knew Anne Lock's name was because he had been involved in her murder.

In his closing speech, Mark Dennis reminded the jury that many of the victims had described Mulcahy as the leader, that he had clearly been 'excited by dominance, and thrived on the total control it gave him', and that the victims had been taken increasingly long distances from the place where they had been abducted, 'reducing them to a state of abject fear'. He said Mulcahy's 'hunger for excitement' is what led to 'ever increasing acts of cruelty'. Following him, Mr Carter-Stephenson reiterated to the jury that the defence's case was simple, 'In a nutshell, he didn't do it.'

Before sending the jury out to consider their verdicts, the judge said:

> We have listened to the most dreadful accounts of what hap-
> pened to those women. The way in which you should deal
> with the evidence is to consider it clinically. Bring a cool mind
> to your consideration of the evidence. Don't allow prejudice
> of any kind to get in the way.

On Monday, 29 January, at 2.30 p.m., the court rose.

Having returned once to check a legal point, four days later, on the morning of Friday, 2 February 2001, the jury filed back into a packed Court Number One, after a total of twenty hours of deliberation. Mick Freeman remembers:

> Caroline Murphy was sitting next to me, and you're so uptight
> it's not true. We'd been over two years on this. And it was the
> usual procedure, 'will your foreman please stand, have you
> reached a verdict?' and so on. And when they were asked for
> their verdict on count one, she grabbed hold of my hand.

Caroline says:

You never know what a jury will do, and we weren't able to sit in court and listen to the victims, so we didn't know how things had proceeded apart from what the barristers were telling us. All of the core team were sat together, and a lot of the victims were there with their husbands and chaperones. I have never been in a courtroom so packed, even compared to other high profile cases. The atmosphere was extraordinary. David Mulcahy was sitting there with a smug grin on his face as the victims waited for the verdicts; after each one was read out, you knew they were wondering what the outcome would be when it came to their case.

This was the end of a £2 million enquiry and more than three years of the team members' lives. These were also the final moments of a nightmare that had begun more than twenty-five years earlier.*

- Count one was the rape of the woman holding the teddy bear, in Burton Road, Kilburn, in October 1982. Guilty.
- Count two, conspiracy to rape, Kilburn, March 1983. This attack was on the restaurant manager who fought back and was brutally beaten as a result. Guilty.
- Count three, the rape of a social worker on Barnes Common in January 1984. Guilty.
- Count four, the rape of a woman at West Hampstead station. After the attack, John Duffy and his accomplice, driving past, had spotted her and joked, 'Shall we give her a lift?' Guilty.
- Count five, conspiracy to rape at Highgate West Hill, in July 1984. Guilty.

---

* The earliest offence the pair are known to have committed was the burglary with intent to rape in 1975.

- Counts six and seven. The rape of two Danish au pairs on Hampstead Heath in July 1984. Guilty.
- Count eight, the rape of a German au pair at Brent Cross in January 1985. Guilty.
- Count nine, conspiracy to rape a 16-year-old girl on Hampstead Heath in January 1985. This was the attack in which Duffy claimed he intervened, alarmed at Mulcahy's violence towards her. Guilty.
- Count ten, conspiracy to rape a 23-year-old au pair in Church Row, Hampstead, in February 1985. She had screamed so loudly that her voice gave out. She sustained severe facial bruising. Guilty.
- Count eleven, conspiracy to rape a 23-year-old woman in Swiss Cottage who had been on her way to buy cigarettes, in March 1985. Guilty.
- Count twelve, the rape of a 25-year-old solicitor's clerk on Hampstead Heath in March 1985. Guilty.

Now the foreman was asked to give the jury's verdicts on the last three counts.

- Count thirteen, the murder of 19-year-old Alison Day, at Hackney Wick, on 29 December 1985. Guilty.
- Count fourteen, the murder, on 17 April 1986, in Horsley, of 15-year-old Maartje Tamboezer. Guilty.

Now the court turned to the final count. The murder of Anne Lock. Caroline Murphy says:

The tension was unbearable. Laurence Lock had gone through hell on earth. He'd been a suspect, and that isn't to criticise what had to be done, but he had suffered so much, with the media surrounding the case, with everything. And we'd had to say to him that we wanted to open this all up again. It hadn't been easy to get him to trust us, he was very reluctant to get on board. As we awaited that verdict, I kept thinking about a 'not guilty' verdict, and thinking 'what if this happens again?'

• Count fifteen. The murder of 29-year-old Anne Lock, who had been married just a month, and who had been preparing to be a bridesmaid at her best friend's wedding. Guilty.

It was over.

Mick Freeman says, 'Each time they came back with another "guilty", Caroline's fingernails dug deeper and deeper into my hand. After the last one came in, I looked down and there was blood pouring from it.' 'I don't think there was a single person on our team that wasn't in tears,' she adds.

The protocols of the courts usually diffuse passions, but on that cold morning, not even the solemnity of the Old Bailey could temper the three victims who wept and hugged each other as the verdicts were announced. Mick Freeman says:

> So many of the victims said, 'I can now put it to bed. I know the second man is caught and is going to prison.' I must confess that it gave me great satisfaction to then add, 'And by the way, he's never coming out.' So many of these women were still looking over their shoulder until that moment, thinking that any man on the street could be him.

One might dare to call it poetic justice that a woman's intuition was what ultimately led to Mulcahy's conviction. For Caroline Murphy, this was not only the conclusion of a journey that had begun with her alone in an office looking at the Operation Loudwater attacks and having a hunch which had led to the biggest joint operation the Metropolitan Police had ever undertaken. It was also the end of three years of journeying into the emotionally scarred lives of the victims of John Duffy and David Mulcahy, of earning the trust of those victims, of supporting them and helping them find the courage to see that justice was finally, exhaustively done. The second of the Danish au pairs, who had told her husband just before the trial, hugged her and thanked her after it was over. Caroline says:

> I said to her, 'I can't believe you are saying that to me, we dragged this all up, it's us who should be thanking you.' But she kept saying, 'Thank you for putting this man away, thank you, and thank you for helping me and my husband.' And then her husband hugged me and shook my hand, and said, 'You have no idea of the impact this has had on my wife. Now she is able to get out of a car and walk down a street at night. In the whole time I've known her … I knew there was something but I never wanted to push it. Just … thank you.'

For these women, this had been a journey from being victims to becoming survivors.

David John Mulcahy stood as the judge told him:

> The offences of rape of which you have been convicted together make this an exceptionally serious set of offences. They contain almost all the aggravating features which may be found in this type of offending. Firstly, violence was offered, which was used over and above that necessary to commit the offence. Secondly, in every case, a weapon, namely a knife, was used to terrify and to subdue the victim into compliance. Thirdly, the offences were repeated, and on occasion more than one rape was committed at the time of the offences. Rape was committed again and again. Furthermore, there were other sexual indignities inflicted on the victims in addition to the rapes.

The judge read out sections of victims' impact statements describing the effects the attacks had on their lives; one said she 'runs away from the good things in life' and another that she was still tormented by nightmares and still required constant medication.[27]

He then focused on Mulcahy's role in the offences:

> These were sadistic killings. Of the two of you, I have no doubt that it was you that derived gratification from killing. These were acts of desolating wickedness in which you descended to the depths of depravity in carrying them out. The punishment for such terrible crimes is mandatory: a sentence of life imprisonment is intended to, and will, reflect society's abhorrence of these crimes.

Hyam then passed sentenced on David John Mulcahy. For each of the rapes: twenty-four years' imprisonment. On each of the five charges of conspiracy to rape: eighteen years. For each of the murders: mandatory life sentences. He was given a total of 258 years' imprisonment, all sentences to run concurrently.

Mulcahy showed no emotion at the realisation that he was going to spend the rest of his life in prison, although at the guilty verdict for the first of the murder charges, Brian Altman later said, 'I think the blood drained from his face.'[28] As he was led away, he looked towards the victims who were in court and smirked.

The judge then paid tribute to Dr Jenny Cutler and all of the Operation Marford team, saying, 'All of the officers involved in that investigation have carried out their duties admirably.' (Dr Cutler would later mourn the fact that the Prison Service was moving away from one-on-one therapy in favour of group therapy, pointing out that Duffy's confessions could never have occurred in such a scenario.[29]) Caroline Murphy says, 'When we looked at photographs of us all afterwards, we realised how exhausted we were. We'd been running on adrenaline for months.' The families of the murder victims were not in court for the sentencing, but seated at the back was Paul Tidiman, the fiancé of Alison Day, who described the jury's decision as 'brilliant'.[30]

In a prepared statement, Alison's family thanked the police for 'their painstaking dedication' and thanked the officers 'who have given us continued support and assistance'. The statement continued:

> Our hearts go out to the rape victims and their families over the trauma they have had to experience of another trial, and can but hope that the verdict today will help to ease their pain in the knowledge that it was their evidence that assisted the outcome.[31]

A close friend of the Tamboezer family told the press:

> It was incredibly difficult for them. I asked them whether this had brought it all back to them. Maartje's mother, Marijka, told me, 'We don't need this to remind us. There is not a day that goes by when I do not think of Maartje.'[32]

Outside the Old Bailey, Andy Murphy told the press:

> In 1986, with the arrest of John Duffy, police brought about the end of a series of the most horrific rapes and murders this country has ever seen. Today's verdicts will ensure that David Mulcahy will never have the opportunity to terrorise the streets of London again.

At a press conference later in the day, Detective Chief Superintendent Dave Cox, who had been in overall command of Operation Marford, said:

The investigations that took place in the 1980s were very competent and professional investigations of their era. They didn't have the technology of DNA, they didn't have modern fingerprint technology. The horror of these offences was magnified because of the fact that the victims were randomly selected. Such stranger attacks are the stuff of horror movies and nightmares, and they diminish the quality of life for all of us.[33]

Caroline Murphy tells me:

Your dad was so helpful to us, and with all the work he did, and the work all the other SIOs did, John Hurst and so on, the fact that they got to see that closure on the case must have been so satisfying for them.

The core team of Operation Marford were awarded a Commissioner's Commendation for their work. Mick Freeman had held off his retirement to see the case through to its conclusion, and now decided to stay a while longer for one specific reason:

I wanted to put the job to bed. Because Mulcahy was still protesting his innocence, even though there have never been any grounds for appeal, I wanted to make sure that if anything ever happened and this all had to be resurrected, that everything was put exactly where it should be, which it hadn't been previously. I'd inherited papers at the start of the case which were in a state and some things had been lost, so I decided to make sure that everything was exhaustively organised so that anyone in the future that needed to examine anything could do so easily.

Also paying tribute to the police was one of the victims, the 16-year-old girl who had been attacked on Highgate West Hill and who had been saved by a passer-by disturbing

Duffy and Mulcahy. She complained that in the 1980s it had taken four attempts for police to take a statement from her. (One thinks of the case of the Danish au pairs as an example of how different women had different experiences of the police at the time, suggesting it was often a problem of individuals rather than a problem of the times.) However, she stressed to the press that attitudes had improved hugely, praising the constant support she had been given by the police and saying, 'Women who have been subjected to such attacks should be made aware that the police and court process today is supportive, caring and understanding.'[34]

On the eve of the second anniversary of his arrest, Mulcahy began his sentence at Belmarsh Prison in South London. He was placed in a special segregation unit, having allegedly been the victim of attacks by other prisoners while on remand.* His wife, who had shaken her head at the verdicts from the public gallery, told reporters that she would fight on to prove his innocence. The press were baffled by the notion of such a man managing to keep such impulses a secret from his family, though they made much of evidence that Mulcahy had regularly boasted to colleagues that he liked to have 'complete power over women' and that his wife was 'completely submissive'.

Sandra Mulcahy gave one press interview, six weeks after the sentence. At the time, she was not only dealing with her husband's life imprisonment, but with another in a long line of personal tragedies. After miscarrying in 1986 and losing a child to leukaemia in 1997, now her youngest son was being treated for stomach cancer at just

---

* The *Daily Express* of 3 February 2001 claimed that while on remand, Mulcahy had been assaulted and 'attacked with bleach and with scalding water', while Duffy had also been 'knocked semi-conscious' after being struck by two heavy duty batteries in a sock at some time in the past. Some years later, on 6 July 2008, the *Sunday Mirror* would claim Mulcahy had again been attacked in prison.

9 years of age. She spoke to Angela Levin of the *Daily Mail*, who remembers:

> She was very focused at the time on one of her sons being seriously ill. I suspect she had to keep herself together in order to cope with her boy and the other children. She was probably in denial for the same reason. She struck me as a tragic figure.[35]

In the interview, Mrs Mulcahy said:

> David has told me he is innocent, and that is enough for me. If, in years to come, he admits he did those crimes, then my sons and I will walk away and never see him again. Meanwhile, I believe him one hundred per cent.[36]

She said that he had told her the DNA was planted because the police had to justify the expense of the enquiry. (What he clearly hadn't told her was that the DNA evidence had in fact *prompted* the enquiry, not justified it.)

On Thursday, 9 March 2001, John Duffy made his last public appearance, appearing at the Old Bailey to be sentenced for the additional crimes he had now confessed to. For his part in eight rapes, seven conspiracies to rape and two burglaries with intent to rape, Hyam sentenced him to seven sentences of twelve years each, one of eleven years, three of nine years and two of three years.[37] Duffy remains to this day a Category A prisoner with no special privileges. And as Mick Freeman points out, 'Although most coppers of your father's generation probably wanted to see the death penalty brought back, if Duffy had been hanged, we'd never have got Mulcahy.'

Although Duffy and Mulcahy were tried for the offences that there was the strongest chance of a conviction on, Operation Hart listed many more as being similar enough to be linked. Duffy told police he believed they had probably committed further attacks, and he also said that Mulcahy had boasted to him of having carried out many attacks alone too.[38] After Mulcahy's conviction, police announced that they would be re-examining other unsolved cases and urged women who may have been attacked by either man to come forward. Mick Freeman says:

> A few women came forward from all over the country, but these attacks bore no resemblance to the ones we knew about. I can't blame them of course, haunted by the knowledge that their attackers were possibly still out there. In the end, Mulcahy was never positively identified for any other offences, before or after Duffy was imprisoned, but who can say?[*]

Detectives planned to examine a national file containing over 180 unsolved murders of women stretching back to the 1980s before questioning Mulcahy again; at the time, Andy Murphy said, 'It would be fair to say that there are around half a dozen other cases in the Hampstead area alone during the eighties which he may have been involved in.'[39] In particular, the murder of Hampstead teenager Yiannoulla Yianni in August 1982[**] seemed to bear basic similarities to the later killings, as did that of Jennifer Ronaldson, a 19-year-old nurse at Guy's Hospital who was raped and strangled, and whose body was dumped in the Thames near Poplar in November 1980.

---

[*] The *Guardian* reported on 3 February 2001 that 'at least one woman … has come forward to allege she was a victim of Mulcahy alone, and is considering bringing a complaint because she feels police did not do enough. She was attacked in 1983 when Duffy was free, but this shows that Mulcahy seems to have been prepared to operate alone.' Nothing more came of this, although it is interesting that the year is 1983, the period when very few offences seem to have been committed by Duffy and Mulcahy together.
[**] A link with this case had been mooted back in the eighties. As this book went to press, a 56-year-old man was finally charged with Yianni's death after a cold case review.

Duffy's claim that Mulcahy had told him he had also committed attacks alone is an interesting one. Although there is no evidence for these attacks, and the claim may have been fantasy on Mulcahy's part, I was struck by a story I came across in the *Hampstead & Highgate Express* of 12 November 1976. The headline was 'Rapist "may live near the Heath"'. It was a report of a vicious attack on Saturday, 6 November, at 5.40 p.m. A woman had been walking down North End Way when a young man had knocked her handbag to the ground, and, as she bent to pick it up, had kicked her in the face.

The youth had then 'punched and kicked her many times again and dragged her 30 yards from the footpath into Heathland scrub. After raping her, he tried to strangle her, then robbed her and stole most of her clothing.'

The attacker escaped on a bicycle, and Detective Chief Inspector George Dent said he believed him to be local, explaining, 'It was a very bad night and had been raining hard. We think he may not have come that far.' The woman was left wearing only a sweater, and ran bleeding to a nearby house.* Dent said, 'She put up a very good fight but took a terrible beating.'[40]

Could this have been Mulcahy? The youth was described as being between 18 and 20 (Mulcahy was 17 at the time). He later owned a motorbike, so it's likely he would have owned a bicycle in his teens (or have stolen one). The scene of the attack, North End Way, would be precisely the site of attacks by Duffy and Mulcahy in 1982 and 1985; a further attempted attack by them on the same road also took place in 1985. Although this attack was nearly six years before the first rape we know the pair carried out, it should be

---

* The house was owned by presenter and actor Nicholas Parsons, who telephoned for an ambulance while his wife comforted the victim.

remembered that the two burglaries with intent to rape had already taken place by now, and both had been at Mulcahy's suggestion. The estimated height of the attacker was 5ft 10in, which fits, as does the long face in the photofit. (The victim did, however, think the attacker had fair hair under his blue woollen cap, rather than Mulcahy's mousy hair.) I showed the report to Paul Dockley. His response was, 'Too many coincidences for my liking.'[41]

We will never know the truth about the extent of Mulcahy's evil or the reason for it. Andy Murphy said at the time of Mulcahy's conviction, 'Both men came from close, hard-working families and had not been abused or subjected to violence when young* … you have to accept that some people are just evil. Mulcahy is such a person.'[42] Murphy believed that, 'Without Duffy, Mulcahy lost that dynamic force that drove both men. They fed off each other and wound each other up. They liked to relive their offences.' Forensic psychologist Dan Wilcox said at the time that the pair had probably been fantasising about rape from as young as 12 years old, saying, 'They change what normality is and justify each other's actions in much the same way as members of a paedophile ring.'[43]

I have already stated how Mulcahy's crimes were clearly procedural more than pathological, both in the meticulous planning (compared to Duffy, who was far more opportunistic and clumsy when attacking alone) and in his ability to stop when the police got too close. Professor David Canter says, 'Sometimes the act of settling down and having children can change an offender enough for him to stop offending,'[44] although Mulcahy was already a married man and a father when the rapes began. In his novella *A Clockwork Orange*, Anthony Burgess saw youth

---

* Unless one counts school bullying.

violence as something which for some was inevitable but also ephemeral; his teenage protagonist, Alex, commits rape and murder purely for excitement, but simply grows out of it, in the same way perhaps that has been seen with many of those who commit acts of violence at football matches. Society finds this concept easier to comprehend in acts of mob violence than in acts of sexual violence or violence towards children, but when one looks at Mulcahy's hyperactive, craze-driven nature, perhaps to him it really was simply an obsession that he lost interest in.

The real clue must surely come from Duffy's recollection of Mulcahy seeing himself as an 'immortal warrior'. The delusion ties in somehow with that intimidating stare down the lens Mulcahy performed when he realised he was in shot during the *Blue Peter* coverage of his roller-skating marathon. Keith Hider says, 'Looking at his life on paper, he was a total non-entity, if it wasn't for being a mass-murderer.'[45] To his neighbours, he was simply a local man who offered to carry an old lady's shopping; like Duffy, people who knew him found it hard to believe the crimes he was proved to have committed. But behind his everyday, unremarkable existence, this was someone who had discovered a way of feeling, in his words, 'God-like'; someone who had experienced 'the power of life and death over others'. His words are tatty derivatives of martial arts fantasy and sociopathy, and it is surely significant that every crime of violence he was convicted of was against either a woman or a child, with the exception of the airgun attacks, which were carried out at a safe distance and from a place of concealment.

One curious fact remains about the last two murders. On both of these occasions, Mulcahy sent Duffy away and returned to the victim alone. In the case of Maartje Tamboezer, he claimed this was to make sure he had left no fingerprints. (It was considered more likely that he returned to make certain that she was dead.) In the case of Anne Lock, he sent Duffy back to the car, supposedly then raping her before killing her. We will never know exactly what happened when he was alone again with those victims, but let us remember also that after Duffy had raped Maartje Tamboezer, he and Mulcahy then marched her across the fields, and when they reached the copse she was found in, Mulcahy suddenly became enraged and struck her. Could this have been because he was sensing that once again he would be unable to perform, and the sudden attack was out of rage or as an excuse not to have to try? Throughout the whole case, his violence seemed more and more connected to his sporadic impotence. Initially it cured his impotence. Later it eclipsed it.

While Mulcahy may have seen his crimes in his own mind as some kind of malevolent odyssey, Mick Freeman says of him and Duffy, 'Leaving aside the rapes and the murders, they were just a couple of little toerags. That's all they were.'

Mulcahy has shown no remorse for his crimes, and instead has spent his time in Full Sutton Prison mostly pestering the legal system in whatever way he can. In 2014, he was one of a number of inmates who lodged a claim with the European Court of Human Rights demanding compensation for every election missed due to imprisonment.[46] (The ECHR ruled in favour of Mulcahy and his fellow complainers in February 2015, but no compensation was awarded to them.) In July 2014, he demanded compensation because a parcel that was sent to him was damaged, and allegedly received £515. After another failed attempt to appeal, he demanded access to 6,000 documents relating to his case, and because a decision on this arrived some weeks after the deadline, he took out an action against the Commissioner of the Metropolitan Police, which was dismissed.[47]

Mulcahy arranged some years ago for his rather tedious and frequently risible protestations of innocence to appear on a website. Obviously hoping that, unlike Duffy, his words will be believed without being checked against the facts, he uses a mixture of lies and muddling to try and throw doubt on his conviction (attempting again the hackneyed, long-disproved alibi of having been ill with bronchial pneumonia on the night of Alison Day's death, for instance). Tellingly, he singles out and libels three women, namely Caroline Murphy, forensic scientist Liz Harris and Dr Jenny Cutler, whom he claims coached Duffy in his evidence (obviously his GP was lying too; the number of disparate profession-als supposedly complicit in the conspiracy is astounding). He also accuses the Recorder of London of partiality, for good measure.

Where Duffy's recollection of events was highly accu-rate, he claims this shows Duffy was lying; unfortunately he also uses examples of Duffy's memory letting him down as proof that he was lying. (In fact, Duffy made a number of natural errors of memory, such as thinking that the Danish au pairs were Swedish, a mistake unlikely to have occurred had he been coached.)

He claims Duffy lied to take revenge on him for not giving him an alibi when he was arrested for raping his wife. If Duffy was feeling vengeful, Ross Mockeridge would have been the obvious target, seeing as it was his evidence that destroyed Duffy's defence of amnesia. Furthermore, if Duffy wanted revenge on Mulcahy, he waited a very long time to do it, and also had the good fortune to have a one in 1 billion DNA match on his side.

Mulcahy's claims that the DNA was planted by the police because they had a vendetta against him (DNA found in semen is not easily doctored) begs the ques-tion of why a team of detectives who had nothing to do with any previous enquires involving him would have such a vendetta; and also, why, if they did, did they not simply incriminate him in Operation Loudwater, rather than then trying to implicate him in a case from a decade earlier? If the DNA was planted on the clothing of the Danish au pair, why is there no other DNA present? And if police planted forensic evidence, why only plant it on one exhibit? Why not build an even stronger case?

The website has led nowhere, understandably. One should be especially thankful for this, since as well as going into extremely graphic detail of the rapes, Mulcahy also maliciously named all of the rape victims* on it (including, with even more gratuitousness, the 14-year-old girl raped by John Duffy alone at Watford, an incident that has no bearing on his case). Naming the victims and publicly disputing their evidence was clearly a final, desperate act of bullying and revenge.

Mulcahy also tried to interest the press in a story that Duffy was paid £20,000 for giving evidence against him, and that Duffy will one day be released and 'repatriated to Ireland'. Ever the attention-seeker, he tried to persuade the newspapers of this idea: the only one that bothered to print it was the *Sunday Mirror*, which quoted Mulcahy's lawyer, Giovanni Di Stefano, as saying the matter 'needs to be investigated'.[48]

Unfortunately for Mulcahy, his so-called lawyer turned out to have no legal qualifications and in 2013 was sentenced to fourteen years' imprisonment after pleading guilty to twenty-seven charges ranging from deception to money laundering.**

---

* The names have now been removed.

** Giovanni Di Stefano (b.1955) has in the past claimed to be acting on behalf of Moors Murderer Ian Brady, paedophile Gary Glitter and Saddam Hussein.

My brother, Martin, who had hoped to follow my father into the police force, an ambition scuppered by colour blindness, spent his career in the Prison Service, eventually reaching the rank of governor. I asked him about the concept of someone who is serving a life sentence constantly trying to bait the authorities. He said,

> This is not a surprise. You do often find that prisoners with little hope of release tend to need something to cling to psychologically, and that can range from either somewhat mundane things like art to the other extreme of pursuing appeals and looking for any avenue to create doubt about their conviction.* This type of arrogance also often has a link to this type of offender's behaviour pattern and manipulative ways anyway.[49]

Professor David Canter says, 'Offenders can get into a situation where they think "that wasn't really me, that was a different person".'[50] Perhaps, if it is true that Mulcahy never offended again in all those years after Duffy's arrest (with the exception of the assault on his son), this may be another reason why he feels justified in protesting his innocence. But Mick Freeman adds, with regard to the disbelief that Mulcahy's friends and family still have for his crimes, 'He is very manipulative and clearly quite good at pulling the wool over people's eyes.'

---

*   Lifers, particularly those convicted of murder, follow a very clear, structured line of management through their sentence. There is regular and significant input from and interaction with forensic psychologists, prison officers, casework officers and sometimes, but not always, psychiatrists. Periodically throughout the sentence there are formal reviews, with interviews and inputs from a number of disciplines, to discuss progress, or the lack of it, and to set targets and objectives for the prisoner. These discussions will inform any significant decisions such as progressive transfers to another prison, recategorisation or perhaps even making a recommendation for release to the parole board. They also consider and make decisions on reversing those processes if there are particular concerns or a lack of progress. Mulcahy's protestations of innocence will have had a major bearing on his management as a 'lifer', preventing his progression due to his denials not allowing him to complete offending behaviour or cognitive skills courses.

Perhaps David Mulcahy's protestations of innocence are also for the sake of his family. Perhaps there, in his role as a father, we can now, at the end, find some glint of humanity in the man. Fatherhood has been an inevitable preoccupation of this book, a book driven by pride for my own father, and so I can barely comprehend the consequences of having to face the fact that your father has committed crimes such as these. When one remembers that Duffy's inability to become a father played some part in his offending, and that his own father being informed of his crimes triggered Duffy's mental collapse, one perhaps has something of a sense that maybe it is with fathers that we should leave this story. And with the words of one father in particular. For as I neared the end of this book, I was privileged to speak with the father of Alison Day.

With great dignity, he spoke to me of his appreciation for the police officers who dealt with the case, and of how, since losing Alison, he has also lost both his wife and his daughter-in-law. Understandably, he spoke of his desire for capital punishment to be reintroduced. 'What frightens me,' he said, 'is the thought that one day I'll get a knock on the door from the police telling me that they are going to be let out.'[51] But that will never happen. Both men will die in prison.

He tells me that every night when he goes to bed, he says goodnight to Alison and to his late wife. And finally, he tells me that he can still hear the last words Alison said to him, that she opened the front door to leave that evening, and from the kitchen he heard her call out in a sing-song voice, 'Bye bye, Daddy.'

A few days later, I take a train back to that town where I spent a safe childhood. It's my first visit there in a very long time. I go to the churchyard, and lay some flowers on Alison's grave.

It's the least I can do.

Tragically, it's the most any of us can do.

★★★

Alison Jane Day (23 May 1966–29 December 1985)

Maartje Tamboezer (22 March 1971–17 April 1986)

Anne Veronica Lock (11 June 1956–18 May 1986)

AFTERWORD

For the women who lost their lives to those two men, the final injustice is that they have been immortalised by their deaths, not by their lives. And though there has been a solution in investigative terms, there can never be a solution in emotional terms.

So many times during the research and writing of this book, I wished my father was there to tell me facts I couldn't determine or just to tell me that he approved of such a book being written. Amazingly, on the day I was delivering the final draft, I was contacted by Monica Weller, who had been in touch with my father when researching her book *Injured Parties: Solving the Murder of Dr Helen Davidson*. It transpired that my father had himself suggested that 'someone should write the story of The Railway Murders'. In March 2010, he had sent Monica an email containing his recollections of the case, an email which I was staggered to find contained information I had given up trying to find. He had signed off by saying, 'I could see a very large amount of work being required to bring it into book form.' Receiving that message at the eleventh hour was almost supernatural.

My father was diagnosed with a brain tumour in 2012. It was a poor, undignified illness, and one of its cruel legacies was that in the years since, images of him in his final days have always been the first recollections of him to come to mind. The priceless, unexpected reward of researching this book, however, is that now I picture him back in his prime.

My father's illness limited his speech. Steroids assisted him, but over the course of a day their effects would gradually wear off, and he would fall silent. One evening, we watched a television documentary about the then-unfolding Jimmy Savile revelations. The programme questioned how various institutions and individuals appeared to have done nothing to prevent a shocking catalogue of crimes being committed.

When a healthy man, my father would always wait for a programme he had been absorbed in to end, and then make one very considered judgement on it. I didn't expect this to happen anymore. But as the credits rolled, he said, with a conviction so strong at that moment that it blasted through his illness, 'As the saying goes, evil men can only prosper if good men do nothing.'

That must be his epitaph. It's a good sentiment to start from in life, and a valuable note to end on.

He asked me for Bach's *Sheep May Safely Graze* to be played at his funeral, because it reminded him of our happy days driving through the countryside of East Anglia. I never knew then, and he couldn't have known, that if one discovers the words of a piece that is usually performed instrumentally, one finds that the opening couplet is charmingly reflective of his life's achievement, namely keeping our streets just a little safer:

> Sheep may safely graze and pasture,
> Where a shepherd guards them well.

REFERENCES

Chapter 1: Dedication

1   SF interview with Dave Cant, 9 August 2015
2   Figures taken from www.metpolicehistory.co.uk
3   Letter from James Rusbridger of St Austell discussing police policy, published *Daily Telegraph*, 19 April 1987
4   'In the Office of Constable', Sir Robert Mark, Collins, 1978
5   *Daily Mirror*, 20 November 1976
6   *Bobby Moore: World Cup Hero*, broadcast 16 June 2002, BBC2
7   *The Times*, 17 October 1973
8   Letter to Mrs Barbara Farquhar from Dick Kirby, January 2013
9   SF interview with Michael Taylor, 24 August 2015
10 SF interview with Gordon Reynolds, 17 August 2015
11 SF interview with Colin Hockerday, 20 August 2015
12 The murder was reported in the *Romford Recorder*, 14 March 1986. The article includes a reference to a door-to-door salesman that police were seeking information about.
13 The most detailed account of the case was published in *Real Crimes*, Issue 42; Midsummer Books Ltd, 1993
14 *Barlow, Regan, Pyall and Fancy*, broadcast 31 May 1993, BBC2

Chapter 2: Collusion

1   Mr Frank Walsh, former workmate of Duffy, quoted in *Daily Mail*, 27 February 1988
2   Mrs Rosie Bolland, quoted in *Daily Express*, 27 February 1988
3   *Hampstead & Highgate Express*, 4 March 1988
4   'Ed Miliband's School, Haverstock, Was Hardly a Model Comprehensive', article by Andrew Anthony, *The Guardian*, 7 October 2012
5   *Daily Mail*, 3 February 2001
6   SF interview with Richard Priestley, 6 January 2016

7   *Daily Mail*, 3 February 2001

8   *Daily Mail*, 27 February 1988

9   Dr Murray Cox, Consultant Psychotherapist at Broadmoor Hospital (1970–97), speaking on *Timewatch: Shadow of the Ripper*, BBC2 documentary, broadcast 7 September 1988

10   Unless otherwise stated, all quotes from John Duffy are taken from interviews conducted by Hertfordshire Police in 1998

11   *Daily Telegraph*, 3 February 2001

12   Ibid.

13   Criminologist Bill Waddell, curator of Scotland Yard's Black Museum, speaking on *The Black Museum*, Central Television documentary, broadcast 6 September 1988

14   *Daily Mail*, 24 March 2001

15   *Hampstead & Highgate Express*, 9 February 2001

16   Interview with victim in *The Guardian*, 5 February 2001

17   *Daily Mail*, 4 November 2000

18   Interview with Margaret Byrne, *Daily Mail*, 14 January 1988

19   *Daily Express*, 5 October 1985

20   Ken Worker interview on *Crimewatch File: The Railway Murders*, BBC1, 17 August 1988

21   *Crimewatch UK*, BBC1, 12 December 1985

22   *Daily Express*, 13 January 1988

23   *Daily Mail*, 4 October 2000

Chapter 3: Alison

1   SF interview with John Manners, 1 October 2015

2   SF interview with Mick Freeman, 24 September 2015

3   Quoted in *Daily Mail*, 7 November 2000

4   *Daily Mirror*, 2 January 1986

5   *Romford Recorder*, 3 January 1986

6   *Daily Mail*, 2 January 1986

7   SF interview with Brian Roberts, 22 October 2015

8   *Romford Recorder*, 10 January 1986

9   SF interview with Barry Fyffe, 22 November 2015

10   *Daily Mail*, 16 January 1988

11   *Crimewatch File: The Railway Murders*, broadcast BBC1, 17 August 1988

12   *Newsroom South-East*, BBC1, 15 January 1986

13   *Crimewatch File*

14   *Crimewatch UK*, BBC1, 27 February 1986

15   *Romford Recorder*, 4 March 1988

16   *Julius Caesar*, Act III, Scene II

Chapter 4: Maartje

1   'The Adventure of the Copper Beeches' by Sir Arthur Conan Doyle

2   *Surrey Advertiser*, 4 April 1986

3   Barry Fyffe interview

4   *Surrey Advertiser*, 15 January 1988

5   *Crimewatch File*
6   SF interview with John Hurst, 27 October 2015
7   *Daily Mail*, 24 July 1986
8   *Surrey Advertiser*, 30 May 1986
9   *Surrey Advertiser*, 25 April 1986
10   *Surrey Advertiser*, 2 May 1986
11   *Crimewatch UK*, BBC1, 22 May 1986
12   *Daily Mail*, 27 February 1988
13   Brian Roberts interview
14   Barry Fyffe interview
15   *Crimewatch File*

Chapter 5: Anne

1   SF interview with Jeremy Bugler, 15 December 2015
2   Email from Peter Basnett to SF via Adrian Allen, Metropolitan Police Intellectual
     Property Officer, 18 January 2016
3   *Glasgow Herald*, 11 June 1986
4   SF interview with Paul Dockley, 26 November 2015
5   *Daily Mail*, 21 May 1986
6   *London Plus*, BBC1, 21 May 1986
7   *Daily Mail*, 27 May 1986
8   *Crimewatch UK*, BBC1, 10 July 1986
9   *Welwyn & Hatfield Times*, 22 May 1986
10   *Newsroom South-East*, BBC1, 23 May 1986
11   *Daily Mail*, 27 May 1986
12   *Daily Mail*, 28 May 1986
13   *Daily Mail*, 29 May 1986
14   *Daily Mail*, 6 June 1986
15   *Daily Mail*, 2 June 1986
16   *Welwyn & Hatfield Times*, 19 June 1986
17   *Daily Mail*, 13 June 1986
18   Brian Roberts interview
19   *Crimewatch File*
20   *Daily Mail*, 6 June 1986
21   *Daily Mail*, 11 June 1986
22   *Crimewatch UK*, BBC1, 10 July 1986
23   SF interview with Edward Stubbs, 24 August 2015
24   SF interview with Keith Hider, 17 December 2015
25   *Body of Evidence* by Professor David Bowen, Constable, 2003
26   *Breakfast Time*, BBC1, 22 July 1986
27   *London Plus*, BBC1, 22 July 1986
28   *Daily Mail*, 31 July 1986
29   *Crimewatch File*
30   Dave Cant interview
31   Former Detective Superintendent John Stainthorpe, speaking on ITV
     documentary *Nightwatch: Mystery* in 2008.
32   SF interview with Paul Dockley at Brookman's Park, 15 January 2016

Chapter 6: Convergence

1   *London Plus*, BBC1, 1 August 1986
2   *Los Angeles Times*, 28 June 1987
3   Barry Fyffe interview
4   *Daily Mirror*, 2 August 1986
5   Mick Freeman interview
6   Brian Roberts interview
7   This story was also covered in the *Daily Mail* on 13 November 1986
8   *Romford Observer*, 23 September 1986
9   *Six O'Clock News*, BBC1, 1 August 1986
10 *Romford and Dagenham Independent*, 11–17 June 1986
11 Paul Dockley interview
12 *Crimewatch UK*, BBC1, 18 September 1986
13 *Crimewatch File*
14 *News of the World*, 28 September 1986
15 SF interview with Professor David Canter, 18 January 2016
16 *Criminal Shadows* by Professor David Canter, HarperCollins, 1994, p.27
17 David Canter interview
18 John Hurst interview
19 *Crimewatch File*
20 David Canter interview
21 *Criminal Shadows*, p.65
22 Professor Stuart Kind interviewed on *Manhunt: The Hunt for the Yorkshire Ripper*, broadcast ITV, 30 September 1999
23 David Canter interview
24 Keith Hider interview
25 *Glasgow Herald*, 20 January 1988
26 *Crimewatch File*
27 Paul Dockley interview
28 *Criminal Shadows*, p.53
29 *Crimewatch UK*, BBC1, 12 December 1985
30 *The London Standard*, 25 November 1986
31 *London Plus*, BBC1, 25 November 1986
32 Taped interview with David Mulcahy conducted by police, November 1986
33 *Daily Mirror*, 27 November 1986
34 John Hurst interview
35 *Crimewatch File*
36 John Hurst interview
37 *Romford Recorder*, 16 April 1987
38 *Romford and Dagenham Independent*, 11 April 1987
39 *Romford-Havering Observer*, 22 April 1987

Chapter 7: Separation

1   *The Guardian*, 27 February 1988
2   All quotes from the trial of Duffy are as reported in the national press on 13–14 January 1988, or the *Surrey Advertiser* on 26 January 1988, unless otherwise stated
3   Obituary of Sir Donald Farquharson, *Daily Telegraph*, 8 September 2011
4   Keith Hider interview
5   Brian Roberts interview
6   *Daily Express*, 27 February 1988
7   *Hampstead & Highgate Express*, 4 March 1988
8   *Daily Star*, 14 January 1988
9   *Glasgow Herald*, 20 January 1988
10 *Daily Mail*, 21 January 1988
11 *Glasgow Herald*, 23 January 1988
12 *The Times*, 27 February 1988
13 Barry Fyffe interview
14 *Daily Mail*, 3 February 1988
15 Keith Hider interview
16 *Crimewatch File*
17 Keith Hider interview
18 *Daily Mail*, 27 February 1988
19 *Daily Express*, 27 February 1988
20 Keith Hider interview
21 *Romford Recorder*, 4 March 1988
22 *Daily Mirror*, 27 February 1988
23 *Daily Mail*, 15 July 1988
24 *The Times*, 27 February 1988
25 *Hampstead & Highgate Express*, 4 March 1988
26 *The Times*, 27 February 1988
27 *Criminal Shadows*, p.52
28 *The Times*, 27 February 1988
29 *Romford Recorder*, 4 March 1988
30 Ibid.
31 *Daily Telegraph*, 27 February 1988
32 *Daily Express*, 27 February 1988
33 *ITN News*, 26 February 1988
34 Brian Roberts interview
35 Keith Hider interview
36 John Hurst interview
37 *BBC News*, 26 February 1988
38 *ITN News*, 26 February 1988
39 *London Plus*, 26 February 1988
40 Ibid.
41 *Daily Mail*, 5 February 1987
42 *Evening Standard*, 7 January 1988
43 *News of the World*, 28 February 1988
44 *News of the World*, 17 January 1988
45 *Daily Mail*, 27 February 1988

46 *Daily Mirror*, 27 February 1988
47 *Daily Mail*, 24 March 2001

Chapter 8: Severance

1   *Body of Evidence*, p.6
2   Brian Roberts interview
3   Dr Jenny Cutler, interviewed on *Witness of Truth: The Railway Murders*, broadcast on BBC1, 11 December 2001
4   *The Guardian*, 3 February 2001
5   *The Times*, 3 February 2001
6   Professor David Canter interview
7   Paul Dockley interview
8   SF interview with Caroline Murphy, 8 January 2016
9   Mick Freeman interview
10 *BBC News Online*, 2 February 2001
11 Les Bolland interviewed on *Witness of Truth: The Railway Murders*.
12 *Daily Express*, 27 February 1988
13 *Evening Standard*, 2 February 2001
14 Keith Hider interview
15 *Daily Mail*, 3 February 2001
16 Keith Hider interview
17 *The Trial of the Railway Rapist*, broadcast on Channel 4, 6 February 2001
18 Ibid.
19 Unless otherwise stated, dialogue from the Mulcahy trial is taken from national press reports on 23 October 2001
20 *News of the World*, 3 February 2001. (Since the victim waved her right to anonymity to tell her story, I am relying on the tabloid newspaper to have been respectful of the facts on this occasion)
21 *Body of Evidence*, p.7
22 *The Guardian*, 5 February 2001
23 Professor David Canter interview
24 *The Trial of the Railway Rapist*
25 *The Times*, 3 February 2001
26 Statement from Mulcahy's GP, April 1987
27 *Daily Express*, 3 February 2001
28 Ibid.
29 *Witness of Truth: The Railway Murders*
30 *ITN News*, 2 February 2001
31 *Romford Recorder*, 9 February 2001
32 *Daily Telegraph*, 3 February 2001
33 *ITN News*, 2 February 2001
34 *Daily Telegraph*, 3 February 2001
35 Email to SF from Angela Levin, 3 January 2016
36 *Daily Mail*, 24 March 2001
37 *Daily Mail*, 10 March 2001
38 *Evening Standard*, 2 February 2001

39 *Hampstead & Highgate Express*, 9 February 2001
40 *Hampstead & Highgate Express*, 12 November 1976
41 Email to SF from Paul Dockley, 3 February 2016
42 *Evening Standard*, 2 February 2001
43 *The Guardian*, 3 February 2001
44 Professor David Canter interview
45 Keith Hider interview
46 *Hampstead & Highgate Express*, 16 October 2014
47 Case No: 3YU22395, Central London County Court, between Claimant David Mulcahy and the Defendant, the Commissioner of the Metropolitan Police
48 *Sunday Mirror*, 22 May 2005
49 Email to SF from Martin Farquhar, 9 September 2015
50 Professor David Canter interview
51 SF interview with Kenneth Day, 17 January 2016

INDEX